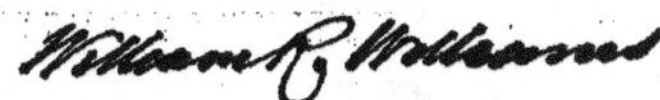

THE

FATHERS OF THE DESERT;

OR, AN ACCOUNT OF

THE ORIGIN AND PRACTICE OF MONKERY

AMONG HEATHEN NATIONS;

ITS PASSAGE INTO THE CHURCH; AND SOME WONDERFUL STORIES OF THE FATHERS CONCERNING THE PRIMITIVE MONKS AND HERMITS.

BY HENRY RUFFNER,

LATE PRESIDENT OF WASHINGTON COLLEGE, VIRGINIA.

VOLUME I.

NEW YORK:
PUBLISHED BY BAKER AND SCRIBNER,
145 NASSAU ST. AND 36 PARK ROW,
1850.

C. W. BENEDICT,
Stereotyper,
201 William st., N. Y.

PREFACE.

The author was led to compose this work, first by reading in the Christian Fathers of the 4th and 5th centuries, some strangely romantic legends of the hermits and founders of monastic societies in their days;—and secondly, by discovering a remarkable resemblance between Christian monachism, and that which has existed from very ancient times among the Hindoos and the Boodhists of Eastern Asia.

The fact of this resemblance struck him as so curious and so interesting, that he determined to investigate it, and see whether he could trace out any connection between religious institutions so remote in place, yet so much alike in form and in spirit. He found that the same principles of religious philosophy, led to the same unnatural practices, among idolators before our Saviour's time, and among Christians in the 4th century. How came these heathenish principles into the Church?—That was the next question. The author has attempted to trace them from their source in the distant East, through Egypt, Chaldea and Persia, into Western Asia and Greece. Thus they got first among the Jews, and finally into the Church, where they produced all the extravagances of monkery, and other kindred errors and superstitions.

The first part of the work is taken up with a brief and plain account of the religious principles of the Hindoos, the Boodhists, and other Eastern nations, and—so far as they existed—of the penances and monkery that grew out of these principles. The reader, if he has not heretofore informed himself on these matters, will here meet with some curious and amusing facts, and in a religious point of view, instructive also.

Some following chapters give a simple and intelligible sketch of those principles of the Grecian and Jewish philosophies which were derived from Eastern Asia,—the monastic sects of the Jews,—the gradual rise of asceticism in the Church, until it ripened into monkery, under the influence of those principles of philosophy which came from Eastern Asia.

The second part of the work consists mainly of legends and anecdotes translated from the Fathers, giving a lively portraiture of the religion of those times, and a strangely romantic view of the wonder-working saints of the 4th and 5th centuries. Strangely romantic their stories are, whether we consider what is true, or what is evidently fictitious, in the accounts which the Fathers give of them.

The author has bestowed much labor and research on the work which he now presents to the American public. He has endeavored to make it amusing as well as instructive. He has therefore avoided dry and tedious dissertations; he has mingled story and anecdote with solid matter, and brought before the American reader in a connected view, what he found scattered in many books, chiefly in foreign languages. As no writer in our language has occupied this field of religious literature, he hopes that the unlearned reader will find in these *Monkiana* much that is new to him; and if it be not also interesting and instructive, the fault must be in the author's mode of presenting it, rather than in the subject matter of the book.

HENRY RUFFNER.

Virginia, May, 1850.

CONTENTS OF VOL. I.

CHAPTER I.

NAMES DEFINED, WITH A GLIMPSE OF EARLY MONACHISM IN THE CHURCH.

Page

What is a Monk ?—Asceticism among early Christians.—The Hermits. Their principles.—Were Anthropomorphists.—Their notions of Demons.—Their manner of life.—Origin of associations of Monks.—St. Pachonius and St. Basil.—Monasteries.—Their Rulers.—Cenobites, Anchorites and Sarabaites.—Orders of Monks in later times. —The Workers and the Mendicants,—their vows, and their wealth and laziness.—Convents and Nunneries.—The name Nun.—Concubinage.—Demons and Demoniacs.—Exorcism.—Dates of the rise and progress of Monachism, ... 1

CHAPTER II.

OF MONACHISM AMONG THE HINDOOS.

§1. *General Principles of the Hindoo Religion.*

Origin of Monachism.—The Vedas and other holy books.—Hindoo Theology; Brahm and the Trimurte.—Metempsychosis.—All souls defiled by matter.

§2. *Hindoo Doctrine of Penances.*

Laws of Menu.—Degrees of sanctity.—The Yogi and the Sannyasi.—Hindoo castes.—The Brahmins.—The four degrees of Saintship.—Fasting.—The Sannyasi.—Story of the Indian Prince.—The Shradhu, a ceremony for the dead.—Atonements.

§3. *Doctrine of Future Judgment, Heaven and Hell.*

Journeys of the Righteous and the Wicked to the Judgment Seat.—Yumu, the Judge.—Degrees of Future Happiness.—Absorption into Deity.—Crimes of some Ascetics.—Future Punishments.—General Principles of Hindooism.

Page

§4. *Practices of Hindoo Devotees.*

Strabo's Account.—Other Ancient Accounts.—Accounts of Modern Travelers.—The various strange Exercises of the Devotees, . . 19

CHAPTER III.

OF MONACHISM AMONG THE BOODHISTS.

§1. *Origin of Boodhism.*

Traditions concerning Boodh.—Ward's Account.—The Burman Legend.—The Account in the Puranahs.

§2. *Doctrines of Boodhism.*

Of a First Cause.—Metempsychosis.—Absorption.—Boodh and his Relics.—Differences between Boodhism and Brahminism.—Boodhist Monachism.—The Moral Law of Boodh.—The Priesthood.—A Fundamental Principle.

§3. *Monachism in Burmah, Siam, and Cochin-China.*

Ceylon.—Rhangoon.—The Talapoins of Siam.—Cochin-China; Borri's Account.—Resemblance to Romanism.—Tonquin.

§4. *Monachism among the Lamaists of Thibet.*

Prevalence of Monachism.—Superstitions.—Resemblance to Romanism.—Theory of the Jesuits to account for it.—Malte Brun's and Carl Ritter's opinions.—Refutation of the Theory.—Nestorian and Boodhist Missions in Central Asia and Cathay.—Reports of Rubruquis and Marco Polo.—Prester John.

§5. *Monachism in China and Korea.*

Chinese Boodhists.—Nieuhoff's Account.—Hamel's account of the Korean Monks.

§6. *Monachism in Japan.*

The Spiritual Sovereign of Japan.—Resemblance to Popery.—The Sentoists,—their Monachism.—The Mountain Hermits, and their mode of Confessing Penitents.—The Boodhists of Japan.—The Tolerance of the Japanese Government, till the Jesuits meddled with Politics and were expelled.—Moral Law.—Doctrine of Purgatory.—Service for the Dead.—Monasteries.—Temples and Worship.—Bonzes.—Hated and Calumniated by the Jesuit Missionaries.—St. Francis Xavier, ... 52

CHAPTER IV.

MONACHISM AMONG THE MAHOMETANS.

Page
Niebuhr's Account.—Other Accounts.—Religious Orders of the Turks, 102

CHAPTER V.

SKETCH OF THE RELIGIOUS PHILOSOPHIES OF ANCIENT PERSIA, CHALDEA AND EGYPT.

Antiquity of the Oriental Religious Philosophy.—The Westward Movement of this Philosophy.—The object of this and some following chapters is to trace the course of this Philosophy into the Church.—1. *The Persian Philosophy* briefly noticed,—its Dualism,—its General Principles.—2. *The Chaldean Philosophy,*—its Leading Principles.—The Chaldean Magii and Astronomy.—3. Religious Philosophy of Ancient Egypt,—its Fundamental Agreement with the Hindoo System.—Its Theology.—Principle of Emanation.—Demons.—Metempsychosis,—why the System did not produce Monkery.—The Druids believed in Metempsychosis, ... 119

CHAPTER VI.

ASCETIC PHILOSOPHY OF THE GREEKS.

§1. Orpheus and his Philosophy.—Imperfectly known.—His doctrines of Oriental Origin.

§2. Pythagoras and his Philosophy.—He traveled in the East.—His Principles Oriental.—His Doctrines,—Ascetic Principles.—Esoteric School.—The Influence of his Philosophy in Greece.

EMPEDOCLES, A PYTHAGOREAN.

§3. *The Stoical Philosophy,*—its Fundamental principles.

§4. *Plato and his Philosophy.*

Its Extensive Influence.—Plato studied the Egyptian Philosophy.—His Doctrines;—God, Ideas and Matter.—Things Sensible and Intelligible.—Matter, its Primary State.—The Demiurge and Logos.—Gods and Demons.—The Mundane Soul.—The Soul of Man, its Threefold Nature.—The Rational Soul,—how Purified.—Metempsychosis.—The Four Cardinal Virtues.—Plato Borrowed from Pythagoras and the Orientals, ... 129

CHAPTER VII.

PLATONISM OF PHILO THE JEW.

Page

City of Alexandria—Its University and Library.—The Alexandrian Jews.—The Greek Septuagint.—Philo, an Alexandrian Jew, a Platonist.—Allegorized the Books of Moses.—Philo's Writings.—His Doctrines,—of God and His Chief Powers.—The Logos.—Angels and Demons.—The Human Soul.—The Human Body.—Virtue.—Ascetism.—The Contemplative Life.—Specimen of his Allegorical Interpretations, ... 144

CHAPTER VIII.

PHILOSOPHY AND MONACHISM OF THE JEWS.

The Jews had no Philosophy, till after the Babylonish Captivity.—Got some ideas of Chaldean and Persian Philosophy in Babylon; and began to learn Platonism in Alexandria.—Book of Wisdom contains Platonic Doctrines.—The Jewish Sects.—The Pharisees.—The Essenes, a Sect of Jewish Monks, described.—The Therapeutes of Egypt, another Monkish Sect, described.—They differed from the Essenes.—Were not Christians, as Eusebius pretended.—Origin of Jewish Monachism, ... 157

CHAPTER IX.

THE LATER JEWISH AND GENTILE PHILOSOPHY.

§1. *Jewish Cabalistic Philosophy.*—Specimen of Rabbinical Philosophy. —The earlier Cabbula was merely the Oral Law.—The later Cabalistical Philosophy,—its Principles.—Its affinity with the Gnostic Doctrines.

§2. *The Later Pythagoreans.*—Maxims of their Philosophy.

§3. *The Eclectics and New Platonists.*—Originated in Alexandria, A.D. 200.—Their Principal Teachers.—Their Doctrines,—of God—Celestial Beings—Apparitions—Theurgy—The Soul and the Body—Ascetical Purification of the Soul.—Remarks on this Philosophy, . 174

CHAPTER X.

IS MONACHISM A SCRIPTURAL INSTITUTION?

The Capuchin Bouldau.—Cardinal Bellarmine defends the Scriptural

Page

Origin of Monkery.—Old Testament Example not Admissible.—Bellarmine's Arguments Stated and Answered, . . . 189

CHAPTER XI.

ASCETICISM AMONG CHRISTIANS OF THE EARLY AGES.

Tendency to Asceticism in the Apostolic Age.—St. Paul forewarns Christians against it.—Notions concerning Virginity, Fasting and Prayer.—Growth of Ascetic Principles and Practices.—Influence of Platonism on Christianity.—Renunciation of Worldly Goods and Pleasures.—Platonizing Fathers.—Growth of Superstition.—Ascetics begin to withdraw into Solitude.—Persecution hastens the development of Monachism.—Fear of Demons and Worldly Enjoyments, drove the Monks to excessive Self-Mortification, . . 197

CHAPTER XII.

SCATTERED NOTICES CONCERNING VIRGINITY, ASCETICISM, &c., COLLECTED FROM THE EARLY FATHERS.

1st Century.—Hermas, Clement and Ignatius, concerning Fasts, Virginity, &c.

2nd Century.—Justin Martyr, concerning Angels, Demons, and Religious Virgins.—*Tatian*, concerning Virgins and Marriage.—*The Gnostics.*—Extract from Neander.—*Irenæus.*—His allusion to the Marcionite Monks.—*Athenagoras*, on Virginity and Monogamy.—*Theophilus*, ditto.—*Epistle to Diognetus*, on the contest between Soul and Body.—*Clement of Alexandria*, on Asceticism, Marriage and Virginity.

3rd Century.—Origen.—A passage on Virginity, Monogamy and "Useful Deceptions," Pious Frauds, Ascetics.—*Apostolical Canons.*—A Canon on Asceticism.—Excessive Fasting.—*Dionysius.*—His Letter to the Gnossians on Virginity.—Answer of their Bishop Pynitus.—*Tertullian.*—His Character and Principles.—Exalts Virginity.—Ascribes Heathen Chastity to the Devil.—Jerome's Account of Heathen Virginity.—Tertullian on Ascetic Mortifications.—His invective against his Admired Virgins.—*Cyprian.*—His Praise of the Sacred Virgins.—His Censures of their Levity, Vanity, and Unchastity.—Some of them Caught Sleeping with Men.

4th Century.—St. Basil on Virgins Living with Unmarried Clergymen.—*St. Jerome.*—His Sojourn in the Desert.—On the Ruin of

Page

Religious Virgins,—their Vanity, and their Practice of Cohabiting with Unmarried Clergymen and Laymen.—*Sulpicius Severus*, on the same Practices in Gaul.—*St. Augustine* accuses Religious Virgins of going about Tattling, and of getting drunk, . . . 208

CHAPTER XIII.

EGYPT.

The Deserts, the Nile, and the Character of the Ancient Inhabitants, 239

CHAPTER XIV.

LIFE OF ST. ANTONY THE MONK; *from the Greek of St. Athanasius.*

1. Preface.—2. Youth of St. Antony.—3. He begins an Ascetic Course of Life.—4. His first Contest with the Devil.—5. Prepares for a Second.—6. Severely Beaten by the Devil.—7. What a hubbub the Devil raised against him in the Sepulcher.—8. His Hermit-Life in a Ruined Castle.—9. Comes forth a Miracle-Worker.—10–12. His Sermon about the Ascetic Life and the Demons.—13. His Boldness in the Persecution, his Miracles, and the Crowds that frequented his Monastery.—14. Retreats far into the Desert; Plagued by Demons.—15. More Miracles and some good Advice.—16. Miracles! Miracles!—17. His Wonderful Vision about the Passage of Souls.—18. Taken to Alexandria to Oppose the Arians.—19. How he Outwitted the Philosophers.—20. Sundry Matters.—21. Antony's Death.—Remarks on his Character, ... 247

CHAPTER I.

NAMES DEFINED, WITH A GLIMPSE OF EARLY MONACHISM IN THE CHURCH.

THE Church had been planted more than 200 years before it produced that moral prodigy—a monk. Idolatrous heathenism had generated this strange form of religious enthusiasm, many ages earlier. Corrupted Judaism had taken of the Gentile seed and planted it in the congenial soil about the Dead Sea and in the fiery sands of Egypt, where it was found growing by Christianity, but for a long time despised and rejected. At last, however, Christianity herself became sufficiently impregnated with heathenish superstition and philosophy, to bear in her own bosom a variegated brood of monks, who strongly resembled their cousins of the elder stock among the idolatrous Gentiles of the East.

But, what is a *Monk*?—According to the primitive idea and the proper sense of his Greek name, *Monachos*, he is a man who leads a solitary life,—who separates himself from human society that he may devote himself to sanctifying exercises. He has renounced all wordly pursuits, property and pleasure. He exercises himself continually in chastity, fasting, watching, prayer, and combats with evil spirits. He macerates his body with hunger and exposure to the elements. He mortifies to the utmost all the desires of his corporeal nature: he denies himself all the pleasures of the earth, and makes a purgatory of the world, that he may gain the paradise of heaven. Such is the primitive idea of a monk. But the modern monk varies from the primitive pattern. We shall see presently how this variation came to pass.

A moral discipline founded on principles similar to those of monkery, was in use among the Greek philosophers before the birth of Christ. They called it *Askesis* or *Exercise.* Some Jewish sects adopted it before the Christian era. They who practiced this discipline were called in the Greek language *Ascetics*, that is, *Exercisers.*

The Ascetics, though they proceeded in the way of the monks, did not always nor necessarily go so far. Their system of *Ascetism* was generally a defective sort of *Monachism.* It contained the germ which by unfolding grew into monachism. But Ascetism, although it was innoculated into Christianity even in the first century, did not expand into monachism until the latter part of the third century.

As Grecian *Ascetism* originated with the philosophers, and was in earlier times practiced by them and their disciples almost exclusively, so they who *exercised* themselves according to the strict rules of the philosophers, were said to *philosophize*, and every system of ascetism was called *philosophy.* The Christian Fathers of the fourth and fifth centuries applied the same terms to the monachism of their days: he who practiced it was said to *philosophize*, and the system of its doctrines and rules was dignified with the name of *philosophy.*

When the Christian life began to vary from the simple purity and social benevolence of the gospel, it first took the form of *ascetism*,—a mild ascetism, which it pushed gradually into monachism, by augmenting the severity of its exercises, and then fleeing from the face of human society into deep, and yet deeper and drearier solitudes. At first the ascetics merely avoided promiscuous company, and spent much of their time in private devotion. But then a private room in the house sufficed, or a secluded place in the neighborhood gave them the requisite secrecy for meditation and prayer. But habits of seclusion, like other habits, would naturally grow upon devout minds, that preferred the secret to the social exercises of religion. As every thing mysterious in religion makes a strong impression upon common minds, especially in a superstitious age, so the very obscurity in which the ascetic involved himself and his devout exercises, invested his character with a sort of awful sanctity in the eyes of the multitude, and made many esteem this manner of life peculiarly holy and sanctifying. Therefore many would be inclined to embrace it, and the tendency would be to carry out its principles to perfection. Then too the bloody persecutions of the third century drove multitudes of Christians into the deserts for safety. The ascetics, and those who were ascetically inclined, found the solitary life agree so well with their notions of spiritual perfection, and become by use so congenial to their feelings, that the return of peace to the church could not recall them to their homes and friends again. Many remained of choice in the deep solitudes to which necessity had driven them at first. Thus monachism began.

The term *Monachism* signifies the manner of life peculiar to monks, and so does the term *monkery;* which is however a disrespectful appellation, and has reference to the superstitions and follies of the monks.

Because the first Christian monks retired to uninhabited places, and especially to the deserts of Egypt,—they were called *Eremites* or *Hermits*, that is, *Men of the Desert.* In modern times a hermit is a monk in the original sense of the term, that is, a recluse or solitary man, in distinction from the monks generally, who since the fifth century have lived in societies of their own profession.

At first every monk sought to be what the name imports, a dweller in solitude. He shunned the company of mankind, even of his wife and children, if he had a family,—even of his fellow monks in the lonely wastes. Of these holy recluses like himself, he might tolerate occasional visits ; but he shunned all habitual companionship with human occupants of mortal clay. By him the face of a fellow man was not regarded as the " human face divine;" it was a thing of vile flesh and blood, a symbol of base animality, of sinful carnality, of decaying mortality. The human voice made no music in his ears; it was formed by organs of dust in the atmosphere of the earth; its melodies were dangerous to the soul because they gave it a carnal pleasure. He despised and hated his body, as the seat of appetites and of senses, which defiled the soul whenever they afforded it a sensible gratification. He felt bound therefore, to war against them, and to sanctify the soul by inflicting on his vile, sinful body all sorts of indignities and mortifications.

Yet, with a strange inconsistency, most of the early monks of Christendom were *anthropomorphists*. They believed that the infinite God had the bodily form and members of a man.* With a wonderful degree of ignorance and irrationality, they took in a literal sense those Scripture phrases which speak figuratively of God as having organs and members like ourselves. A well-instructed child of seven years old has sufficient intelligence to understand such phrases aright. But the monks took everything in a literal sense, which they read or heard in the Scriptures; and this ignorant simplicity of theirs was the ground-work of their monachism.

They conceived also that angels and demons had bodies of a fine, elastic material, which these spiritual beings could expand, contract, metamorphose, and render visible or invisible to human eyes, just as they pleased. They imagined that these heaven-born spirits could lust after earthly things; and had so much of the grossness of human nature, as to prove dangerous sometimes to the flesh and bones of men, and even to the chastity of women. These silly notions about angels and demons were not peculiar to the monks, however; learned Fathers of the Church, and even reasoning philosophers, entertained fancies of the same sort; and there yet lurks even in the Protestant mind a remnant of these old superstitions.

Most of the monks—especially if they were monks of note—

* See Sozomen's Ecclesiastical History, Book viii. chap. 11.

thought it necessary to let a servant or friend,—who was always an admirer and reporter of their sanctity and their miracles,—approach them once in a while with a supply of indispensable food for their contemptible bodies. But some considered this custom an imperfection that called for amendment. The solitude of such monks had a flaw in it; and the bread which they received, though it might be like a stone, was yet made by art and man's device, and had about it the look, if not the savor, of human comfort. Therefore these scrupulous brethren would have no such thing. Aiming at a perfection as nearly angelical as could be attained whilst they had any remnant of flesh and blood, they made themselves superior to vulgar humanity by going stark naked, and feeding—when they must feed or die—upon the raw plants which they happened to find in the desert. They thought, and others thought also, that it was a miraculous token of divine favor, when their bare bodies grew all hairy like the wild beasts of the same desert. Having thus made wild beasts of themselves, they had no objection to the company of bestial hermits like themselves—lions, hyenas, and wolves. We read of their associating occasionally with these, which they seemed to prefer to the wild goats and wild asses that roamed through the same vast solitudes. But they had no particular aversion to any sort of beasts. What they dreaded was the sight of men—and above all, of *women*, whom they esteemed more dangerous than lions, or serpents, or the devil himself.

One reason why these saintly savages preferred beasts of prey to others of gentler kind, was probably because the ravenous eaters of flesh became very meek and pious, and learned to eat raw vegetables, like good monks, when they associated with one of these hairy men of God: and one reason—but not the only one—why they shunned human society, was, that it spoiled their conversation with heaven and made the angels shy. These heavenly messengers would not visit them familiarly—(I speak as a monk)—until they had weaned themselves thoroughly from all human attachments and human society, and had renounced everything in the world that was grateful to the natural feelings of man.

Let not the reader suppose that we are drawing an imaginary picture of enthusiasm run mad. We delineate the very image of the saintship most in vogue and most admired in the fourth and fifth centuries of the Church's history—those pattern centuries of a perfect Christianity in the estimation of Puseyites and other pretended Protestants, in whom the old leaven of Popish superstition is yet fermenting. We draw our sketch from the writings of the revered Fathers of those centuries, whose admiration of this monkish saintship knew no bounds, and whose graphic descriptions and high praises of it will appear in the following documents which we have translated from their works. This is the sort of sanctity which was believed to confer miraculous power, and to entitle the practitioner to the very highest place in the kingdom of heaven. Of its ten thousand wonderful doings on the earth, in those days, the reader will find many recorded as indubitable facts in the documents just alluded to. If he can believe the tenth part of them, his faith must be founded upon the presumed infallibility of the holy Fathers, who recorded them for the edification of believers.

We said before that some of the hermits retained so much of the dregs of humanity, as to have settled abodes and to eat bread. These were obliged in the course of years to relax somewhat of their exclusiveness. The fame of their extraordinary fastings, prayers, psalm-sayings,* and combats with the devil and his legions away out in the deserts, soon spread through half the villages and cities of Christendom. Admiring multitudes, especially from the populous valley of the Nile, were soon attracted to their places of exercise, eager to behold such spiritual heroes, and to enlist in the holy war under their victorious banners. In vain did they refuse admittance to those who beset their doors, and watched day and night about their hiding places. In vain

* We had written it *psalm-singings;* but the low monotony of their solitary repetitions did not amount to sing-song.

did they fly from one solitude to another; in vain, attempt to conceal themselves in the most dreary wastes, in the most secret dens of the most desolate mountains, or the obscurest retreats of distant islands: still their secret found vent;—the faithless companion or two that waited on them in their wanderings, or the silly demons that infested them everywhere,—would blab, and draw an admiring crowd of candidates for discipleship around them.

Overcome at last by such persevering importunity—now when their fame was at its height and wondering curiosity at its utmost stretch—they yielded finally to what seemed to be the will of heaven, or to the express command of an angel;—they emerged from their caves, or whatever else had concealed them from human eyes;—vouchsafed to take charge of their waiting followers, and to instruct them in the mysteries of their wonderful sanctity. In such way it was that St. Antony, St. Pachomius, St. Hilarion, and other fathers of monachism, first came to establish schools of associated monks. At first however, the disciples were not congregated in one building. This would have been too great a departure, all at once, from first principles,—solitude being the essence of primitive monachism. Neither had Antony's monks and others like them, any formal vows or written regulations. Those of the same school only lived so near to one another in separate cells, that they could assemble once in a while in the open air, to hear the instructions of their holy father, and perhaps to join in some act of devotion. Then every man to his cell again, and to his solitary exercises, apart from every other. Solitude was still the general rule: social meetings were the exception, and that restricted to the utmost: no conversation, no, not a word nor even a look,—not even so much as "how do you do, brother."

The next step was to organize these fraternities under an established system of rules. This was done first in the Upper Thebaid (the uppermost province of Egypt), by St. Pachomius. So important a change in the primitive system of monachism could not be effected without divine interposition. An angel appeared to the saint, who had now attained a high degree of sanctity,—handed him a board with a system of rules engraven on it, and ordered him to organize monastic associations under that system. This occurred some years after Antony had taken charge of the first school of monks in the Lower Thebaid. Other experienced masters soon founded other schools and associations in other parts of the country, chiefly on the loose plan of the great St. Antony, who, of all the fathers of monachism, retained most of the original solitary principle. But the *angelic* system of Pachomius ultimately prevailed in Egypt, and was adopted with improvements in other countries. It allowed three monks to occupy each separate cell; but forbade conversation, and made them hide their faces from each other by veiling them with a sort of hood.

Not many years later, Saint Basil the Great, in Asia Minor near the Black Sea, first established *monasteries* in the modern sense of the term.

At first every single monk's place of exercise was his *monastery*, were it den, hut, hole in the ground, or old ruined house. Antony made his disciples build their monastic cells so far apart, that one could not hear another at his exercise. But as Basil's monks lived in a rather cold climate, the founder had them congregated in rather large buildings, with adjoining cells like a modern monastery; though each brother's cell was still his private monastery, in which he spent the most of his time. In Antony's schools, each monk did his little eating and drinking in his own cell, and provided for himself according to the primitive plan. Pachomius, as we have said, clubbed his monks. Each club had a common table in their cell, but then they were to be mute at table, and each to have his hood so drawn over his eyes that he could see his food, but not his fellow's face. Eating was a base affair at best; to season their mean, scanty meal with friendly looks and words, would have made it a social pleasure—the very thing that a true monk should abominate. But St. Basil's monasteries had not only a *chapel* for social worship, but a *refectory* for social meals, at which all sat down together. But to correct the evil tendency of this sociability, all had during the simple meal to give mute attention to something sacred, that was spoken or read in their hearing; and while their ears were occupied with the edifying sounds, their eyes were to be bent upon the table where their food lay.

In Palestine, and thereabouts, there was in those times a peculiar sort of monastic establishment called *Laura*, which consisted of a central church or chapel, surrounded at some distance by a circle of monastic cells, standing separate, and each occupied by a monk. This arrangement was designed to unite the original solitary system with periodical assemblages for instruction and worship.

The head of a monastic society was called *Abbot*, which is the Syriac word for father. But as this was a title of respect often given to private monks of advanced age, the head of a society in Egypt came to be called *David;* and the common Father or head of many societies, was called *Archimandrite*, that is, the chief of a mandra, or sheepfold, as the term signifies. In the western countries of Europe, where Latin was spoken, the head of a monastery was often called *Prior*, though the building might be called either *Abbey* or *Priory.**

The primitive hermits and founders of Christian monachism, were in after times distinguished as *The Fathers of the Desert.*

Many of the primitive monks did not approve of the social system of monachism, even in its most restricted form. They regarded it as a corruption of the perfect way of holiness. Though solitude might still prevail over society in the ratio a hundred to one, still there was something of society, and that of the worst kind—*human* society; and thereby something in the likeness of worldly comfort, which was not to be endured by a holy man. Many, therefore, adhered to the primitive pattern; they hid

* See for the signification of these several terms Du Fresne's Glossary, and Fosbroke's British Monachism.

themselves in deep solitudes, and rejected all society except that of beasts, which was innocent ; of demons, which was unavoidable ; and of angels, which was unattainable until they had divested themselves of all earth-born humanity.

Now as monachism branched off into diversity, new names had to distinguish the several classes of monks. Those who lived in communities under an abbot, were called *Cenobites*, from their living together in common ; the solitaries were called *Anchorites* from their living apart, each one to himself. Between these two was a third class called *Sarabaites*, who lived two or three together in a cell, but apart from all other society. Their plan was generally disapproved by the Fathers of the Church, because there was less absolute solitude than among the Cenobites, and no rule or government.

There was still a fourth class who arose after monkery had gotten into general repute as the most perfect way of life, and the profession itself, independently of the moral character of the professors, began to be esteemed a holy thing. This, the least respectable class, were called *Gyrovagi* or *Vagrants*. They took up the trade of saintship as an easy way of living at the expense of others. They went about from monastery to monastery, and from house to house in the garb of monks, seeking hospitable entertainment, and like stray dogs, staying longest where they were best fed. Beggary and occasional robbery among those vulgar and unholy beings, the married working people of the world, afforded them supplies, often of better quality than the meagre food of the monasteries. They resembled the vagrant Fakirs of India and the vagrant Santons of Turkey.

Occasionally the Cenobite monks would become troubled in spirit, lest even the silent and joyless company of their fellow-monks at table and in church should defile them. Then they would get leave of their abbot to retire from the monastery into the neighboring deserts, where, in perfect solitude and extreme destitution, they would labor and watch and pray for months or years, to expiate the sin of their poor enjoyments in the flesh.

In process of time the Cenobites came to be distinguished into different orders, as new founders would arise and establish what they conceived to be more perfect rules of the monastic life. The orders were named sometimes after their founders, as the *Benedictines* from Saint Benedict, the *Dominicans* from Saint Dominic; and sometimes the name had reference to some place or some peculiarity of dress, as the *Carmelites* and the *Capuchins.*

These orders were distinguished externally, as they still are, by the color and fashion of their costume: but their chief distinction was that between the working orders and the *mendicants* or beggars. The primitive hermits and the Cenobites generally, for a long time, professed to depend on their own labor for support. The Egyptian and Syrian monks employed their hands in weaving baskets and mats out of the palm leaves and rushes of the desert, whilst they occupied their minds with prayers and meditations, and sometimes their vocal organs with psalmodian dronings. It was partly the fear of the devil that kept them so piously busy; for they judged rightly, that whilst their hands were occupied with good works and their minds with holy exercises, the omnipresent and ever-watchful fiend could not find a single point of their spiritual fortress unguarded, nor a single cranny or loophole where the smallest of his imps might creep in. But these worthy hermits considered manual labor as a matter of religious duty also, according to the apostolical maxim, If any man will not work, neither should he eat.

When we say that the good old superstitious hermits labored so worthily for their bread, we mean of course to except those savage perfectionists who went naked and ate grass, and those lazy parasites who went in monk's clothing from place to place, feeding upon the product of other men's labors. With these exceptions all the monks for centuries—Cenobites as well as Anchorites—held like honest men and good Christians, that saintship did not exempt a man from the obligation of supporting himself by his own industry. The Cenobites of those best ages of monkery, such as the Tabennians of Pachomius, the Basilians of Basil, and the Benedictines of Benedict, all adhered to this principle ; and where the inmates of a monastery had a community of goods, as all the later orders of Cenobites had, there each brother was bound by rule to do his share of labor for the benefit of the community.

But in later times St. Dominic and St. Francis founded their orders upon a different principle. They considered productive industry as a worldly thing, and inconsistent with perfect saintship. They made it a rule, therefore, that no friar or brother of their orders, should defile himself with any sort of manual occupation : they were to devote themselves wholly to what was called the work of God,—such as fasting, praying, psalm-singing, preaching and begging. They built their monasteries in or near cities for the convenience of preaching, and of levying contributions on the wealthy and the industrious, by begging in the name of God and Saint Mary from door to door. Being esteemed the holiest of the holy, they were abundantly supplied by the pious ; nor were the wicked less liberal when their consciences troubled them ; for they were made to believe that giving to the monks was the surest way of purchasing the favor of heaven.

o easy a way of gaining spiritual honor and corporeal comforts, could not fail to attract many followers. Beggar-monks soon swarmed like summer flies in every Roman Catholic country. Thousands of them were continually going about as beggars, preachers, pardoners, and traders in saints' relics, in which they drove a very large and a very lucrative business.

All the monks of later times, both workers and beggars, were under a solemn vow of poverty ; which meant originally that they were to have no property, except a daily supply of necessaries for their daily wants. But it came to mean, that while the individual members could have no private property, the order or community might have any quantity of any sort of wealth. Thus the vow of poverty did not prevent the members from making interest in all possible ways for their monasteries. So well did they ply the consciences of the superstitious—and all were superstitious during the Middle Ages when monkery reigned—that the poor and the rich, the righteous and the wicked, all contributed to the lands and chattels of the monasteries, until the most of them became immensely wealthy. Then the brethren had no need to work or to beg any more. They could be as fat and as lazy as they pleased upon the princely revenues of their monasteries. And fat and lazy did the greater part of them become, and luxurious and profligate withal. Hospitable they were to strangers, and charitable, as they could well afford to be, towards the beggarly poor: and now and then a brother's peculiar turn of mind led him to employ his abundant leisure in literary exercises. As their lands and buildings were held sacred, even by warring barbarians; they preserved a portion of every country in Europe from desolation, during a 1000 years of ravage and of revolution. Thus did a wise Providence, through their means, preserve a remnant of civilization in the midst of barbarism and superstition, until Christendom was prepared for a new course of improvement, whose brightening ages shall not cease to roll, until they bring forth the glory of the latter days.

The term *Convent* is applied to both monasteries and *Nunneries*. In many places the same system of walls and buildings included both a monastery at one end and a nunnery at the other, with a chapel in which both monks and nuns met for worship, between them. This was a very convenient arrangement in more respects than one. The prying eyes of the world could not penetrate the sacred enclosure. We read without surprise that in many, if not most, of these establishments, an abominable licentiousness prevailed. It was the natural consequence of the celibacy, the wealth, the luxury and the laziness of these degenerate communities.

Before ascetism had ripened into monachism, the church had a class of sacred virgins, who professed to live chastely for Christ's sake, and who were cherished and lauded as the brightest ornaments of the church. These generally resided privately in the houses of their relations; or several together in a separate house; until Cenobite monachism led to the establishment of nunneries, which were regulated upon the same principles as the communities of the other sex.

These sacred virgins were called by different names, such as *Moniales* and *Sanctimoniales* among the Latins, and *Ascetria*, female exercisers, among the Greeks; but the term *Nona* or *Nonis (Nun)*, finally prevailed over all the rest. This term seems to have been originally Egyptian, and to have signified an elderly woman or mother; but it came to be applied to consecrated virgins as a title of respect, as the term Father was to priests and monks.*

We are sorry to say that some—perhaps in justice we ought to say *many*, if not *most*—of these darlings of the church, as early as the beginning of the third century, and for ages afterwards, disgraced their profession and the cause of virginity, by vain and licentious conduct. Would you believe it, reader, that, when it became disgraceful for priests to marry, and most meritorious for Christian females not to marry; just then it should become customary for unmarried clergymen and consecrated virgins to live together in the same house, sit together in the same private room, and *sleep together in the same unconsecrated bed*—yet under the profession of chastity all the while? Yet all this we shall hereafter prove from the writings of the holy Fathers of these purest ages of Christianity,—as Puseyites and very high churchmen esteem them to have been.

Nearly all the ancient nations believed that the air around us, and the circles of the heavens above us, were inhabited by countless numbers and various orders of spiritual beings, both good and evil. The Greeks called them all *Demons;* but the Jews called only the evil spirits demons, whose prince they called

* If the reader would investigate the origin and signification of this term, he may consult the writings of Jerome, Palladius, and Hospinian, and especially Bingham's Ecclesiastical Antiquities, book vii. chap. 4. § 8; and Du Fresne's Glossary on the word *Nona*.

Beelzebub or *Satan*, in Greek the *Devil*. The good spirits they called *Angels* or *Messengers* as Moses called them. The Christians imitated the Jews in the application of these names.

It was also the common belief of Jews and Christians, that whilst the demons were everywhere on the earth and in the air, the dry deserts were filled with legions of them. These waste and desolate places being scarcely habitable by man, were claimed by these malignant spirits as their own patrimony. They might with some reason claim it, on the ground, that as they did not, like man, need sustenance from the fruits of the earth, those desolate regions which yielded no sustenance for human flesh and blood, fell naturally to their lot. Whether such was their reasoning or not, certain it is—if we may believe the holy Fathers—that whosoever ventured to take up his residence in the deserts,—especially if he went for religious purposes—was sure to be infested by them in all possible ways; with all manner of alarming sounds and fearful shapes and threatening actions and deceptive allurements. Nowhere would a spiritual warrior have so hard battling with the fiendish hosts, as in those hot and dreary solitudes which were naturally a sort of hell on the earth. But so much the greater was the merit of living there; so much more the glory of defeating the Devil and his legions upon their own ground.

It was also the common belief of Jews and Gentiles, both before and after our Saviour's time, that demons took possession of the bodies of living men, producing madness and epilepsy, and so controlling the man's faculties as to speak and act with his organs. Those so possessed were called *demoniacs*.

Both Jews and Gentiles had also among them certain men who professed to have the power of *exorcising* the demons, that is, of driving them out of the bodies of the possessed, and thus curing the demoniacs of their madness, or epilepsy, or hypochondria, or whatever mental or corporeal disease these indwelling spirits had produced. Our Saviour cured all such cases immediately without form or ceremony, thus exerting what was obviously divine power. But the *exorcists* pretended to produce the same effects by means of certain charms and drugs, administered with much form and ceremony.

The Christians of the third century and after ages, believed that demons still possessed madmen and epileptics, as they had done before; that certain holy monks had, by a long course of ascetism and fighting with demons in the desert, gained such miraculous power over them, as to be able to cast them out like our Saviour. They believed also that pious persons duly authorized and instructed, could expel demons by the forms and ceremonies of exorcism, as the Jews had formerly done. The Christian forms were believed, however, to be much more efficacious than those in use among the Jews and unbelieving Gentiles, because the Christian *exorcists* employed the sign of the holy *cross*, of which the demons were terribly afraid—the name of the Trinity, which they could not bear—and profuse sprinklings of holy-water, which was much more efficacious than that of the Gentiles who were its inventors. Besides these powerful intruments, the Christian exorcists, like their Jewish and heathen predecessors, used sundry forms of prayers to God, adjurations to the demons in every sacred name, and execrations and revilings of these mischievous spirits; who, it was believed, would often retreat from sheer vexation, when they found that the exorcist could out-curse and out-rail them, that is, beat them with their own weapons. By means of this sort, the exorcists could expel the demons not only from persons, but from places and things infested by them. Among the different officers of the church from the fourth century downwards, was the exorcist or devil-driver. He continued to be an established officer in the Roman Catholic Church after the Reformation in the sixteenth century, and bishops occasionally exercised their genius in devising more powerful and demon-terrifying forms of exorcism, long after modern science and biblical knowledge began to be diffused through the nations of Christendom. Why have the Roman Catholic priesthood dropped this part of their infallible system in this country? Or if they have not dropped what Fathers and Popes held for so many ages, why do they keep their exorcists and exorcisms so completely out of the view of the public, that we hear and see nothing of them?

We have mentioned this system of demonology, because it occupies a conspicuous place in the history of monachism, as the reader will see. But we must add that the early Fathers of the church were not unanimous in respect to the efficacy of the *exorcisms* practiced in their time. Origen of the third century and Chrysostom of the fourth, had the good sense to disbelieve in the power of exorcists to cast out demons, though they believed in the existence of demons and in demoniacal possession. But in their opinion demoniacs could be cured only by miraculous power. Thus Origen (Tract 35 in Matth.) says, "If any one ask whether it be proper to adjure demons, we answer, He who sees Jesus commanding demons, and giving [miraculous] power to his disciples, will say that to adjure [exorcise] demons is not according to the power given by the Saviour. It is a Jewish practice." He means that the power given by the Saviour to the apostles, was the power of working miracles; whereas the adjuration of the exorcists was borrowed of the Jews, and was a sort of magical operation. Chrysostom says, "We poor wretches cannot drive away the flies, much less the demons." Some centuries later, however, the great St. Bernard arose, who had power over the flies as well as over Beelzebub, the lord of flies.* The legend concerning him relates, that the flies once proving troublesome in his monastery, he solemnly cursed and anathematized them; and lo! within twenty-four hours, every fly of them was dead.

Ascetism arose in the church early in the second century, and grew by degrees, until it became monachism about the middle of the third century. By the end of this century solitary hermits had begun to multiply in Egypt. By the middle of the fourth century, Cenobites and Anchorites, male and female, had increased

* This is the meaning of the Hebrew name Beelzebub.

in Egypt to a host estimated to number 100,000. Some of them, ere long, became fierce and turbulent, and learned to fight men as well as demons. By this time, too, the monks of Syria and Asia Minor were counted by tens of thousands, and monachism had taken firm hold in Western Europe where Latin was spoken. Shortly afterwards, it had penetrated every nook and corner of the Church. In the sixth century monasteries were established in Britain and Ireland, and even in the Western Isles of Scotland.

After the year 400 it was no longer safe for any man to oppose the monastic system, as some had done before; for the monks were terrible enemies to deal with. They did much to overthrow heathenism and to establish Christianity. They did more to mix heathenism with Christianity, to promote every kind of superstition, and to bring in and sustain the monstrous system of Popish tyranny and persecution. Though in the dark ages of barbarian violence and confusion, they exerted a conservative influence; yet when the dark ages began to pass away, the monastic system became the chief obstacle to the reformation of religion and the general improvement of society.

CHAPTER II.

OF MONACHISM AMONG THE HINDOOS.

§ 1. *General Principles of the Hindoo Religion.*

MONACHISM originated in Eastern Asia a long time—probably fifteen hundred years—before the birth of Christ. Its fountain-head is the ancient superstition of Hindostan or India, one of the primitive seats of human civilization. The people of this country have sacred books, which must be nearly if not quite as ancient as the books of Moses; besides other books of their religion, written after the first, from time to time, in the ages of remote antiquity.

The language of these ancient books is called Sanscrit. Like the Hebrew, Greek, and Latin, it has been for many ages a dead language, and is the parent of most of the living dialects of Hindostan, as the Latin is of several modern languages of Europe.

The most ancient of the Hindoo books are four in number, called Vedas. They are filled, for the most part, with religious precepts, prayers, and hymns. They appear to have been the books of devotion used by the Hindoos in the primitive times of their religion. Like the books of Moses, they bear in their language, style, and matter, the strongest internal evidence of great antiquity.

Next in age to the Vedas, is a book entitled, The Laws of Menu, which unfolds the rules of this ancient religion. Then come a succession of books called Puranas and Shasters,—besides divers more which need not be particularly mentioned.

These books form altogether an extensive library. They teach the doctrines, worship, mythology, and practical rules of this ancient system of religion. This system is on the whole very extensive and complex, and requires the study of many years for one to become thoroughly acquainted with it. We shall give a sketch of its leading principles, so far as may be necessary to show the primitive source of ascetism and monkery. It will be found among the principles of this ancient system of religious philosophy. All the monachism that has appeared in the world may be traced to this one heathenish source. In this and the following chapters, we shall trace these principles with their practical effects, over Eastern Asia and through Egypt and the Greek philosophy into the Jewish, and finally into the Christian, religion, where we see them finally developed into the monachism which exists to this day, and forms a remarkable feature of the Roman Catholic system of Christianity.

Hindoo books teach, that there is *One Infinite Eternal God*, who is the original source of all other beings, and comprehends them all in his universal essence. He is called *Brahm*, which, like Jehovah in the Hebrew, signifies *The Self-existent.*

But this sublime original Godhead is not the object of Hindoo worship. He is thought to be too great for human knowledge. He is hidden from the human understanding in the infinitude of his spiritual nature. He possesses no conceivable attributes, exercises no agency in the affairs of the universe,—but, unconscious of passing events, reposes in the eternal enjoyment of his own existence.

Brahm revealed himself in three forms or persons, called *Brahma*, the Creator, *Vishnu*, the Preserver, and *Siva*, the Destroyer. These three divine persons, considered as emanations from the infinite unknown Godhead, or as distinct unfoldings of the Universal Being,—constitute the *Hindoo Trinity*, or *Trimurti*, as they call them. Each of them has several names descriptive of his attributes; and each is of both sexes; for every Hindoo god has his female counterpart, who is essentially one with himself. These three gods with their united goddesses, are the supreme objects of Hindoo worship, sometimes under one name and sometimes under another. It seems that the worshippers were in early times divided into sects; some preferring the worship of one, some, of another, of these divine persons, to the exclusion of the rest. Each sect assigned to the favorite god certain attributes originally appropriated to another. Hence no little confusion appears in the modern accounts of their distinct attri butes.

Besides the supreme Trimurti, the Hindoo mythology embraces many gods and godessess of divers ranks and characters; and these all have their worshippers—at least the more distinguished among them have;—each individual choosing the particular objects of his worship, according to his fancy or the custom of his family or sect.

About their gods, their actions and transformations, the Hindoos of old invented a thousand allegories and fables, monstrous and absurd; of which we need say nothing more, except that Vishnu, the Preserver, the second person of their trinity, is said to have gone through nine incarnations or births as animal or man, each time to effect some work of salvation on the earth, and that he will become incarnate once more, for the purpose of delivering mankind from their sins, and of renovating the world.

The Hindoo books teach that *all living creatures have immortal souls*. Some also assign souls to vegetables and even to minerals, as the ancient Egyptians did. All souls are considered as emanations or particles drawn from the universal spirit of Brahm; which have been separated for a time from the common source of being, as drops from the ocean; but all will be finally absorbed into it again, and thus loose their separate existence as individuals.

They teach, but somewhat obscurely, that some of the spirits of the heavenly world revolted and fell to the lower regions;

where they are condemned to punishment, like the fallen angels of our theology. Certain it is, however, that spiritual beings of different ranks are believed to inhabit the regions above and below the earth, and that the lower ones are more or less malignant.

The doctrine of the *Metempyschosis*, or *Transmigration of Souls* from one body to another, is a leading doctrine of the Hindoo theology. As every living creature on the earth, is supposed to have an immortal soul; so it is supposed, that souls after death pass into new bodies, of the same or different kinds from those which they left. A brute's soul may become a man's,—or, contrariwise, a soul may be degraded from a human body to that of a brute or an insect, or as some books teach, even that of a vegetable or mineral. Of course the faculties of the soul are more or less unfolded, according to the nature of the body which it occupies; its powers of reason and sentiment can be exercised in a human body, but are more or less cramped, or entirely suppressed, in bodies of inferior organization.

All souls were originally pure, when they emanated from the Universal Spirit; but *became defiled with sin by imprisonment in material bodies*, and by subjection to the passions which spring from their connection with earthly things. All the gross matter of the world, is believed to have a polluting influence upon the spirits that are invested with it; unless they overcome this evil influence by a resolute resistance and a severe mortification of the flesh. But few or none avoid defilement in their first incarnation, or imprisonment in a human body. Therefore, when they die, they transmigrate into other bodies of brutes or men, according as their sins are greater or less. Those who have been great criminals, are punished in hell for a time, and then become snakes, toads, or other loathsome animals—perhaps many of them in succession—before they gain admission into human bodies again, and have another trial as men.

Every human soul is now defiled with the sins of a former state, as well as with those which it may have contracted in its present body. *Human life in this world is a state of probation, in which the soul has opportunity to work off its pollutions*, and exalt its future condition, in the manner prescribed by the holy books. Its defilement comes from the body, and from the material world through the bodily senses. It must labor to purify itself, therefore, by counteracting the influence of the body and of the sensible world. It must subdue the bodily appetites and desires—mortify all the senses—deny itself the pleasures of the world—separate itself as much as possible from material things—keep the body still—forget, if it can, all the things of time and sense—shut itself up in silent abstraction—float away in spiritual contemplations; and endeavor to lose its individual consciousness, by melting into the infinitude of its parent Godhead, as a vapor loses its distinct existence in the viewless expanse of the serene atmosphere.

When by such exercises the soul has purified itself from carnal defilements, and spiritualized itself into its original nature, it is released at death from further wandering through bodies; it ascends to the superior heavens, where it bathes in the pure essence of light; and finally reaches supreme beatitude, by losing its individual existence in the universal source of being; as the rain-drop is lost on the ocean from which it originated.

§ 2. *Of the Hindoo Doctrine of Penances or Ascetic Purification of the Soul.*

Learned writers differ in respect to the principle, on which the Hindoo ascetic performs his acts of austere devotion.

The Hindoo devotee, when he tortures his senses, is generally understood to be doing penance, or making atonement for sin. But some late writers, especially Ward, the missionary, affirm, that the Hindoo does not consider himself as a penitent, when he does these acts of self-mortification—but as a meritorious saint, who thus exalts himself above the common lot of mortals, and that on the ground of these performances, he assumes a proud superiority over the vulgar herd of his fellow men.

These views are not essentially inconsistent. The ascetic devotions of the Hindoos may be, and are probably considered to be, both penitential and meritorious. So far as they remove guilt and liability to punishment, they are penances; so far as they purify the soul, exalt its dignity and promote its spiritual happiness, they are meritorious. The devotee who both atones for his sin and merits happiness by voluntary sufferings, may on both accounts esteem himself holier and worthier than others, and assume a proud superiority over them.

We shall now proceed to give some account of the ascetic doctrines taught by the ancient Hindoo books.

The laws of Menu, written probably a thousand years before the Christian era, give the following directions to the man who would purify himself from sin, and become a saint of high degree.

"Let him seclude himself from the world, and gain the favor of the gods, by fasting, subduing the lusts of the flesh and mortifying the senses."

One would think on comparing this general direction with the early monachism of the Church, that the Christian monks of the fourth century had been trained under the laws of Menu, and were ambitious to become saints of the Hindoo religion.

But Menu gives more particular directions to the candidate for high saintship.

"Let him crawl (says Menu) backwards and forwards on his belly;—or let him stand all day long on his toes. Let him remain always sitting or always standing; only at sunrise, noon, and sunset, let him go to the water and bathe himself."

There we discover a remarkable difference between the ancient Hindoo ascetics and their Christian successors. The Hindoos associated holiness with personal cleanliness; the Christian monks despised the body too much to give it the honor of ablution. Hence they grew filthier without, as they grew holier within. But the modern Fakirs of Hindostan have learned to be as filthy as the monkish saints of the fourth century.

But says Menu in continuation, "Let him in the heat of summer kindle five fires about him. When it rains let him bare himself to the storm where it pelts the hardest. In the winter, let him wear a wet garment. So let him rise by degrees in the strength of his penances."

Here is monkish ascetism in perfection, differing slightly in mode, but agreeing perfectly in spirit, with that of the Fathers of the Desert, glorified by the Fathers of the Church in the fourth and fifth centuries, as the perfect pattern of the Christian life.

But, as the last sentence quoted from Menu implies, there were degrees of saintship among the Hindoos.

A man might become a Yogi, or common saint, by withdrawing into solitude at forty or fifty years of age, either for life or for a term of years. If he began young, he might, after a certain number of years, return into the social world, and enjoy the respect and profit of his sanctity during the remainder of his days. But he who consecrated all his remaining years to monachism, and became what was called a forest-anchorite, attained to a higher degree of sanctity. One of the sacred books teaches, that he was too holy to be touched without sacrilege, and that his curse and his blessing had miraculous power.

The highest degree—that of a Sannyasi—could be attained only by twenty years of total seclusion from the world, and the complete abstraction of the mind from worldly thoughts and affections. Then the soul was prepared, without farther transmigration, to ascend to heaven, and after bathing in celestial light until the last tinge of earthly defilement was purged away, to consummate its destiny by absorption into the Divine Nature. A saint of this degree had such power with the gods, that they would instantly comply, not only with his formal prayers, but even with his slightest wishes.*

Having given this general sketch of the subject, we shall now give a more particular account of the Hindoo system of ascetical

* The above sketch is from Bohlen: Das Alte Indien. ch. ii.

sanctification. To make the account more intelligible, we shall first notice the Hindoo institution of casts, to which the people have adhered from the remotest times until this day.

The whole population were originally divided into four casts or orders, of which the higher possessed privileges that the lower durst not exercise. By intermarriage of the people of different casts, a large number of mixed casts were formed, each of which, like the original four, had certain employments assigned them, and had certain privileges and disabilities.

Of the four original casts, the Brahmins are the highest. They are the sacred cast; and they have the exclusive privilege of exercising the priestly office, and superintending the affairs of religion and learning. From them the Hindoo religion is called Brahminism. They pretend that they were formed out of Brahma the creator's head, and are therefore entitled to rule and guide the whole people. The three inferior casts, namely, the military cast, that of the husbandmen and artisans, and lastly, that of the servants,—were formed respectively from the breast and arms, from the thighs, and from the feet of the creator.

Ascetic saintship, as might be expected, has been found chiefly, though not exclusively, among the Brahmins. Many Yogis or common saints have been of other casts; but the Sannyasis are generally, if not exclusively, Brahmins.

The Hindoo Shasters, or holy books, describe four degrees or states of probation for the Brahmins who aspire to regular saintship. These degrees are adapted to the age of the probationer. They are as follows:

First degree; Brahm Charee.

This is entered by the young Brahmin, sometimes, in early boyhood. Under an experienced preceptor he studies the Vedas diligently; exercises himself in prayer, and learns to discipline his passions by abstaining from women, from anger, envy and revenge, and by acquiring the love of truth and other virtues. At night he accustoms himself to sleep little and that upon straw, or upon the skin of an animal, under the covert of a tree. His food is of the plainest sort, and he avoids pleasant amusements, such as singing, dancing, and games of every sort. Morning and evening he practices ablution by dipping and sprinkling himself, and repeating many prayers. He wears also a particular sort of plain dress.

In this state of initiatory saintship, the young devotee continues from five to twelve years, before he enters upon the

Second degree; called Gerishth.

When the probationer has completed his first degree, he may either return to his father's house, or proceed to this higher degree of sanctity, in which he can acquire much additional merit.

In this degree the exercises of the former were aggravated: the ablutions with their prayers and ceremonies, were increased. Most of the night was spent in contemplating the moon and stars and vault of heaven, with longing to mount up to the region of those bright orbs. In the first degree the devotee lived sparely on charity: in the second degree he lived on what he could glean from the fields, or in failure of this, he begged a little rice, a part of which he threw into the fire as an offering to the Deutah (deified saint) and to the dead. The dress was somewhat changed.

Third degree; called Banperisth.

When a Brahmin advances to this degree, he gives up all family cares, and retires finally from the world into some solitude, where he builds himself a cell or a grotto. If his wife through affection desire to accompany him, she may; but then all sexual intercourse is at an end, and they become as cold as the rocks on which they repose.

"Here the hoary devotee—wraps his aged limbs in a vestment made of bark or leaves. He never cuts his hair or pares his nails. His ablutions with their attendant ceremonies are now trebled. Solitary and forlorn, he hangs down his head, bending under the weight of imaginary crimes. With reverential awe he reads and meditates, silently and assiduously on the holy Vedas. At night he lies on the bare ground. In the summer he sits often for days and weeks beneath the broiling sun, with four fires built around him. In the rainy season he sits exposed to the weather. In the winter he sits all night in cold water. He fasts all the day and eats only in the evening. His only food is dried fruits and grain that grows wild, and these prepared by merely soaking them in water. If his supply fails, he goes to a town and begs a little rice, and then returns to his solitude.

"If worn down with labors, he desires to end his life, he may travel east or north, until he falls down and expires, or he may hang or drown himself at once. He is then sure of eternal happiness."

Fasting is one of the chief exercises of the Hindoo saints. The Holy Books prescribe a great variety of regular fasts, some of which are of long duration and intensely severe. In one of these fasts, the devotee is neither to eat nor drink during twelve days and nights. In another, he drinks only warm water. In another, he builds a fire before his cell-door, where he sits and inhales the hot air and smoke. There is another of fifteen days, during which he lives only upon leaves, seeds, &c.; and another of a week, during five days of which he lives on the produce of the cow, to wit—first, the milk; second, the curds; third, the ghee or clarified butter; fourth, the urine; fifth, the dung.

While fasting, every votary, must abstain from all sensual indulgence, all amusements, and all personal comforts, such as shaving, anointing himself, lying on anything except the bare ground.

We come now to the highest, which is the fourth degree, called Asherum.

This is the state of the Sannyasi, who has reached perfect saintship by regular degrees, according to the precepts of the Holy Books. It is the sacred cast of Brahmins, especially, to whom these precepts are given. The Yogi is a voluntary or amateur saint. He does not confine himself to any prescribed form, but exercises his own genius and fancy in the adoption or invention of such modes of self-torture, as will best satisfy his enthusiastic aspirations after holiness, or give him most eclat among the multitudes to whom he exhibits his feats of saintly endurance.

The ancient Greeks called both Sannyasis and Yogis by the general name of Gymnosophists. But the Brahmin Sannyasi does not wander about, naked and filthy; nor display himself to the public gaze like the mad Yogi, who treats his vile clay with all possible contempt as the prison of his soul. The Sannyasi is distinguished by a calm, silent dignity, and by his secluded manner of life in woods and solitudes, where the world sees him not.

He aims to subdue the passions by subduing the body. He has discarded all connection with family and friends. He throws off all clothing but a wrapper about his waist. With a staff in one hand, and a pitcher in the other, he hies to the desert, never to return. Fasting and miserable he is absorbed in contemplations of the Deity, and never speaks except to pronounce the mysterious word Awan, which is the commencement of the Vedas. His food is wild fruits, his drink water. The business of his life is mental prayer and intense contemplation, by which his soul is abstracted from material things, and so united to the Deity as to endue him with a degree of divine power. He exercises an energy that is felt through the universe. By means of this divine energy he can call down the stars, and raise demons from the lowest hell.*

The Sannyasis believe that they could even disembody the soul, and taking an ethereal flight as pure spirits, could return again at pleasure to the body. When we consider the enthusiasm of these men, and their habits of intense contemplation, we are not surprised that they should take a fit of mental abstraction, in which the body and all visible things around them were forgotten, for an actual flight of the soul into the regions whose imaginary scenes were conceived with the vividness of reality.

Father Bouchet in the *Lettres Edificantes et Curieuses*, tells a remarkable story founded on this notion.

An ancient Indian prince, who possessed the power of volun-

* This notion of the miraculous power acquired by means of extraordinary mortification of the body and exercises of devotion, came with Monachism into the Christian church. Every great monkish saint became a miracle-worker.

tary metempsychosis, used, when he took his voyages through the heavens, to leave his body in the care of a servant. The servant, by close observation, at last was able to learn the form of prayer, called Mandiran, by which his master disengaged his soul from his body. He soon took advantage of this discovery. The next time that his master took a flight, he disengaged his soul from his own body, and transferred it to that of his master. To prevent a dangerous use of his forsaken body by the soul of his master on his return, he cut off the head and carried it away. Thus secured, he took possession of the prince's throne and bed; no one being able to detect the imposture.

When the hapless spirit returned and perceived how he had been defrauded of his throne and his queen, he retired full of grief and dismay to a grove, which he filled with his desolate wailings. The goddess of his former devotion, probably Bhavani, the Indian Venus, took compassion on him, as the story has it, though it was an ill-judged compassion, and prepared him the beautiful body of a parrot, in which he flew away to court, where to his sorrow and vexation he beheld his servant in possession of his rights and of his lovely queen. The hapless bird flew about through the palace, until he was caught by a servant and presented to the queen, who admired his splendid plumage and kept him in her chamber. This only aggravated his sufferings; for now he was imprisoned where he had to behold the caresses bestowed by the queen upon his treacherous slave, and all the mortifying circumstances of his irremediable loss.

The secret was not discovered till some ages afterwards, when a Sannyasi, who, by the power of absorption, could penetrate into the past, the present and the future,* revealed it as a warning to the sovereigns of India, not to trust implicitly to their servants.

The Sannyasi, when at his devotions, beholds all the alluring and all the appalling objects of nature with unmoved indifference

* This wonderful power of penetration, acquired by the Hindoo Sannyasis, was also attained in later ages by some Christian Sannyasis, or monks of the highest order of sanctity.

His soul is fixed on the supreme Brahm. He sacrifices every human feeling to devotion. The pouring rains of the tropic, and the freezing snows of the Himmalayah are alike unfelt, when they beat upon the anchorite's naked body. Emaciated with hunger, he is not tempted by delicate viands. Sweet odors, and sweet sounds of earth, yield him no pleasure. Voluptuous nymphs may display their wanton attitudes before him, without exciting the slightest desire in his heart. His soul has become insensible to all earthly delights and sufferings. Corporeal sensations affect not his soul, he has mortified his flesh till it can feel no more; and his soul can now soar undisturbed to the celestial regions, and bathe in the essence of Deity. Insensible of change, abstracted from material things, and immersed in the Divine infinitude, it has reached the summit of spiritual sanctification, and awaits only its final release from its clay prison, to ascend to the regions of bliss, where it has heretofore dwelt in contemplation. There it will bathe its ethereal essence in uncreated light, until it is finally absorbed in the Divine source of all being. This is the Hindoo's idea of supreme felicity.

After having gone through the four degrees of penance, the Sannyasi sometimes resolves to burn himself as a sacrifice to the Deity. This is permitted by the Holy Books, and is deemed highly meritorious in a Sannyasi. The sacrifice is made with great pomp and ceremony.

Many drown themselves, or are drowned by their friends, in the purifying waters of the Ganges.*

Ward says that there are no such ascetics now as those above described, if there ever were such. At present there may be no Sannyasis in the woods and deserts of India; but we shall produce evidence hereafter, that they did exist in ancient times.

* The foregoing account of the degrees of Hindoo saintship, is taken chiefly from Maurice's Indian Antiquities, Chapters 3 & 5 of vol. iii. On the Hindoo religion, his chief authority is the Ayeen Akbery, one of the holy books.

We add some further particulars from Ward,* respecting the Hindoo religion.

The Hindoo Shasters teach what the Christian Scriptures do not—that is, *certain rites for the repose of the soul after death.*

The soul after death takes a little body not larger than one's thumb, and remains in the custody of Yumu, judge of the dead. When the time of punishment arrives, this little body is enlarged and made capable of enduring torments.

The performance of a ceremony called Shradhu, delivers the deceased sufferer at the end of one year, and transfers him to heaven, where he receives the reward of his meritorious actions, and afterwards transmigrates to another body, of the sort for which the general character of his former life has fitted him. Without the Shradhu the deceased remains in his suffering state, and cannot transmigrate until the term of his punishment is fulfilled.†

The ceremonies of the Shradhu begin on the eleventh day after the decease; are continued monthly, and concluded at the expiration of a year. The service consists of offerings and prayers for the dead, with certain prescribed forms and ceremonies.

Hence it appears that the notion of purgatorial torments after death, and of shortening their duration by prayers and offerings for the dead, was not an invention of the Christian Fathers of the fourth and fifth centuries, but was borrowed, like most other corruptions of Christianity, from the heathen nations of antiquity. The most important of them originated in the East Indies and in Egypt. How they came thence into the Church, we shall attempt to show in some following chapters.

In the ancient Hindoo books we find also the doctrine of ceremonial uncleanness by contact with certain persons or things

* Ward's View of the History, Literature, and Religion of the Hindoos, vol. ii. book iv. ch. 2.

† If the reader will pay attention as he proceeds, he will be surprised to find nearly all the Roman Catholic superstitions among the more ancient idolators of Eastern Asia.

deemed unclean, and by the occurrence of certain states of the body, by which it was supposed to be defiled. An unclean person could not partake of any religious worship or ceremony, until he was duly purified in the manner prescribed by the holy books.

The ancient common law of the Hindoos also designated a multitude of offences, for which the offender was bound to make atonement. Some of the designated offences were violations of common morality; others were founded on the distinction of cast, and on superstitious notions and doctrines of religion taught in the sacred books, such as killing an insect or a cow, eating onions, &c. The atonements were various, such as paying fines, restitution of property gotten by theft or fraud, religious offerings, voluntary mortifications of the body, penitential prayers, and repetitions of the name of God, &c. The ancient Hindoo penances were therefore similar in principle and in practice to those prescribed to penitents now by the Roman Catholic priests. The penalty of omitting to perform these penances was also the same, namely, punishment in a purgatorial hell, with the addition among the Hindoos, of transmigration into the body of some noxious animal or miserable man. For example he who kills an animal by strangling, or laughs at a Puranah at the time of its recital, will, after enduring infernal torments, be born a snake, then a tiger, then a cow, a white heron, a crow, and a man having the asthma.

The Ugnee Purana assigns to those evil men who lose human birth, eight millions of inferior births before they can become men again. They are to pass through millions of states of minerals and vegetables; then they gradually ascend through fishes, insects, birds and beasts to the dignity of men again.*

As our works on Christian theology agree in fundamentals, but differ more or less in details; so do the Hindoo Puranahs; which being works of the Hindoo fathers, expound in different ways the fundamental doctrines of the Vedas. In this Puranah we find the doctrine that every being, minerals not excepted, has a soul.

* Ward's View, book v. ch. 1.

In this as in many other particulars, the ancient Egyptian philosophy agreed with that of the Hindoos.

A consequence of this doctrine of transmigration is, that the Hindoos consider the sufferings of the present life as punishments for sins committed in a prior state. Hence, when they become diseased, many of them sit down in despair, supposing human remedies to be vain for an evil sent by divine justice.

§ 3. *Of the Future Judgment, Heaven and Hell.*

The doctrine of *judgment after death* is taught in the Pudnu Puranah after this manner.*

Yumu is judge of the dead. He dwells on a floating island at the southern extremity of the earth. The meritorious are led to his seat by a delightful road. On the way they are entertained with the songs and dances of the heavenly courtesans, and with choral hymns chanted by inferior Gods in praise of the superior. At intervals are houses of refreshment, where cool fountains play, and delicious viands are set out for their entertainment. Along the road-side limpid waters are adorned with lilies, and tall trees, embowering the ways, drop showers of odorous blossoms along their path. The road is frequented by heavenly beings marching in splendid processions, accompanied by bands of singers, who make the woods and waters vocal with their hymns of praise and of gladness. Such are the entertainments of the saints on their way to the judgment seat.

The wicked have on the contrary a long and painful journey to undergo.

Sometimes they have to travel over burning pavements;—then to wade through hot embers or scorching sands;—then to tread over beds of glowing sharp-edged gravel. Now and then showers of cutting and piercing instruments, or of red-hot cinders, or of scalding rain, pour down upon them. Hot winds blister their skins and scorch their lungs. They drop into dark wells, or stumble through gloomy passages over rough stones, amongst

* Ward; book v. ch. 2.

which serpents crawl and nestle. Another while, they must force their way through a dense thicket of spiny shrubs; and then again over heaps of gory clods, rotten bones and putrifying flesh, alternating with piles of thorns and iron burs. They meet tigers, jackals, wild elephants, terrible giants, and other fearful monsters. They travel naked, with disheveled hair, parched lips and throats, covered with blood and dirt; wailing and shrieking as they go, with faces of horror and despair. Sometimes they are dragged along by thongs tied round their wrists, or fastened by holes in their noses or heels, or knotted in their hair. Sometimes they are dragged along with head and heels tied together. When at last they arrive, they behold Yumu clothed with terror. He is two hundred and forty miles high: His eyes are like two fiery lakes: Rays of dazzling splendor shoot from his body: A flame issues from his mouth: The sound of his breathing is like the roar of a tempest. In his right hand he grasps an iron club; and when he utters the sentence of punishment, his voice is like the thunder that dissolves the universe. Then having reproved them for their crimes, he drives them with his club to the different hells to which they are condemned.

Future Happiness,* is, according to the Puranahs, of four degrees: 1st. That enjoyed in the heaven of the inferior gods: 2d. Deification, by which a saint becomes a Deutah or inferior god:† 3d. Dwelling in the highest heavens among the superior gods; and 4th. Absorption in the universal spirit of Brahm.

The descriptions of heaven in the Puranahs are in the oriental style; full of gold and precious stones, cool waters, shady bowers of bloom, and images of sensual delight.

The meritorious works that carry a man to heaven, are chiefly such as profit the Brahmins on the earth—says Ward;—such as ceremonial observances, some of which, as exhibited in the temples, are unmentionably obscene. This statement is true, so far as it goes. But missionaries who write of the religion and of the

* Ward; book v. ch. 3. † Like the Roman Catholic saint-gods.

priests that they are laboring to overthrow, can seldom represent them impartially. The Hindoo superstition is bad enough, when justly considered; but Ward should have in this place remembered the ascetic mortifications of the Brahmins. If they impose on others for their own benefit, they also punish themselves severely by their monkish austerities.

As to *Absorption*, the highest state of Hindoo felicity; it is considered as the only state which secures the soul against farther transmigration; because the soul then ceases to have a separate or individual existence. It is lost in the universal spirit of Brahm; and like him, or as a reunited portion of him, enjoys eternal sleep without ideas or consciousness.

In a sacred book entitled Bhagavat Gheeta, Krishnu—that is Vishnu under another name—praises the man "who forsaketh every desire of his heart, is happy within himself, without affection, indifferent to good or evil, to whom pleasure and pain, gold, iron, and stones, are alike." The person whose very nature, as they say, is absorbed in divine meditation,—whose life resembles a sweet sleep, unconscious and undisturbed;—who desires nothing, not even God, and who is thus changed into the image of the ever-blessed, obtains absorption into Brahm.

There are, however, some followers of Vishnu, who do not seek absorption, but a conscious happiness with him.

The practices leading to absorption, have been already mentioned—such as retiring from the world, seclusion in a forest, fasting, prayer, undivided contemplation, &c.

The ascetics did not always succeed in killing their passions, for the Puranahs relate many instances to the contrary. Vashisthu, one of these saints, inflicted on himself incredible severities; yet in the midst of his devotions, (says the Mahabharatu,) he fell in love with one of the heavenly courtezans, and lived with her five thousand years. Purasheru, an ascetic, violated the daughter of another ascetic, while she was ferrying him over a river. From this act sprang the famous Vyasu, author of the Mahabharat. Other instances are related of their committing acts of rage and violence. Brigu, for example, kicked the god Vishnu on the breast. Javalee, an ascetic, stands charged with stealing cow's flesh at a sacrifice, and when search was made for the beef, changing it into onions, to avoid detection. Hence onions are forbidden food to the Hindoos.

Future Punishments are described in a book called the Shree-Chaga-vutu. There are various hells for the punishment of different classes of transgressors. The following sketches of a few will suffice.

Adulterers, thieves, &c., are to be cast into the hell Tamisru, and continually famished and beaten. Defrauders are to be put into a hell of darkness; gluttons are to be cast into a hell of boiling oil. Contemners of the Vedas and of the Brahmins are to be plunged into a hell of burning metal, for three and a half millions of years. He who injures a man of superior order is to be torn by swine. The unmerciful are to be tormented in a hell of snakes, flies, lice, and other vermin. A Brahmin or king who drinks spirits, is to be cast into pans of liquid fire. He who despises a religious devotee, shall stick fast in mud, with his head downwards. He who causes sorrow to others, is to be bitten by snakes with five heads, &c.*

From these specimens the reader can judge of the Hindoo notions of retributive justice, and of the comparative demerit of crimes. As the Hindoos had no idea of eternal punishment, they considered those of all the hells as purgatorial.

We have now put the reader in possession of so much of the Hindoo system of religion, as will enable him to understand the grounds on which the Yogis and Sannyasis practice those ascetical austerities, which have struck the attention of foreigners for more than two thousand years past. If we examine this system philosophically, we shall discover that the whole resolves itself into the following fundamental principles:

* Ward; book V. ch. 4.

1. Matter and spirit are essentially distinct and incompatible substances.

2. Matter is essentially evil and impure; spirit is essentially good and pure; but capable of defilement from contact with material bodies.

3. All spiritual beings, from the highest to the lowest, are emanations or individualized portions of the eternal and universal spirit called Brahm, which has no personal properties, no action nor consciousness, but is the essence of all beings that have them.

4. Individual spirits become souls by assuming material bodies; and every such body is endued with a soul, which may transmigrate from one body to another.

5. By inhabiting an animated body, the soul is subjected, more or less, to the impure desires and passions generated by material objects, operating upon the soul through the bodily senses. Thus the soul contracts impurities; it is debased by earthly affections, and the spiritual repose which constitutes its true happiness, is destroyed by the agitation of its corporeal desires and passions.

6. All true happiness consists in a calm, unchanging repose of the spirit.

7. To attain this state of blessed repose, the soul in the flesh must purify itself, and atone for its offences, by mortifying the corporeal senses, subduing the desires which disturb it, and dwelling in fixed contemplation of the divine essence from which its being is derived, and in which alone it can find a pure and undisturbed repose.

These principles can be further reduced to two, which run through the theory and practice of the whole system.

1. Matter is essentially evil.

2. The happiness of the soul consists in repose, or exemption from all the affections and passions that spring from matter, and disturb the repose of the soul.

Hence to reduce the body to insensibility by suffering, and thus to deliver the soul from its influence, is the Hindoo way of sancti fication. All that is done for this end is meritorious, purges the soul from sin, and procures the favor of the gods.

§ 4. *Practices of the Hindoo Devotees, as observed by Foreigners in all ages.*

Let us now see how the ascetic doctrines of the ancient Hindoo books have been carried out in practice, both in ancient and in modern times.

The earliest accounts by foreigners have come down to us from the Greeks.

When Alexander the Great, three hundred and thirty years before Christ, conquered the western parts of the country called India, from the river Indus, he found several sorts of monkish ascetics there. Some Greek scholars who accompanied his army, or who conversed afterwards with persons who had been in the country, wrote accounts of the wonderful things seen in that distant region, of which the Greeks had previously heard nothing but vague reports. Some things which these writers related from hearsay, were certainly fabulous; but they gave unquestionably true accounts of the Hindoo monks, whom they called *Gymnosophists* or *Naked Philosophers*. Both the ancient Hindoo books, and the notices of travellers in later ages, fully confirm their accounts, however strangely they sounded in Grecian ears.

From these writers of Alexander's time, whose works are now lost, Strabo, the Greek geographer, about three hundred years later, compiled the account which we shall quote pretty fully from his pages. We have to remark, however, that the Greeks never penetrated as far as the valley of the Ganges, where the Hindoo religion originated, and where its institutions flourished in their highest perfection. Their accounts are, therefore, less full and satisfactory, than otherwise they might have been. Yet they are substantially accurate, and highly interesting from their antiquity. Few modern travellers have taken such intelligent views of these Naked Philosophers.

The Greek writers dignified these oriental monks with the title of philosophers, as they did every class of men who professed to live by rule. So did the Greek Fathers of the Church many ages afterwards call Christian monachism by the honorable name of philosophy.

But we now proceed to give the substance of what Strabo relates from preceding writers concering the Hindoo monks.*

"Megasthenes says that there are two sects of Indian philosophers, the Brachmans† and the Garmans. The Brachmans live in the woods not far from cities. Their manner of life is simple. They sleep on straw or skins, use no animal food and abstain from women. They attend to serious instructions, and impart them to such as desire to hear. But the hearers, while the speaker is addressing them, must not speak, nor hawk, nor spit. When they have lived thirty-seven years from boyhood as anchorites, they return to their possessions, live pleasantly, dress well, and, if they choose, marry wives, that they may rear children for the same mode of life."

"Aristobulus, another writer, says that he saw two Brachmans; the elder had his head shaven, but the younger wore his hair. Both were followed by disciples. They spent a part of their time in the market-places, where, on account of the esteem in which they were held for their counsels, they received plentiful gifts of oil, honey, and corn. When they came to Alexander they ate dinner, standing at his table; and to give a specimen of their patience, they withdrew to a neighboring place, where the one lay upon his back and exposed himself to the sun and the rain. The other stood upon one leg, holding in each hand a billet of wood three cubits long. When he got tired, he stood upon the other leg; and so he continued the whole day This one said that he intended to persevere in his ascetic life during forty years."

"Onesicritus says that he was sent by Alexander to visit some of these philosophers who went naked, as he had heard, and were much respected. He found them two or three miles from the city. Each was naked, motionless in one position, sitting or lying

* Strabo, Book xv., ch. 1.

† Brahmins.

the whole day exposed to the sun, though it was too hot for others to bear."

Such, according to the authors quoted by Strabo, were the Brachmans, or Naked Philosophers. We easily recognize in them the Sannyasis of the Hindoo books.

Of the Garmans, or, as others call them, Sarmans or Samaneans, the more respectable sort were called by the Greeks Hylobioi, or Woods-philosophers, because they lived in the woods upon plants and wild fruits, and had no clothing but leaves of trees. They also abstained from women and wine.

Next in respectability to the Woods-philosophers were the Physicians. These were simple but not wild in their manner of life. They fed on rice and cornmeal, which was freely given them. They were hospitably entertained in the houses of the people; *for they could make women bear many children, and male or female, just as they pleased, with their medicines.** Both these sorts of Garmans exercised themselves in voluntary pains and sufferings. They would continue the whole day motionless in one posture.

But there were others who practised soothsaying and charms, and were skilled in the use of incantations for the dying. These went about the villages and cities begging. Some were more decent in person and manners than the rest. These like the others preached about hell; but in a way to promote religion and virtue. Some carried women along to philosophize with them, but they had no sexual intercourse.

Such is Strabo's account of the Hindoo ascetics or monks, taken from writers who lived about six hundred years before monachism appeared in the Christian Church. They agreed in every essential particular with the Christian monks of the fourth century. They professed abstinence from women and wine.

* Some of the Christian monks even as early as the fourth century. and many of them in the fifth century, as the Fathers tell us, had this same gift of making barren women fruitful. Many longing wives resorted to them for this purpose. But it does not appear that the holy men used any artificial medicines.

They rejected all pleasant food, and lived abstemiously on the spontaneous products of nature. They wore little clothing, and lay on the ground. Most of them lived in solitude, exercising themselves in patient suffering and silent devotion.

But some of the sects mentioned by Strabo were composed chiefly of roguish impostors, who practiced beggary and quackery, —who debauched credulous women, and plundered both men and women under hypocritical pretences of devotion, and knavish pretences of medical skill and magical power.

After the time of Strabo, the Greeks acquired little additional knowledge of the Hindoo philosophy. About two hundred years later, Clement of Alexandria, a Platonic Christian writer, speaks of the same two classes of ascetics. In his Stromata, Book I., he says, there are two kinds of Indian philosophers, the Sarmans and the Brachmans. Of the former some are called Allobioi, who inhabit no cities nor houses. They are clothed with the bark of trees, eat acorns and wild berries, and drink water with their hands. They know nothing of marriage, nor of the procreation of children.

In the third book of the same work, Clement says,—" Many Brachmans, eat no living creature and drink no wine. Some of them take food daily, some only every third day. But they set no value on life, and despise death, believing it to be a regeneration. Those of the Indians called Semnoi—that is, venerable—go naked all their lives. They exercise truth, predict the future, and worship a certain pyramid under which they believe the bone of a certain god to repose. But neither the Gymnosophists no those called Semnoi use women, thinking this to be unnatural an iniquitous. Hence they keep themselves chaste. They hav also virgins called Semnai. They appear also to observe celestia phenomena, and from them to predict certain future events."— So far Clement.

The term Semnoi which he uses, is a Greek word signifyir venerable. He evidently confounds this word with the nan Samanæi or Sarmanæ, which are but other forms of the nan

Garmanæ, which Strabo applies to the second class of Indian ascetics. The mention of the monumental pyramid, or tomb of a god, worshipped by the Samaneans, indicates that these were Boodhists, of whom we shall give an account in the next chapter.

The Greek philosopher Porphyry flourished in the third century, about sixty years after Clement. He says that the Brachmans live, some in the mountains, and some on the banks of the Ganges: the former eat fruits, milk, and herbs; the latter fruits and rice. —Palladius and Ambrose, two Christian Fathers of the fourth century, say, that they undergo the severest philosophical exercises, study frugality and piety, sing hymns to God, contemn transient things, and renounce all the pleasures and conveniences of life.

The other sect are called Samanaei by Porphyry, Garmans by Strabo, and Sarmans by others, as already mentioned. Bardesanes relates that persons admitted into their community, renounced their worldly goods, left their wives and children, if they had any, to the care of others, shaved all the hair from their bodies, and wore a monastic gown. They lived without the city in houses and temples. They had stewards who provided for their wants. At the ringing of bells they assembled in the house for prayer, after which each had his dish of rice given to him, with the addition, if he desired it, of some herbs and fruits.

This description applies to the modern system of Cenobite nonachism among the Boodhists of Eastern Asia, and seems to emonstrate, both that the Samaneans were Boodhists, and that heir monastic system existed before the time of Bardesanes, bout the year 172 of the Christian era. But it should be bserved, that Diodorus Siculus, a Greek historian, who lived few years before Christ, relates in his second book substantially e same thing of the Brachmans. If he did not err in applying to them, as he probably did, then it would appear that the rachmans had also, at that early period, a regular system of nobite monachism. But as neither the Hindoo books, nor any other ancient or modern writer recognises such a system as existing among them, the reasonable conclusion seems to be, that Diodorus ascribed to the one sect what properly belonged, even in his time, to the other.

We come now to the reports of travellers who have visited India since the Christian era. The earliest of these on record are the travels of two Mahometans of Western Asia, probably Arabia. They were translated from the Arabic by Renaudot, and may be found in the seventh volume of Pinkerton's Collection of Voyages and Travels.

The earlier of these travellers visited India about the year o our Lord 850. He gives the following graphic sketch of th Hindoo ascetics.

" There are in the Indies men who profess to live in the wood and mountains, and to despise what other men most value. The abstain from everything but such wild herbs and fruits as gro in the woods. The put iron buckles on their privy parts to pre serve their chastity. Some of them are quite naked, or hav only a leopard's skin thrown over them. In this plight they kee standing with their faces towards the sun. I formerly saw one this posture ; and when, sixteen years afterwards, I returned the Indies, I found him still in the same posture, and was a tonished that his eyes had not been put out by the sun's heat."

Here we find unchanged the naked philosophers of Alexande time, nearly twelve centuries before.

About the year 1280, Marco Polo, the famous Venetian t veller, found them still unchanged. Speaking of the Hin Brahmins (the Brachmans of Strabo) he says : " They are great abstinence and long life. There are some devotees am them, called Tangui, who go altogether naked, live austerely rub their bodies with an ointment made of burnt ox-bones. T neither kill nor eat any living creature, nor any herb or r until it is dried, esteeming everything to have a soul. They no dishes, but lay their victuals on dry leaves, &c."

After the Mahometans conquered Hindostan, the fanaticism of the conquerors seems to have infused itself into their Hindoo subjects, and to have incited them to a wilder and more savage fanaticism than formerly; as the following accounts of modern travellers will show. Besides the Yogis, who are a purely Hindoo sect, we read of a class of religious savages called Fakirs or poor men, who are partly Mahometans and partly of the Hindoo religion.

Bernier, a French traveller, about the year 1670, thus describes them:

"Amongst the great variety of Fakirs, &c., of the Indies, there is abundance of them that have convents, wherein they naintain vows of chastity, poverty, and obedience,* leading so dd a life, that I doubt whether you can give credit to it. These are ommonly called Jaguis, (Yogis) as if you should say, *united to od.* You shall see many of them sit stark naked, or lie days nd nights upon ashes, and commonly enough under those large ees that are about the water-tanks, or else in the galleries that e about their idol temples. Some of them have their hair nging down to the middle of their legs, and that wreathed into veral parcels, like those who have the disease called in Poland e plica. Of these I have seen some who held one arm or both rpetually above their heads, and that had at the ends of their gers wreathed nails, that were longer by measure than the half my little finger. Their arms were small and lean, as of hecti- persons, because they took not sufficient nourishment, in that ed posture, and they could not let them down to take any- g with them; wherefore, also, they have young novices, who e them, as holy men, with great respect. There is no ara in hell so terrible to look upon as these men are, all d, with their black skin, long hair, dried arms in the posture re mentioned, and with long crooked nails."

I have often met in the fields whole squadrons of these rs, altogether naked, dreadful to behold. Some held their

* These are the three vows made by the Roman Catholic monks.

arms lifted up in the posture before mentioned; others had their terrible hair hanging about them, or else they had wreathed it about their heads; some had a kind of Hercules club in their hands; others had dry and stiff tiger skins over their shoulders I saw them pass thus quite naked, without any shame, through the midst of a great borough. I admired how men, women, and children, could look upon them so indifferently, and how *the women brought them alms with much devotion, taking them for very holy men, much wiser and better than others.*"

On the top of a mountain in Cashmire, in the north of India, Bernier saw an old hermit, "whose religion was not known, though it was said that he did miracles, caused strange thunders when he would, and raised storms of hail, snow, rain, and wind. He looked somewhat savage-like, having a long and large white beard, uncombed. He asked alms somewhat fiercely; suffered us to take up earthen cups of water which he had ranged on a great stone; made a sign with his hand that we should speedily march away; and grumbled at those who made a noise; because, said he, (when I had come into his cave, and softened him by humbly putting a rupee into his hand,) a noise raiseth furious storms and tempests."

Hamilton, in his account of the East Indies, dated about the year 1700, says—"There is another sort of Banians called Yougies (Yogis) who practice great austerities and mortifications. They contemn worldly riches, and go naked, except a bit of cloth abou their loins; and some deny themselves even that, *delighting i nastiness and a holy obscenity*, with a great show of sanctit They never cut nor comb their hair; but besmear their bodie and faces with ashes, which makes them look more like devi than men. I have seen a sanctified rascal of seven feet hig with a large turband of his hair wreathed about his head, and h body bedaubed with ashes and water, sitting quite naked und the shade of a tree, with a gold ring through his prepuce. *Th fellow was much revered by young married women, who prostra ing themselves, &c.*"

Papi, a later traveller,* thus describes a Fakir:—"Picture to yourself a fanatical madman, whose face and whole body, which is naked except a small wrapper about the privy parts, is thickly besprinkled with a white powder—whose tangled hair, never touched by a comb, stands out in a hundred bushy tufts, like the snake's on Megara's head, who from time to time bellows frightfully, who behaves like one possessed by the devil, walks with long hasty strides, setting all shame and decency at defiance, his fiery eyes rolling fearfully in his head; and you will see in the person of this disgusting, filthy madman, the lively image of a Fakir. I frequently saw them lying on their backs in the open street, perfectly motionless with their eyes closed, when the sun shone with a scorching heat, and the sand under them was burning hot. In this position they would hum through the teeth a sacred hymn, and pretend that they were so absorbed in heavenly contemplations, that they did not notice the passers by; yet, for all that, they kept glancing round to see whether some one was not throwing them a gift."

It is related of the Indian Emperor Aurengzebe, that he once invited the Fakirs of southern India to his court, because he had heard that they kept gold and jewels sewed up in their ragged garments. When they came, he gave them a royal feast in his palace; and, after the feast, ordered a new suit of clothes to be brought forth for each of them, which he then presented to them with these words: "It is just and meet that men so entirely devoted as you are to the service of God, should be better clothed. Therefore lay aside these ragged garments, and take, each of you, one of these new suits. In vain did the frightened Fakirs make all sorts of objections. They had to make the exchange, and went away grievously dissatisfied with the discovery of their hypocrisy, and the loss of their treasures.

Niebuhr, the celebrated traveller, says—"The Musselmans (Mahometans) of Surat, in India, have among them a great many Fakirs of their own religion, who are the most insolent beggars in

* Quoted by Bohlen, Das. Alte Indien. Ch. 2.

the world." Again he says of the Hindoos: "They have two orders of Fakirs among them, the Bargais and the Gusseins, who travel about armed, in troops of some thousands. These orders are sworn enemies, and wherever they meet, fierce combats ensue. The stories of the ridiculous penances of the Fakirs are well known. Their fanaticism has not yet become cold. There died lately at Surat, one of these madmen, who had lived shut up in a cage for twenty years, with his arms constantly raised above his head."

Those dangerous fanatics who go about in troops, always create alarm when they approach a town. The men fly, *but the women generally welcome their coming, expecting a blessing from the private visits and prayers of these holy men.* When a pilgrim of this sort enters a house, in the absence of the husband, he leaves his staff or his sandals at the door, to warn the good man, if he should happen to arrive, that the saint is engaged in private prayer with his wife. Seeing this sign, he takes care not to enter, knowing that if he did, he would get a good beating for his impious intrusion.*

Frequent mention is made of the long filthy hair of these fanatics. Dr. Fryer, in the seventeenth century, saw at Surat a Yogi whose hair was four yards long, and trailed upon the ground. This confirms a remark of Ward, that the Yogi's lengthen the natural growth of their hair by artificial additions, which they could easily combine with their uncombed, clotted, and inextricably-tangled locks.

The reader has seen what the Hindoo books say of the Sannyasi's purgatory of five fires. We find in Maurice's Indian Antiquities, a modern instance of this. It is a proof not only that the ancient rules of Hindoo ascetism are yet practiced to some extent, but that human nature can, under the influence of fanaticism, endure voluntarily, the most intolerable sufferings.

A Yogi resolved for forty days to endure the purgatory of five

* Picard. Ceremonies et Coutumes Religieuses de tous les Peuples du Monde. Tome 1, Religion des Brahmes.

fires, the blazing sun being one of the five. This solemn act was to take place *during a public festival, before an innumerable crowd of spectators.* He seated himself early in the morning on a quadrangular stage, with three ascents to it. He fell prostrate and thus continued his devotion until the sun grew hot. He then rose, stood upon one leg, and fixed his eyes steadfastly upon the sun. Four fires, each large enough to roast an ox, were then built at the corners of the stage, the devotee counting his beads the while, like a Roman Catholic penitent. After increasing the heat of the fires by putting incense into them, he bent down with his eyes still on the sun, and stood on his head during three hours. He then sat cross-legged the rest of the day, roasting between the fires, and bathed in the exudations of his own grease. So he did, or was to do, continually, until the forty days were expired.

Fryer saw others who had vowed to keep a standing posture for sixteen years. One had fulfilled his term. The legs of all were dreadfully swollen and ulcerated.

Sonnerat says, that some stand on the toes of one foot, the other foot being lifted up, and both arms elevated, in the midst of four fires, and with their eyes intently fixed on the solar orb.

Others (says Sonnerat) appear in public quite naked, to show that they are no longer susceptible of any passion, and have returned to the state of primeval innocence.

Sonnerat agrees with Ward in saying that the devotees are characterized by pride, self-love, and an inflated conceit of their superior sanctity. They avoid the touch of the common people and of foreigners, as a defilement. They have a sovereign contempt for all who are not sanctified like themselves.*

The class of Yogis called Tapasvinas, exercise their genius in devising strange modes of self-torture. Some bury themselves in pits with only small breathing holes at the top. Some stand buried up to the chin, with their heads only above ground. Others disdaining to touch the vile earth, have themselves sus-

* Maurice's Indian Antiquities, as before referred to.

pended in cages from the boughs of trees. Some condemn themselves to imprisonment for life in iron cages, with some painful contortion of the body annexed. Purchas relates on the authority of the Jesuit missionaries, that one of them had his body enclosed in an iron cage, with his head and feet outside, so that he could walk, but neither sit nor lie down. At night his pious attendants attached a hundred lighted lamps to the outside of the cage, so that their master could exhibit himself *walking as the light of the world*."* Some instead of cages wear heavy iron collars or fetters, like certain Christian saints in the fifth century. Some give an expressive sign of their chastity, by dragging a heavy chain fastened by one end round their privy parts. Others keep their fists hard shut, until their finger nails grow through the palms of their hands. Others support their arms above their heads by grasping the branch of a tree, and there they stand motionless, until their arms stiffen and dry up, like dead tree limbs. Others stand perpetually on one leg, only at night supporting themselves in a leaning posture, by holding the end of a stretched rope. Others keep their faces turned over one shoulder, until they cannot turn them back again. Others lie on wooden beds, bristling all over with iron spikes an inch long above the wood. Others have themselves fastened for life to the body of a tree by a short chain. Others suspend themselves for half an hour at a time, feet uppermost, over a hot fire. Others have themselves suspended by a chain from the end of a long lever balanced by a pivot on the top of a post fifteen feet high, a hook at the lower end of the chair being thrust through the muscles of their naked backs; and thu they are whirled round like a stone in a sling, by men at th other end of the lever. But it would be tedious to enumerate a the ways in which these heroes of a false sanctity torture then selves for the good of their souls, and *the applause of the spectator* It does not appear that these mad devotees practice their feats solitude. Their devotion must be stimulated by the presence a crowd.

* How different from him who was truly the Light of the world!

All these ascetics profess abstinence from women, wine, and delicate food. They live on the charity of their admirers—especially the women, who will do anything for such holy men. Few of the Hindoo saints appear now to be anchorites, like the ancient Gymnosophists and woods-philosophers. They seem to have discovered that holy contemplations are aided by the presence of witnesses.

Popular applause has a wonderful influence on the human mind. The Yogi feels its invigorating power. The Christian hermit of old felt it in his secret cell, knowing that his deeds of self-denial would come to light, and that ten thousand tongues would utter his praise. We shall find instances of this in the lives of the hermits.

Alexander Von Humboldt found at Astracan, in Russia, where some Hindoos had settled, a Yogi who was described to him as having for twenty years long withstood the severe winters of that climate, naked, in the vestibule of the temple. Humboldt saw him there, sitting where he had always sat, shrivelled up and overgrown with hair like a wild beast. He sat in the open vestibule, where people could see him, *and admire!*

Devotees, after they have signalized themselves by such achievements as above described, become first-rate saints: they enjoy the reputation of being almost divine: they are nurtured in the temples as beings whose presence is holy and diffuses blessings on all around them. They are venerated whilst living, as the Roman Catholics venerate the relics of their dead saints, and attribute a miraculous virtue to them. We know not which leserves the palm of superior sense and piety,—the Hindoo or he Roman Catholic.

The Hindoos have also an order of holy virgins in their temples. 'hey are devoted by their parents to the service of the gods. 'heir office is to weave garlands for the festivals, to adorn the tars and to sing and dance in honor of the gods. These holy rgins of the heathen nations, may be considered as the protopes of the consecrated virgins of the church in the third and ırth centuries, and of *the nuns of later ages.*

CHAPTER III.

OF MONACHISM AMONG THE BOODHISTS OF EASTERN ASIA.

§ 1. *The Origin of Boodhism.*

We mentioned in the preceding chapter that Vishnu, the second god of the Hindoo trinity, had, in a long course of ages, gone through nine incarnations, to effect some work of salvation on the earth. In the ninth he appeared as Boodh, or Budhu, as it is sometimes written. This name signifies *The Wise*, and is rather a title of honor than a proper name. He is also called Gaudama or Gotama, which is supposed to have been his proper name.

Great obscurity rests upon the history of Boodh. There are no authentic records of his life, either in Hindostan, where he lived, or among the three hundred millions of people who follow his religion in Eastern Asia. There are some old legends concerning him; but these are evidently mixed with fabulous traditions, disagreeing with one another, and, except a very few particulars, are founded on no reliable authority. The historical traditions of Ceylon, one of the primitive seats of Boodhism, say that there were several different Boodhs in divers times and places A similar tradition exists in Burmah. It is probable, therefore that much of the confusion and inconsistency of the legends aros from this circumstance, just as the confusion of the mythologic traditions of Hercules, Bacchus, &c., among the Greeks, aros from not properly distinguishing several personages of the same name.

The following outline of facts, embraces what learned men have generally considered, as in the main, authentic, concerning the founder of Boodhism.

At sometime between six hundred and one thousand years before Christ, a distinguished religious philosopher, whose name was Gaudama, and his title of honor Boodh, appeared on the banks of the Ganges, and was believed by the Hindoos to be an incarnation of their god Vishnu. It was afterwards reported that he was born of a virgin. His doctrine differed in some particulars from that of the Vedas, which the Brahmins taught. He gathered many followers of his new system of religion; but for some reason not easily explained—perhaps his retired mode of life, and his mild, unassuming manners—the Brahmins still paid him great respect, and regared him as an incarnation of Vishnu; though they did not embrace his peculiar doctrines—an inconsistency scarcely credible. After his death, however, his disciples incurred the enmity of the old party, and were expelled from Hindostan by a bloody persecution. They took refuge in the island of Ceylon, and in the countries north and east of Hindostan; where they propagated Boodhism with so great success, that when Europeans began, in modern times, to visit those countries, they found Boodhism prevailing in Ceylon, Burmah, Siam, Thibet, Eastern Tartary, China, and Japan. In the two last-named countries only, were the people still divided between their old religions and Boodhism.

Such is the account most generally current respecting the origin of Boodhism.

But Ward gives an entirely different view of the origin of Boodhism. He thinks it doubtful whether this was not the primary religion of Hindostan, and Brahminism a later system, raised to pre-eminence by the superior influence of the Brahmins.

He says that, according to the Hindoo writings, two of the six primative schools of Hindoo philosophy, inculcated the atheistical doctrines concerning a First Cause, which Boodh afterwards taught.

According to the Hindoo history, about seven hundred years before Christ, Veru Vahoo of the race of Goutuma or Gaudama, a follower of one of these sects, destroyed his sovereign, and seized the throne of Delhi. This king and his three successors reigned one hundred and eight years. The last of them was Moohee Pootoo; and as most writers agree in placing the era of Boodh in the sixth century before Christ, we may suppose him to have been the son of Moohee Pootoo, whose family name was Goutuma, one of the family names of Boodh.

In the Temoo Jetoo, a history of one of the incarnations of Boodh, he is said to have been the son of a king of Benares, and to have persevered in choosing the life of an ascetic against the will of his parents. Accounts agree that he was of royal descent, embraced an ascetic life, and adopted a system of philosophy already prevalent; we may, therefore, suppose, (says Ward,) that he became the patron and idol of the sect already existing, and which was afterwards distinguished by his name, and supported by the reigning monarchs, who were connected with him both by agreement of opinion and by ties of blood. Thus the Boodhist philosophy predominated during a number of succeeding reigns over the religion of the Brahmins.

But the Brahmins still contended earnestly against the doctrines of Boodh, which they esteemed to be atheistical; but whilst the Boodhist kings reigned, they could contend only with words. But three hundred years before the Christian era, Dhooranduru dethroned Adytyu, the last of the Boodhist dynasty, and assumed the sovereignty. From this time we may date the commencement of the persecutions by which the Boodhists were finally expelled from Hindostan, about one hundred and twenty years before Christ.

The learned Burmans hold that Boodhism was introduced into their country about four hundred and fifty years after Boodh's time, which agrees with the date just given.*

* Ward's View; book vi., ch. 2.

As a curious and interesting specimen of the legendary stories concerning Boodh, we shall give an abridgement of Carey's translation of the Temoo Jetoo, the Burman legend above mentioned.

In the kingdom of Kasheeku, and the city of Varanusee, (Benares,) reigned Kashee Raja, an excellent king, who had sixteen thousand wives, but no child. The people came and begged the king to supplicate for a son. The king ordered his sixteen thousand wives to feast the gods and supplicate for a son. They did so, but without effect. The Queen Chundra was perfectly versed in holy rites. The king asked her particularly to supplicate for a son. When the moon was full, she fasted; and, reflecting upon her virtuous deeds, she relied upon her perfect devotions to procure her a son. When she performed them the second time, the divine messenger determined to fulfil her desire.

Looking around for a proper person to become incarnate in her womb, he beheld Boodhu-sutwu, who had once reigned over the kingdom of Varanusee during twenty years, but after death had fallen into a hell, and been punished for the space of eighty thousand years. He was then born again in the country of Tavutingra, and at death desired to ascend to the higher heaven of the gods. The divine messenger said to him—"O thou great one! The queen of Kashee supplicateth for a son: wilt thou consent to be incarnate in her womb, that thou mayest perform meritorious works and make the people happy?"

He consented, and was conceived in the womb of Chundradevu. At the same time five hundred sons of the gods were conceived by the wives of the nobility. All were born on the same day.

The king was delighted at the birth of his son, and of the five hundred sons of the nobility. He selected faultless nurses for the prince. [He had need to be particular on this point, for the legend says,]

"If an infant sit upon the lap of a very tall woman, to draw the breast, its neck grows long; if on the lap of a short woman, it grows hump-backed; if the woman be lean, her thighs injure it; if very fat, it straddles or staggers when it walks; if the woman's breasts be very long, they flatten its nose; if she be very black, her milk is cold; if asthmatic, it is sour; if she has a goitre, it is bitter. Therefore rejecting all faulty nurses, he gave the child four times sixty *small-breasted*, *honey-like-milk-producing* nurses."

When the child was named, the king summoned the prognosticating Brahmins to declare its destiny. They examined its marks and found every sign propitious. The king was pleased, and proceeded to name the child.

When the young prince was a month old, he was brought before the king. It happened that four thieves were at the same time brought in to receive sentence. The king ordered cruel punishments to be inflicted upon them. The child was filled with horror and dread at his father's cruelty. He remembered his former sufferings in hell, and expected to be cast into hell again for his father's sins. He resolved, therefore, to adopt forthwith a system of ascetic austerities. By fasting he made his body feeble and lame. He affected to be deaf and dumb and idiotic. As he grew up, they vainly endeavored to excite his desires by tempting fruits and all sorts of pleasant things. They endeavored also to excite his faculties by frightening him: but it was all in vain.

The soothsaying Brahmins were called in a second time; and now declared that the prince's condition foreboded evil to his parents and to the kingdom. By their advice, therefore, the king resolved to send him "in the unfortunate carriage through the unfortunate gate" to the burial-ground, and there have him interred alive. But through a mistake, resulting from the merit of Boodh's austerities, "the fortunate horses were put into the fortunate carriage," and thus the young prince—now sixteen years old—was conducted to a distant forest. Here Boodh assumed more than mortal strength: he slung the carriage whirling through the air: he possessed strength enough to go eight hundred miles in a day. The god's arrayed him in a divine dress, and adorned him with such beauty, that when he addressed the charioteer, who was digging the grave, to bury the poor helpless boy, he was not recognized. But the charioteer being convinced at last of his identity, besought him to return to the palace as heir of the kingdom. He refused and declared his resolution to abide in that forest, as a mendicant hermit. Then the charioteer announced his intention to follow his example. But the prince sent him to inform his royal parents of what had happened. The queen mother, when she was told of the wondrous change in her son, and his resolution to become a hermit, sent a son of the gods to the forest to provide for him accommodations suitable to his purpose. This mighty genius soon made in the forest a house of leaves and a pool of water, and caused trees to grow, which bore fruit at all seasons of the year.

Here the princely hermit took up his abode. Casting off his splendid vestments, he girded himself with a coat made of bark, and threw a leopard's skin over his shoulders. He covered his head with his long twisted hair, and laid a bamboo across his shoulders. Then taking a staff in his hand, he walked about in his woodland bower, exclaiming, This indeed is bliss! How happy am I! In the evening he took of the fruit of the trees, and boiling it in tasteless water, without salt or acid, he fed on this as immortal food.

The king first, and then the queen, visited Mahee (for so the prince was named) in his forest hermitage, taking with them a great retinue. Their object was to persuade him to return and inherit the kingdom. He gave them a taste of the boiled leaves which he often ate. The royal parents did not relish the diet, and expressed their astonishment, that with such food he should be so beautiful and so happy. He accounted for it by saying, "It is my serene repose that makes my countenance so beautiful. I feel no remorse for the past and no concern for the future, and I am prepared for whatsoever may happen. Therefore my countenance is so gay. The foolish, because they are anxious about the future, and sorry for what is past, wither away like a green reed plucked up by the roots."

The king offered him all the delights of royal luxury, if he would return ;—elephants, chariots, footmen, horsemen—lovely maidens for wives, and dancing girls for amusement; or, said he, you shall, if you choose, have them here in the forest: kings' daughters shall come, that you may have posterity by them. Then you can be a hermit-priest during the remainder of your years.

" Oh, (said Boodh in reply) a man ought from his earliest youth to perform the virtuous acts of an ascetic life. He may become a priest: that is my choice. I have seen a youth, the beloved son of anxious parents, die as soon as he could say father and mother. I have seen maidens in the bloom of youth and beauty, perish like the uptorn sprout of a bamboo. Therefore, since the young die, who can confide in life? The life of mortals shortens every night. Of what avail then is youth? Men are continually harrassed, and continually surrounded with cares. They pass away without seeing good. Why then should you instal me in the kingdom?"

The sovereign Kasheeku said, " O son, inform me who it is that harasses, and who agitates mankind, and what it is that passes away without profit?"

Boodh replied, " Death harasses mankind, increasing age gathers around them. This know, O, sire, that as the thread is shortened by every flight of the weaver's shuttle, so dwindles away the life of man. As the waters of the flowing river never re-ascend, so the days of man's life never return. As the overflowing river sweeps away the trees on its margin, so do increasing age and death bear away the generations of mankind."

The king, when he heard the virtuous sayings of Boodh, became dissatisfied with human life; and being desirous of becoming a hermit, he resolved to cause his son to go and reign in his stead. He therefore repeated his magnificent offers, and presented every allurement that he could imagine. To show his disregard of the kingdom, Mahee replied, "O, sire, why temptest thou me with perishing wealth, dying woman, and the fading bloom of youth! O, king! What to me is love—the smile of beauty—transitory pleasure—the anxious pursuit of wealth—sons and daughters and wives—to me who am released from the bonds of iniquity? I know that *death will not forget me.* Of what use then are pleasures and riches to me? As the fall of ripe fruits is a constant evil, so to mankind death is a source of constant anxiety. Of the many people seen in the morning, a diminished number is seen at night; and when the morning comes again, still fewer of them are to be found. *Virtuous deeds ought to be practiced to-day, for who can tell but that we must die to-morrow:* the arrows of death are continually flying, nor can we possibly escape them O, king! thieves long after riches, but I am freed from the bonds of iniquity. Return, O, king, for I desire not thy kingdom."

When they heard these sayings, the king and queen, and all their retinue, maidens and noblemen, desired to become mendicants. The king then sent a proclamation to the city,—Whoever will, let him come to my son and be a hermit-priest. The inhabitants of the city then left their merchandise and their houses open, and went out to the king, who with many of his subjects immediately embraced a forest life with Mahee. The hermitage which the genius had prepared was filled with occupants for the space of six miles.

All lived on fruits and performed the duty of ascetics. Mahee by the power of his devotions was lifted up in the air, and thence delivered virtuous and mellifluous discourses.

A neighboring king, having heard that the king of Varanusee had abandoned his kingdom, went to take possession of it. But learning from the drunken remnant of the inhabitants, how the king's son had drawn the king and the people to the forest to share his hermit life, he was so impressed, that he too went with his attendants to see; and when he heard the mellifluous words, they all embraced the same forest life. So did three other kings in succession. The elephants and horses became wild; the chariots decayed and fell to pieces; the coins of the treasuries dropped neglected into the dust, and the whole concourse of the people, after accomplishing their austeries, died and went to heaven. Even the elephants and horses, having had their souls enlightened in the society of sages, were reproduced in the six abodes of the gods. Mahee closed his earthly career as Boodh, with the declaration, "I who was deaf, dumb, and lame, am declared to be a god."

Ward gives some account of what the Brahminical Puranahs say of Boodh. One Puranah says that he was born in the district of Magudhu. The Boodhu Puranah says that Boodh had sent his attendant gods to be born of noble families, but he himself entered the womb of Maya-devu. Immediately after his birth, he gave signs of divinity. At school he showed wonderful knowledge, and instructed thousands of his school-fellows. After leaving school, he took up his residence under a tree.—Next he married Gopa, a virgin of pure family, and kept eighty-four thousand concubines besides. Afterwards he fled from them all and became a Sannyasi. He practiced great austerities, and made many converts. He became so abstracted in holy contemplation, that the boys ran sticks up his nose without awakening him to consciousness.

The gods were filled with such admiration of his sanctity, that they came down and worshipped him. But a certain man came and upbraided him so loudly for his austerities, as to rouse him to reply, "O, wicked friend! knowest thou not that I am performing Yogu,—which requires the body to be purified by austerities? Death is better than continuance in a body so vile that meritorious actions will not proceed from it. I will subdue my evil desires."

He finally seated himself on a rock with the vow;—"On this rock may my body, blood, and bones become dry. Though my life depart, I will not abandon this Yogu." The attending god, smitten with admiration at this vow, worshipped him.

Some Brahminical writers charge, that several sects arose among the Boodhists, some of whom denied the existence of any spiritual being. Other writers charge the whole sect of Boodhists with this perfect atheism. But the charge is false.

§ 2. *The Doctrines of Boodhism.*

Boodh has been generally regarded as a reformer of the religion of the Vedas. Certain it is, if the old traditions are correct, that he appeared long after the Vedas were written, and long after the religious system taught in them prevailed in Hindostan. Yet he may have adopted, as the foundation of his system, the doctrine of a pre-existing sect.

Colebrook, who is high authority in this matter, thought the religion of the Vedas to be the most ancient in Hindostan.

The fundamental difference between Boodhism and Brahminism, is in relation to a *First Cause.* According to Ward and some other late writers, the Boodhists deny the existence of an eternal God, and the creation of the world, and are therefore essentially atheists.

The following summary of their religious philosophy, is taken chiefly from Ward's View.

Matter is eternal. Every part of nature has its own rise, tendency and destiny. The condition of men on the earth is regulated by their works of merit and demerit. Works of merit raise individuals to happiness and the world to prosperity; but the predominance of vice produces degeneracy and tends to general ruin. Men raise themselves to the dignity of gods by meritorious deeds, and the greater the merit of their works, the higher are the glory and power of their godhead after death. But not even the highest of these self-made gods has the government of the world in his hands. Four supreme but not infinite gods, have presided in succession over the celestial hosts, since time began. Gotoma or Boodh now reigns: his period is 5000 years, 2356 of which had expired in the year of our Lord 1814; which carries us back to the year 542 before Christ for the commencement of his era. When his 5000 years have expired, another saint-god will obtain the supremacy.

The Boodhists, like the Brahminists, hold the doctrine of Metempsychosis or Transmigration of Souls, and believe in the existence of divers hells, in which the wicked are temporarily punished according to their deserts. The next lowest state of souls is that of brute animals. These are states of punishment. The next is that of man, which is a probationary state. Above this are divers ranks of deity to which human saints are exalted according to their degrees of merit. Above the earth is a succession of heavens, differing in elevation and glory. In these the different ranks of gods have their habitations. All these were once men on the earth, and raised themselves to divinity by the merit of their works on earth—like the saint-gods whom the Roman Catholics worship.

The Boodhists hold also the doctrine that absorption is the highest state of glory and felicity. Among the Hindoos absorption is conceived to be a reunion of the soul with the infinite godhead, from which it emanated. But what can the atheistical Boodhists mean by it? If there be no universal spirit, no infinite God, from whom souls originally proceeded—into what can they be absorbed? Yet do the Boodhists, as all agree, hold the same doctrine of absorption, which we described in the foregoing chapter, as being held by the Brahminical Hindoos, and as constituting in their view the highest state of felicity and the supreme object of desire. Now if the Boodhists are atheistical unbelievers in the existence of an infinite unchangeable spirit, then the absorption for which their spirits are willing to sacrifice all earthly enjoyment, is absorption into nothing; absolute annihilation is to them the state of supreme felicity and the object of supreme desire; the highest of their gods in the most glorious of their heavens are yet in a state of inferior bliss; to be perfect they must be annihilated! The Hindoo idea of absorption into the universal spirit of Brahm, attended with the loss of individuality and consciousness, is an absurd conception of happiness; but the doctrine of absorption into nonentity as the completion of happiness, is philosophy run mad, and so superlatively ridiculous, that Ward is staggered by it, and professes not to understand this part of the Boodhist doctrines. It is not for us who have never seen a Boodhist book, to explain what was obscure to him; but we may signify a doubt, whether those who accuse the Boodhists of atheism be not mistaken. They have listened perhaps too readily to the accusations of their enemies, the Brahmins, and too hastily, perhaps, inferred from their doctrine of the eternity of matter and of the innate powers of nature, that they deny the existence of any spiritual being above that of a human soul exalted to divinity. We rather suspect that they are a sort of Pantheists, supposing that there is in nature itself a Divine intelligence and virtue by which all things are governed: for how else could they imagine the existence of migratory souls, a moral order and government of the universe, and an absorption of individual souls into a universal essence? Probably they differ from the Hindoo notion of a universal, quiescent Brahm, separate from nature and unconcerned in the affairs of the world, and place the essence of Godhead in nature itself, as the animating, moving, and governing spirit of the whole.*

Dr. Buchanan says that Nirvaree or absorption means among the Burmans exemption from all misery, but by no means annihilation. Common sense dictates that such must be the true account of the Boodhist doctrine.

The divine Boodh is the chief object of worship among his followers. His relics, or reputed relics, receive as profound a veneration from the Boodhists, as those of the saints do from the Roman Catholics. A king of Pegu once gave an immense sum

* This view of the Boodhist doctrine concerning the original Godhead, is suggested by Captain Mahoney in his account of Ceylon and the Doctrines of Boodh. See Asiatick Researches, vol. vii., p. 34.

for one of Boodh's teeth. It is supposed to be an elephant's tooth.* This reminds us of the trade in relics so common in Europe during the middle ages.

Inferior gods are honored with images in Boodhist temples, and with a subordinate worship. They occupy the same place in Boodhism which the deified saints do in Romanism: only the former are more ancient than the latter;—the heathen saint-gods being the originals: the *Christian* (if we may so call them) the copies.

The Boodhists acknowledge the Hindoo Trimurti,—namely, Brahma, Vishnu, and Siva, and assign them honorable offices in the highest heavens, but not the supremacy ascribed to them by the Brahmins.

The orders of the priesthood, and the rites of worship vary in different countries where Boodhism has been established. We shall notice some of these variations hereafter.

Besides the doctrines concerning the gods, already mentioned, the Boodhist religion differs from the Brahminical chiefly in the following particulars:

1. The Vedas prescribe certain bloody sacrifices of animals, though in general the Hindoo religion forbids the killing of living creatures. Boodh forbade the taking of life on any occasion, and confined his followers to vegetable offerings, such as flowers and fruits of the earth.

2. Boodh abolished among his followers the old distinction of casts, to which the Hindoos still tenaciously adhere. We mentioned these casts in the preceding chapter.

3. Among the Hindoos the Brahmins are the sacred cast. They have the exclusive privilege of teaching religion, and conducting its services. This privilege being hereditary, is common to all Brahmins, who need no ordination and are all of equal rank. On the other hand the Boodhists have regular orders of priests, who differ in rank, but are taken from the people at large.

* See Carl Ritter's Erdkunde von Asien, vol. iv., p. 1168.

4. The Brahmins marry at discretion. When they engage in ascetic exercises, each one chooses his own time and mode of procedure. He is not bound to others by any vow, nor subject to the rule and government of any order or superior officer.

The Boodhists on the contrary have connected a regular system of monachism with the priestly office. Their monastic system bears a wonderful resemblance to that of the Roman Catholics; but as it is much the older system, we may be sure that it was not borrowed from them. But the Boodhists have not quite so many varieties of monastic orders among them. Their monks for the most part live in monasteries, are bound by vows, and are subject to rule and government. Monastic discipline is strict, and great pains are generally taken by the abbots and the older monks, to keep the younger ones out of temptation, especially from women.

The Boodhist monks are less fanatical and extravagant in their penances, than the Hindoo Yogis. They adopt in great part the same principles of ascetic severity against the body, but their practice is more sober and moderate. They depend mainly on fasting, prayer, psalmody, and the use of the whip, to keep their rebellious flesh in subjection. Like the Hindoo Sannyasis, they endeavor by intense contemplation to raise their souls above all earthly thoughts and cares, and to prepare themselves by divine meditations for the felicity of heaven. Some monks, in order to give themselves more undisturbed to these beatifying exercises, leave their monasteries, and shut themselves up as anchorites in solitary places, like the Christian anchorites of the fourth century. Dark forests and lonely mountain tops, are the favorite places of retreat for these holy day-dreamers.*

* For a general account of Boodhism, see Guignaut's French edition of Creutzer's Religions de l' Antiquité, book 1. ch. v., and Bohlen. Das Alte Indien, ch. ii. For notices of Boodhist monks, see Syme's Embassy to Ava ch. iv. ix. and xi. Turner's Embassy to Thibet, *passim*.

The moral law of Boodh is fundamentally comprised in five precepts, forbidding, first, The killing of animals ; second, Theft ; third, Adultery ; fourth, Falsehood ; and fifth, The use of spirituous liquors. These prohibitions apply to all classes of persons. Devotees who aim at sanctity, are moreover to abstain from dancing, singing, instrumental music, festivals, perfumes, elegant dresses, high seats, &c.

When a man enters the priestly office, he moreover renounces all the pursuits and customs of the world,—shuns women, lives on alms, eats nothing except at noon, possesses but three garments, a begging dish, a girdle, a razor, a needle, and a straining cloth to take insects out of the water which he drinks, lest he should kill them, contrary to law.

The monks are schoolmasters, and teach gratuitously as a work of merit. In this they differ from the generality of Christian monks—in the gratuitous part, from the whole race of them, ancient and modern. Boys of fine parts are, if the parents consent, liberally educated for the priesthood, but may choose at a certain age whether they will be priests or not. Boys of five years and upwards are admitted into the seminaries as students, and are trained to observe the five precepts, and those also which prohibit pleasures and amusements. Those who obey the rules may be ordained priests at twenty years of age. Then if they obey the law of two hundred and twenty-seven precepts, to which priests are subject, they may at the expiration of ten years be promoted to the rank of priests of the first order, who are empowered to have colleges and disciples under them.

The ordination of a priest is a very important ceremony. It requires the presence of a priest who has been twenty years in orders, and of five others who have been ordained ten years at least. Spectators are excluded from this ceremony.

Religious festivals are regulated by the moon. The Boodhists of Ceylon observe every quarter of the moon, so that their sacred days occur about once a week. The Burmans keep holy only the days of full moon and change, having but two festivals a month.

On these days common business is suspended, people resort to the temples to worship Gotama or Boodh, with offerings of rice, flowers, fruits, candles, &c. Old people often fast during the day. The priests do not officiate in the temples, but give religious instruction out of their sacred books to those who attend their colleges, or monasteries, for that purpose. This account is from Ward and applies chiefly to the Burmans.*

There is a fundamental principle of the religious philosophy of both Brahmins and Boodhists, that will explain much of what may seem obscure.

Saints, especially those of high degree, are reverenced as having a portion of divine energy dwelling in them, and as partaking, so far, of the divine nature. Brahm, the supreme god of the Hindoos, though supposed to be generally quiescent and even unconscious, is believed however to have periodical fits of energy, from which all spiritual beings, and all extraordinary manifestations of spiritual power, proceed. When, therefore, a human saint exhibits a high control over his corporeal and mental system, in the voluntary endurance of sufferings, and in abstraction of mind from all earthly things, he is supposed to be energized by the universal spirit of Brahm, and to possess a portion of divinity.

The divine energy attributed to Brahm by the Hindoos, is by the Boodhists supposed to reside in nature. This energy, when imparted in an extraordinary degree, to human souls, is therefore supposed to raise them to the rank of gods, and to make them proper objects of religious worship after death, when they ascend to the heavens, and reign in subordination to the supreme power of nature.

§ 3. *Monachism in Burmah, Siam, and Cochin China.*

The island of Ceylon was one of the earliest seats of Boodhism

* Ward's View, book vi. ch. ii. as before cited.

after its expulsion from Hindostan: but its monastic institutions present nothing peculiar or remarkable, except it be that the monk-priests were formerly, and perhaps are yet, exceedingly ostentatious in their devotions. Like many of their Christian brethren, they walked the streets with their lips and their beads in constant play, muttering and counting their prayers, as if entirely absorbed in their devout exercises;—an infallible sign that they were hypocrites, like the Pharisees of old, and sought the praise of men rather than the praise of God.

The empire of Burmah comprehends the countries of Aracan, Ava, and Pegu. We have already given a general account of Burman monachism. We add some particulars, taken from modern books of travels.

In Aracan, "there are three classes of priests. Their chief, who resides in the Island of Munay, has the direction of the public worship. His orders are seldom disobeyed. The respect which he inspires, approaches to adoration. The king, absolute, as he is, never disputes the precedency with him at ceremonies, and is never covered before him."

So, here we find a little pope among the Boodhists—one almost as God-like in power, as his holiness of Rome was five hundred years ago. But we shall find a much greater Boodhist pope after a while.

"All the priests," says a traveller, "condemn themselves to eternal celibacy. Whoever transgresses on that point, is immediately degraded, and thrown back among the profane. Though all obey the same chief, they do not all observe the same discipline. Some live retired in private abodes, at their own expense. Retired from the world, and despising the pleasures of life, they are forgotten by mankind, and inhabit only rocks in gloomy forests or deserts. When the wants of life oblige them to appear in public, they have an humble aspect and downcast eyes; but their modesty seems to be an artifice to command admiration. Others, more happy and less solitary, inhabit magnificent palaces, (that is, monasteries,) where they indolently enjoy the wealth that the king and princes bestow on them, *with the view of ingratiating themselves with heaven.*

"These idolatrous priests are intrusted with the education of youth, as if men dedicated solely to prayer and mortification, were qualified to form magistrates, warriors, artists, and ministers of state. There are, also, hermits—a sort of wild men, who are esteemed in proportion as they are fantastic. They, like the priests, are divided into three orders, who all renounce the strongest passions of our nature, with an idea of thereby pleasing the Creator, who wisely bestowed these very passions on us, to be enjoyed, but not abused, nor wholly neglected."*

Every trait in this description has its exact counterpart in the ancient and modern monachism of Christendom.

At Rangoon, in Pegu, are many convents, a little way out of the city. The number of Rhahaans and Phongis—the senior and junior orders of priests—was formerly estimated at one thousand five hundred. "Like the Carmelite monks of Europe, they have their heads close shaven."

These clerical monks, like the mendicant orders of Europe, have no need of storehouse or barn; for the pious working people feed them daily, with food ready cooked. All that the brethren have to do, is to detail certain of their number, who shall travel the streets every morning, with an open provision box. They have no need to beg; the good people watch opportunities to drop their offerings into the box, believing that these charities will be richly rewarded with spiritual blessings. Thus the monks always have a plentiful dinner.

The monk-priests wear yellow clothing. This is the distinguishing color of the Boodhist priesthood, and so it was five hundred years—possibly fifteen hundred years—ago; though in Cochin China and Japan, other colors were also worn to distinguish several orders of monks. The Burman monks, as well as those of other countries, profess to abstain from every sensual indulgence. To prevent the brethren, especially the younger,

* Pinkerton's Collection of Voyages and Travels, vol 9, p. 762.

from falling into temptation, no one may go out of the cloister without leave of the prior.

A Rhahaan detected in a violation of chastity, is punished by daubing his face with white and black, mounting him on an ass, drumming him through the streets, and out into the commons, where he is turned loose, and told to go and shift for himself.*

In ascending the great river Irrawady, Syme noticed, in a tall, perpendicular cliff, by the water side, some apertures, resembling doorways. He was told that these were the entrances of cells cut into the rock in former times by hermits, who spent their lives in those inaccessible dens. Their food had to be let down to them with cords from above.† The same sort of fantastical monkery formerly displayed itself in the church. It found practitioners enough, while the vain devotees drew admiring crowds about their dens, and were duly fed by obsequious attendants. But when the fashion changed, and they were left to enjoy their wolf-like solitude unvisited, their holes were left untenanted, except, perhaps, here and there by one Troglodyte, whose melancholy mood drove him into gloomy seclusion; like those madmen described in the gospel, who dwelt in the tombs, because they were possessed by a legion of demons. But we never read of these solitary devotees having suffered themselves to starve outright, much as they hated to eat and drink.

In Siam, the monk-priests are called Talapoins. They live, for the most part, in large cloisters about the towns. Within the walls are separate buildings and cells for the inmates. There is an anchorite class of Talapoins, who retire into the gloomy recesses of the forests, and there lead a purely contemplative life, where a luxuriant tropical vegetation casts a perpetual twilight over the earth, and tigers and serpents share the dismal solitude These melancholy Talapoins, remind us of the ancient woods-philosophers of India, in the days of Alexander the Great.

The profession of a Talapoin is thought to have such sanctity

* Syme's Embassy to Ava, chap. 4. † Chap. 9.

and such merit, that all the Siamese are desirous of sharing its advantages. Hence, be it only for two or three days, they get themselves admitted into a cloister, and invested with the sacred costume. Being, thereby, sanctified, once for all, they live and die more contented. Thus, in the days when Popery was absolute in Europe, a superstitious villain died happy, if he could breathe his last, and be buried, in the coarse rope-girded habit of a Franciscan beggar-monk. Then he thought the devil would not dare to touch him. The infallible church did not condemn prevailing notions of this sort. They were useful to her. They gave, not only to herself, bodily, but to every rag and rope of her trumpery, a precious sanctity in the eyes of her subjects—the wicked no less than the righteous.

The regular Talapoins carried the doctrine of the evil nature of the body, and its pleasures, a little farther, we think, than other Boodhists. They held, and, we presume, do still hold, that marriage is always sinful, and that it is sinful even to look at a woman. No wonder, then, that they burn to death without mercy, every brother who is convicted of unchastity. But the Talapoinesses, or nuns, who occupy separate cloisters, are not so rigorously punished for this crime.* Whether the priests regard female chastity as less important, or the frailty of the sex as a palliation, we cannot tell. The Talapoins, when they denounce the smelling of perfumes—even those of flowers—as sinful, only follow the laws of Boodh ; but where did they learn that it was sinful to make a hole in the ground, or to shed one's urine upon water, or fire, or the lap of mother earth ?

Like the Roman Catholics, they hold the doctrine of confession to a priest, and the penitential efficacy of fasting, and such like austerities. Pilgrimages to holy places, they deem meritorious. They devoutly worship their dead saints. Their worship in the temples consists of ceremonies and entertainments. The Talapoins in the cloisters must not work, but meditate, pray, sing, preach, &c. They are zealous preachers, holding forth,

* Picard, Ceremonies et Coutumes, Tome I. Siam.

sometimes, nearly all the day long. They have the priestly tonsure, and practice frequent ablutions.*

The superstitious people hold the Talapoins in great reverence, as we may infer from the zeal with which they feed them. Gothard Arthus, (quoted by Hospinian,) mentioned, some centuries ago, another and more striking proof of the fact. The Talapoins —more cleanly than Christian monks—frequently bathed themselves. The common people deemed that the water that took off their carnal impurities, was not only sanctified by the process, but endued with a sanctifying virtue.

Therefore, they eagerly got it, and used it as a salutary drink.

Carl Ritter says that Boodhism was introduced into Siam, in the year of our Lord, 638.†

Cochin China, south of the great Chinese empire, is another country in which the religion of Boodh has been established for many ages. Here the Jesuit missionaries found it about three centuries ago, and found, to their astonishment, that it was a religion, which, though thoroughly heathenish, was most wonderfully like their own. In proof of this, we shall give the authority of Borri, one of these missionaries. The following long extract is taken from a translation of Borri's Account of Cochin China. The reader may find it in Pinkerton's collection, vol. ix. p. 762.

"There is," says Borri, "such a variety of Omsaiis (or heathen priests) in that country, that it looks as if the devil had endeavored among the Gentiles, to represent the beauty and variety of religious orders (that is, of monks) in the Catholic Church; their several habits answering their several professions: some are clad in white, some in black, and some in blue and other colors: some live in community, others like chaplains, canons, and prebendaries. Others profess poverty, living on alms; others exercise works of mercy, administering to the sick, &c.

* Carl Ritter, Erdkunde von Asien, Band. IV., Sec. 1170.

† Erdkunde, Band IV. S. 1155.

Others, again, look to the monasteries of women, who live in community, and admit no man among them, but the Omsaii who looks after them, and *they are all his wives.*"

We fear that the zealous missionary was too hasty in imputing such unchaste practices to his Boodhist brethren and sisters, though the charge is not incredible; such monastic concubinage having been rather usual among the monks and nuns of the Jesuit's own church. But hear him further—

"There are vast temples with beautiful towers and steeples. The idols are generally very large statues, with abundance of gold and silver shut up in their breasts or bellies. What is remarkable, the priests have chaplets and strings of beads about their necks, and make so many processions, that they outdo the (Roman Catholic) Christians in praying to their false Gods. There are also among them persons resembling bishops, and abbots, and archbishops; and they use gilt staves not unlike our croziers; insomuch, that if any man come newly into that country, he might be easily persuaded there had been Christians there in former times; *so near has the devil endeavored to imitate us.*"

Here Borri has reversed the truth. If Boodhism be of the devil, then, since it is older than Romanism, he should rather have said, "so nearly have we endeavored to imitate the devil." We do not adopt this language; we only say, that if there be imitation in the case, the Romanists were the imitators.

But Borri proceeds to say, that the Boodhists of Cochin China believe in future rewards and punishments. He charges them with error in not distinguishing between the human soul and demons, and in assigning transmigration as one of the rewards of the soul. The reader is aware that these errors are common to the Brahmins and the Boodhists.

Another error, or rather superstition, that he imputes to them, is, that the souls of the dead stand in need of corporeal food; for which reason the friends of the deceased set out food for them. In answer to the objection that spirits have no mouths, and that the food set out for them remains unconsumed, these ingenious

4

heathen said that "the meat consisted of two parts, the one substance, the other accidents of quantity, quality, smell, taste, and the like. The immaterial souls of the dead, (say they,) take only the *substance* of the meat, which being immaterial, is proper sustenance for the spirit, and left only the *accidents* in the dishes, as they appeared to our corporeal eyes."

We admire the subtlety of this answer. It would have done credit to the angelic doctor Thomas Aquinas; and we are astonished that a believer in the Romish doctrine of transubstantiation, should reject it as unsound, when he himself believes—or professes to believe—that when a priest says *Hoc est corpus* over the bread and wine of the sacrament, the *substance* of these meats is taken away, and the *accidents* remain. Even in this, the subtlest philosophical theory ever invented to give seeming possibility to an infinite absurdity, the heathen Boodhist had anticipated the atom-splitting schoolman of Rome. Or if the former did not *anticipate* the latter, so as to give the devil the credit of the invention, then let Boodhist and Romanist alike share the honor of devising this philosophical absurdity of supposing the accidents or sensible properties of a body to exist without any substance, or with the substance of an entirely different body! It is equivalent to supposing that by the evidence of sense a thing *is*, when in fact it is *not*. But if our senses give fallacious evidence, then nature and nature's God may be all an illusion. The foundations of belief are subverted, and nothing can present itself with evidence of reality, but our own thoughts and feelings. But let us hear what more Borri has to say of the Cochin Chinese.

"They also err (says he) in respect to the souls themselves, adoring those of men who were looked upon as holy in this world, adding them to the number of their idols.

[Listen ye saint worshippers of Rome, to your Jesuit Borri!]

"But the high altar, (says he—and Roman Catholics know very well what is meant by the high altar—) being the most honorable place in the temple, is purposely kept empty, behind which is a vacant dark space, to express him whom they adore as God.

Such a multitude of idols, by them accounted gods, giving us occasion to endeavor to demonstrate to them, that there can be but one God, *they agreed to it*, saying that they whose images they placed along the sides of the temples, were not they that had created the heavens and the earth, but *holy men whom they honored as we do the holy apostles, martyrs, and confessors*, with the same distinction of greater and lesser sanctity, as we assign among *our saints*. And therefore, to corroborate their assertion, they added that the vacant dark place about the high altar was the proper place of the Creator, who being invisible, could not be represented by visible images; but that under that vacuity and darkness the adoration was to be given to him as to a thing incomprehensible, using the *intercession of the idols*, (or saints,) that they may obtain favors and blessings of him (for their worshippers.")

If Borri does not here describe a Boodhist saint-worship precisely similar to that of the Roman Catholics, then we know not what can be like it. Indeed the Boodhist doctrine and worship in this country, so far as he describes them in the above extracts, are even, in his own opinion, the exact counterparts of the Romish system.

Their doctrine concerning a divine creator of the world, was either misunderstood by the missionary, or the Cochin Chinese have, on this point, varied from the doctrine of Boodh, as late writers have generally represented it.

Tonquin is a country lying between Cochin China and the empire of China. Here, likewise, Boodhism is the predominant religion, and still carries all the leading features of its resemblance to Romanism—namely, its convents of monks and nuns, confession of sins to the priests, with priestly absolution; holy water; temples and altars lighted, and holy flambeaux; rosaries on which to count repetitions of prayers; religious festivals and jubilees; sale of dispensations or indulgences, &c. Their monk-priests are said to promise themselves plenty of wives in heaven for their continence upon earth; for what is a sin here, they think will be a virtue there. The monasteries are reported to be places of debauchery; if so, the priests must act upon the principle, that a bird in the hand is worth two in the bush.

§ 4. *Monachism among the Lamaists of Thibet.*

In the cold mountains of Thibet, the religion of Boodh has assumed the form of Lamaism; the peculiarity of which is, that there is an order of superior priests called Lamas; whose supreme head is the Grand Lama, worshipped as an incarnation of the supreme God, and also has several provincial subordinates, worshipped also as incarnations of secondary gods.

Nowhere in the world does monachism prevail as it does in this poor wintry region of mountains and lakes. Monasteries are found occupying choice situations in all the inhabited parts of the country. These are filled with hale, hearty fellows, who show by their looks, that they are well fed and live much at their ease. Once a-week, they march in procession to bathe themselves in the nearest water. Thrice a-day they assemble for prayer. They have their fasts and their festivals, their instrumental music and their hymns, and when they celebrate worship in the temples they make a prodigious noise. As far as Turner and other travellers in the country observed their conduct, they appeared to be gentle, orderly, and strictly chaste. Although, to the transient eye of a stranger, only the fairer side of their character would appear; yet from all accounts, there seems to be no reason to doubt, that they live as inoffensively as any monks in the world. Turner observed that they shut up their cloisters every evening, that the young friars and novices might have no opportunity of intercourse with women. Sometimes, however, "love laughs at locksmiths:" but then, let us not suspect evil, when all appearances are good.

In Thibet the Boodhist priests constitute a complete and regular hierarchy. Besides the Gylongs, or common monk-priests, they have Lamas of different ranks, human and divine; and at the head of all is the Grand Lama, who is the Pope of northern Boodhism, and of higher dignity than even the Pope of Rome, who is God's vicegerent; for the Grand Lama is the great God himself, incarnate. He never dies; he only transmigrates from an old body into a new one. No sooner has he left one human body, than the priests of his court search for him in some new-born infant, and never fail to discover him by infallible marks. What those marks are, we know not: but what does it matter? The priests know them, and that is sufficient. The same remarks apply to the secondary divine Lamas, who rule over provinces in subordination to the supreme god incarnate, who resides in the city of Lassa.

The Lamaists of Thibet have some remarkable superstitions among them. We shall mention two things, in which they have gone beyond even the Romanists.

The one is a singular contrivance, which they have made for the purpose of expediting prayers. It is a barrel-formed cylinder, balanced on an axis, and easily turned by a touch of the hand. It is covered with written prayers and characters of mysterious import. It is placed near the doors of temples and by road-sides. Every devout passer-by gives the cylinder a turn, and thus puts all the prayers in motion at once. This is considered as equivalent to an oral repetition of them all, which would require no little time and labor. We commend this prayer-saving machine to the notice of our Roman Catholic friends, when they have to repeat hundreds of Paternosters and Ave Marias daily as a penance for their sins, and have to mumble them over with all possible haste, and to count them on the beads of the rosary. We submit it to their pious consideration, whether they might not as well turn them on a wheel.

The other matter concerns the Grand Lama's excrements; which being those of a god upon earth, are believed to have in them a divine virtue to heal the ailments of poor mortals, and to guard them against evil spirits and evil accidents. Therefore the priests preserve them with intense care, and deal them out in small portions to the faithful. The faithful reverently mix the precious substance with their food, as a divine medicine; reserving a small part, which they inclose in a little sack, and wear as an amulet suspended from the neck.

The Roman Catholics have equal faith in the relics, sound or rotten, of their *dead* saints; and so far they are as devout as the Boodhists of Thibet; but we do not think that they carry their devotion to the relics of the *living* Pope to the same extent. They seem to think that there is beatitude enough in kneeling before his holiness and kissing his BIG TOE.

When the Jesuit missionaries, a century or two ago, entered Thibet for the purpose of converting the people to Romanism, the were amazed to find a religion established there which they could scarcely distinguish from their own.* The resemblance was even more complete than it was in Cochin China and Tonquin.

There, as we have already stated, was a hierarchy of priests corresponding with their own;—and there a complete system of monachism, with monasteries, nunneries, and hermitages, and monks by thousands and tens of thousands,—all under the same vows as the Roman Catholic, and subject to the same government and discipline;—and all, up to the Grand Lama himself, with shaven heads, like their own priesthood, and clothed in similar showy sacerdotal robes and caps.

There was a chief holy city like Rome with its Pope, and inferior holy cities with their grand dignitaries, like the metropolitan archbishops and patriarchs of Christendom;—all, but especially the holiest of all, full of priests, temples, monasteries, ceremonies, festivals, processions, and pilgrims from distant lands.

In the temples, they saw a showy ceremonial worship like their

* See the description of Thibet in Pinkerton's Collection of Voyages and Tavels, vol. vii. The author took his account of these things from the published letters of the Romish missionaries.

own;—an altar for sacrifice, and a mass of bread and wine offered upon it; images of saint-gods, before which the worshippers bowed—holy water with which they were sprinkled—prayers in a dead language, and rosaries or strings of beads on which to count them.

There too they found sins confessed to priests, and penitents fasting, repeating prayers with the rosary, and whipping themselves:—there the doctrine of purgatory, prayers for the dead, and extreme unction for the dying.

The Romish missionaries were so confounded by the general appearance of conformity between Lamaist Boodhism and Romanist Catholicism, that they did not know what to think, or what to do. They had nothing, or almost nothing, to convert, except some doctrines and some names and titles.

The most mortifying circumstance was, the claim of this religion to a higher antiquity than that of their own Church—" The Mother and Mistress of all Churches." This claim, if admitted, would make " Holy Mother," in her most distinguishing features, the *image*, if not the *offspring*, of heathenism. They could imagine no other way of evading this humiliating conclusion, than by supposing that these people were a sort of bastard Christians, who had once been a part of the true church, but had somehow, most strangely and unaccountably, substituted the Boodhist theology for the Christian, while they retained the forms and institutions of the Catholic Church.

The supposition is egregiously absurd, not only in itself, as a sort of thing unheard of amongst men and morally impossible, but in relation also to the fact, that neither the country nor the religion of Thibet exhibits a remnant or a trace of the religion of the Bible; not a tradition, not a name even, nor a token of any sort, except the points of resemblance to Romanism above-mentioned; and not one of these appertains to Scriptural Christianity—they are all of heathenish origin.

The only historical fact that could give the slightest plausibility to this supposition is, that a thousand years ago, more or less, the

Nestorians sent missionaries into Eastern Asia, and planted churches in Tartary, Northern Thibet, and Northern China.

On this foundation the Romish missionaries endeavored to build their theory of the Christian origin of those Boodhist doctrines, institutions, and forms of worship, which give such a Roman Catholic appearance to Boodhism.

The learned Malte Brun, in his geography, adopts this theory; and Carl Ritter, in his great German work on Asia, supposes that the Lamaists borrowed some religious forms and ceremonies from the Nestorians, who formerly existed among them. This opinion differs much from that of the missionaries before-mentioned; yet even of this Ritter himself produces no evidence, except the mere presumption arising from the conformity of Romanism with Lamaism. But this presumption is overthrown by the fact, that nearly the same conformity exists in Cochin China, in Tonquin, and, as we shall hereafter show, in Japan—countries far beyond the bounds of the Nestorian missions. No Christian church was ever planted within 1500 miles of them. The only Boodhists with whom the Nestorians came in contact were the Lamaists of Thibet, Tartary, and Cathay, or Northern China. But the Boodhists of Cochin China, Tonquin, and Japan are not Lamaists. If any of them derived their religion from Thibet, it must have been at a period antecedent to the rise of Lamaism, and to the existence of Nestorian churches in Northern Thibet or Cathay. The opinion that the Lamaists were once Nestorian Christians, and retained their forms of worship when they embraced Boodhism, is as contrary to historical facts, as it is to rational probability. Ritter's opinion, that the Lamaists embellished their ceremonial by adopting in part the practices of the Nestorians among them, is founded, as he says himself, upon the conformity observed by the Romish missionaries in later times between the Lamaist worship and their own.* He seems not to have been aware that the missionaries observed almost the same conformity

* Ritter's Erdkunde, vol. 2, page 283, &c.

in Cochin China and Japan, and in like manner ascribed it to the malice of the devil.

Though it is not, and cannot be, pretended that the Boodhists derived their monachism from the Nestorians, yet we deem it interesting, both in itself and for the illustration of our subject, to pursue the argument somewhat farther. The religious history of Central Asia, where different systems met and mingled for centuries, is curious and little known. We have room for only a few facts.

Nestorius, Bishop of Constantinople, was condemned by a Council in the year 431, for denying that St. Mary was *God's mother*. The Catholics persecuted his followers, who took refuge in Persia, where they were protected by the king. This opened Asia to their missions. By the year 500 they had spread as far as Bactria and India. By the year 636 their missions extended to China, according to an inscription on a marble slab found in that country about two hundred years ago. The inscription was partly in the Syriac language, and purported to have been made in the year 781. Its genuineness is very doubtful. Setting that aside, it does not appear that the Nestorians penetrated into Cathay or Northern China till after the year 1000. But they had previously planted churches in Tangut, or Northern Thibet, and in Tartary. Such was the progress of Nestorianism.*

In the seventh and eight centuries the Mahometans extended their missions into Central Asia. They interfered seriously with the progress of Christianity.

The Magians, or Persian fire-worshippers, were, at the same time, advancing their missions eastward into the same extensive regions.

Before all these, the Boodhists of Thibet had been pushing the missionaries of their religion into Tartary and China. As early as the year 400 of our era, they had planted Boodhism in the Chinese

* Mosheim. Ch. Hist. Centuries X., XI., XII. Ritter, Erdkunde, vol. 2, p. 283, &c.

province of Shen-si on the upper waters of the Hoangho.* Before the Nestorians had penetrated to the borders of China, the Boodhists had already established one hundred monasteries in the city of Khotan, upon the high table-land of Tartary, and upon the waters of the great river that flows north and east into the Lop Sea. This was the route by which the caravans passed through Central Asia, between Cathay and Persia, or India. By the Lop Sea and its river Yarkiang, did the missionaries of four religions meet on their way to the great valley of the Hoangho, and the populous cities of Cathay. It is certain that the Boodhists were the earliest and the most successful of them all. For some time, however, the Nestorians flourished and, in some parts they became the prevailing denomination. In the twelfth century arose the great Tartar chief, Ginghis Khan, a Mahometan, who reduced all Tartary under his dominion, and greatly injured Christianity. From that time Nestorianism began to decline in Eastern Asia.

In the thirteenth century, Rubruquis, a monk, was sent by Louis IX., of France, into Tartary; and Marco Polo, a Venetian merchant, went to Cathay. Both of them found Nestorian Christians in Tartary, and Polo found them in Cathay, mixed everywhere with Mahometans or Boodhists, often with both, and in a few places with Magian fire-worshippers. These travellers usually called those idolaters, who were not Christians or Mahometans. We should remark that *the Nestorians rejected the use of images in worship, while the Boodhist, like the Roman Catholic, used them.* This made a notable difference between the Christians and the Boodhists of Asia; though it was afterwards a feature of resemblance, when Romanism came into contact with Boodhism.

Both these early travellers in Asia agree in representing the monastic institutions which they met with, as exclusively belonging to the idolaters—that is, the Boodhists. This is an important fact in the present investigation. Another important fact is, that between the Christians and the idolaters, though there seems to

* Ritter, Erdkunde, vol. 2, p. 205, &c.

have been peace, there was nothing like fraternization or amalgamation. The line of separation was strongly drawn, and there was no appearance of the one melting into the other. No such change appears to have been going on as the hypothesis which we are examining supposes. Nestorian Christianity afterwards became extinct in those countries; that is certain; but it must have come to pass by the destruction or conversion of its professors, not by the amalgamation of two religions.

We shall now confirm these statements by quoting from these early Christian travellers.

Rubruquis, describing the rites and ceremonies common to the idol temples at Cailac in Tartary, says that the priests had their heads and faces shaven, and were clad in yellow garments, with yellow hoods or caps—(the Boodhist uniform)—that after being shaven, they lived unmarried, one or two hundred together in a cloister. They also carried about with them strings of nut-shells, much like the beads of the Roman Catholics, and often repeated the same form of prayer. Such precisely are the Boodhist priests of modern times.

Again, says Rubruquis, speaking of the nations that inhabit Northeastern Asia, " They are all given to idolatry. The Nestorians live among them as strangers, and so do the Saracens—or Mahometans—as far as Cathay. The Nestorians inhabit fifteen cities of Cathay, and have a bishop there in a city called Segin. But if you proceed further, they are mere idolators. The priests of the idols of those nations have all broad yellow hoods—(that is, they are Boodhists.) *There are also among them certain hermits, living in woods and mountains, of an austere and strange life.* The Nestorians there know nothing; for they say their service out of holy books in the Syrian tongue, which they do not understand. They are great usurers and drunkards; and some of them also, who live among the Tartars, have a plurality of wives. The bishops visit them only once in a long time. *By their evil life and covetousness, they drive the idolators farther from*

Christianity; because the life of the Moguls and Tuinians, who are idolaters, is more just and upright than theirs."

But enough of Rubruquis; let us now take some quotations from Marco Polo.

"In the province of Chesmur (Cashmere?), the inhabitants are idolators above all others, cunning enchanters, forcing their idols to speak, and darkening the day. *There are certain hermits in this province, who, in monasteries and cells worship idols, honoring their gods with great abstinence of meat and drink, and observe great chastity. They live long. Many of them are reputed saints, and the people show them great reverence. The men of this province kill no living creature, and shed no blood.*"

"In Sachion, a city of Tangut, a few Nestorian Christians are found among the worshippers of Mahomet. Many idolaters are, also, there. The city hath *many monasteries consecrated to idols.*"

Again, he says, "Campion is a great city, the principal of the country of Tangut. In it are Christians, who have three great and fair churches. The rest are Mahometans and idolaters. *The idolaters have many monasteries*, where they worship their idols. The monks live more honestly than other idolaters, abstaining from whoredom and other base things."

Again, speaking of Jangamur, in Cathay, the place

> "Where Rublai Khan
> A stately pleasure dome decreed,"

whose beauties so fired the imagination of Coleridge, he says "there are two sorts of idolaters, called Chebeth and Chesmu, who, in the midst of storms ascend the palace, and suffer no rain to fall thereon, which they make the people believe comes to pass by their sanctity, and, therefore, *they go slovenly, and negligent of their persons, never washing nor combing themselves.* They are also called Backsi, which is the name of their order, as Friars Predicants, or Minors, with us. They have *great monasteries, some of the bigness of a city, in which are about two thousand monks, who serve an idol*, and are sequestered from the laity, as appears from their shaving their heads and beards, and wearing a religious garment. There are some called Sensim, who observe strict abstinence, leading an austere life; for they eat nothing but meal mingled with water, till all the flour be gone, and then they eat the bran. These worship the fire; and the men of other rules say that they are heretics, because they worship not idols as they do. They shave their head and beard, and wear hempen garments, either black or of a bright yellow. They sleep on mats, and live the severest life in the world."*

Again, speaking of the great city of Quinsai, in China, he says that the people are *idolaters*, and have *monasteries with many monks*. He describes all the southern parts of China as being filled with idolators, and makes no mention of Christians and Mahometans there.

He speaks of the great province of Mangi as abounding in *monasteries of idolatrous monks*, but no Christians except a few lately sent there by the great Rublai Khan.

Prester John.

During the Middle Ages, while the Crusaders were warring in Palestine, they heard a rumor of a Christian sovereign somewhere in the far East, who was called Prester John,—that is, Presbyter or Priest John. The rumor was soon carried through Europe and excited a lively curiosity to learn something definite respecting this mysterious priest-king, whose name was John. As always happens when people are eager to hear, rumor after rumor was spread respecting this Prester John; some placing him in one eastern country and some in another; but all agreed in attributing to him great power and a magnificent court. Still no one in particular could testify that he had seen him or visited his country. In those ages of war between Christians in Europe, and Mahometans in Asia, rarely did it happen that a Christian traveller was venturesome enough, or successful enough, to penetrate to

* From this it appears that the Magian fire-worshippers had their monks, too. But no mention is made of Christian monks.

Eastern Asia, where it was supposed tnat Prester John reigned among surrounding nations of infidels. Though many years had elapsed from the beginning of the rumor, before Marco Polo succeeded in traversing the vast and little known regions of the far East, still it was supposed that Prester John was reigning in that quarter of the world, and Polo was resolved, if possible, to discover the place of his kingdom. But, although he traversed Asia east and north and south, still Prester John, like the horizon, seemed to fly from his approach. At last, however, though he did not find him, he imagined that he obtained information of where he was to be found.

He heard of a province called Tenduc or Tandach, lying eastward of Tangut, which is nort-east of Thibet. "Here," says he, "Prester John resides, who now pays tribute to the Great Khan. The king of that nation is called George, and is a Christian priest; and most of the people are Christians. All the Great Khans, since the death of Prester John, who was slain by Ghingis Khan, —give their daughters to these Christian kings to wife. But this king George holdeth not all that Priest John before held. He is the fourth of that family. There is a nation there called Argons, descended of idolaters and Mahometans. There are also two regions where they dwell, called Gog and Magog; but they which dwell there call them Ung and Mongul. In Ung are Gog and in Mongul are Tartars. Riding east seven days towards Cathay, are many cities peopled by idolaters, Mahometans, and Nestorians."

Such was the report that Polo heard and was fain to believe, for the want of something better. By the aid of his imagination, he also discovered the Gog and Magog of the Scriptures in the Chinese name Ung and the Tartar name Mongul. Ritter thinks that the name of Prester John might be derived from the Chinese title *Ung Khan* or *Oan Khan*, meaning over-king or great king, the title by which the great Tartar Khans of those times were distinguished. The resemblance of Ung, or Oan, to Joan (pronounced Yoan), connected with the report spread by the

Nestorians of the conversion of an eastern king to Christianity, might in those times give rise to the whole story of Prester John.

In the year 1046, the Nestorian Archbishop of Samarchand published an epistle, announcing that multitudes of converts had been made in Thibet and Khotan, and that the Nestorians had seven kings and 70,000 horsemen, and that their king was called Nasarat.* Carl Ritter thinks that these must have been the Turks, who then began to bestir themselves in Central Asia, and ruled over countries in which many Nestorians lived. It was one of their princes who was said to been a few years before this time converted to Christianity. A confused report of all these matters may have originated the story of Prester John.

As to Polo's Prester George in the province of Tandach or Tenduc, he was never found; though the enterprising Venetian pursued all the great routes of travel through the eastern parts of Central Asia, in which this visionary priest-king must have been, if he had a local habitation as well as a name. He traversed the whole of Tangut; he describes the more southern country of Thebet or Thibet. He says that the people of this region were idolators, and prostituted their wives and daughters in honor of their idols. He mentions the great city of Cainduc on the eastern border of the country,—also of the great lakes that are laid down on our maps, and of the great extent of the country westward from Cainduc; yet, with the exception of a few Nestorians and Mahometans on the western border, the whole population of Thibet was composed of idolaters; that is, of Boodhists. It is evident, therefore, that no Prester John ever exisited in Thibet; and what is directly to the point of our present investigation, Christianity never obtained a footing there; nor could it have exercised any influence in forming the Lamaist system of Boodhism, which had its chief seat and probably its origin at Lassa, where Christianity does not appear ever to have

* This epistle is found in the Syrian Annals of Abulfardi. See Ritter's Erdkunde, vol. ii. p. 283, &c.

had a church or even a missionary, before the Roman Catholics found there the exact counterpart of their own corrupt system of heathenish Christianity.

Polo did not travel through this part of Thibet, and does not mention the Grand Lama. He travelled nearly six hundred years ago, and the power of this Boodhist pope may have been in its infancy, though his brother at Rome was then in the full magnitude of his vicarious godhead.

Nestorianism, though it carried with it some of the early corruptions of Christianity, came yet far short of the Roman Catholic system, to which Lamaism in Thibet was found to bear so striking a resemblance. Romanism and Lamaism are more nearly alike than Romanism and Nestorianism, in everything except their Christian theology, in which Boodhism differs from both.

It is evident from the reports of Rubruquis and Polo, that Christianity was declining in Eastern Asia in the thirteenth century. Boodhism on the one hand, and Mahometanism on the other, were pressing it down; its fall was hastened by the ignorance and the vices of its professors, and by the want of support from the West, where Mahometanism was bearing down all denominations of Christians in Asia. About two hundred years later, when the Romish missionaries began to penetrate the interior of Eastern Asia, not a remnant of Nestorianism was found in the countries where it had flourished a few centuries before.

Here we close our investigation of a curious and obscure part of the religious history of Central and Eastern Asia. We have thought it to be sufficiently interesting in itself, and sufficiently pertinent to our main subject, to justify the space which we have given to the examination of a hypothesis, resorted to, in the first place, by Romish missionaries, and too hastily adopted by some learned men to account for the close resemblance between Romish Christianity and Boodhism, as it exists in several countries, but especially among the Lamaists of Thibet.

§ 5. *Monachism in China and Korea.*

The Chinese are divided in their religious sentiments; some adhering to the doctrines of their ancient philosopher Con-fut-see, or Confucius, whilst the greater number, especially among the common people, profess the religion of Fo, which is, in fact, the Lamaism of Thibet. The name Fo is nothing but the name Boodh modified, so as to adapt it to the Chinese habits of pronunciation.

Boodhism was introduced into China as early as the first century of our Christian era. Lamaism is probably of later origin even in Thibet; but it is now the only form of Boodhism known to exist in the empire. It prevails most in the northern provinces and among the Tartars inhabiting the vast steppes of Upper Asia, as far as the Chinese dominion extends.

The extracts already given from Marco Polo demonstrate the flourishing state of Boodhist-Monachism in China six hundred years ago. Two centuries ago the Dutch sent an embassy to China. Nieuhoff, the secretary, wrote an account of the journey of the ambassadors from Canton to Pekin. From this account we take two significant extracts.

"On the Maw-wha, near a delightful valley, stands a monastery with a spacious temple. It was built by Lu-zu, a reputed saint, who spent all his time in grinding and sifting rice for the monks, and wore iron chains day and night on his naked body. These made holes in his flesh, which, for want of dressing, putrified and bred nests of worms; yet Lu-zu would not suffer them to be removed, but when one dropped off, he would pick it up again and say, '*Have you not sufficient to feast yourselves left? why then forsake you my body, where you are welcome to feed?*'"

Here was a consistent saint. Holding the Hindoo and Boodhist principle that the body is evil, he punished this vile part of his nature as a sinful thing. Holding that worms had souls like his own, though cramped for the present in mean bodies, he fed them liberally on his flesh, which he conceived to be put to its best use, when it was eaten by worms.

But says Nieuhoff in another part of his work:

" In view of the city (Nankang) stand several stately temples; the chief of them are built upon mountains, where dwell a great company of priests and friars, each in a little hut or cell, where they discipline themselves every day with lashing, which the people believe to be very meritorious in another world, for they hold the transmigration of souls. They told us that on Quanlyu (one of these mountains,) there were as many cloisters as days in the year."

These pious monks might have passed for good Christians; especially of the sort formerly in vogue among the Roman Catholics, and not yet extinct, called Flagellants or Whippers, if the author had not mentioned their belief in the transmigration of souls.

There are in China many sorts of fanatical monks—generally beggars—similar to the Hindoo Fakirs. The generality of these seem to be arrant impostors, who resort to various modes of self-torture, real or apparent, for the purpose of extracting alms from the people. Wherever there is superstitious credulity enough among the people, to reward such feats of pretended saintship with gifts and admiration, there we may be sure to find fanatics and impostors enough to turn this popular credulity to their advantage.

The peninsula of Korea has been rarely visited by Christians, and is little known. It is a dependency of the Chinese empire, and the religion of the country is Boodhism. Of course it has the monastic institutions that constitute an inseparable, if not an essential part of this ancient and wide-spread religion.

Nearly two hundred years ago, the Dutchman Hamel, was shipwrecked on the coast of Korea; and afterwards wrote the best account that we have seen of this inhospitable country. He represented the people as having little except the form of the religion which they professed. But they had numerous monasteries, built chiefly, as in China, upon the tops of mountains. The early Christian monks of Asia followed the same custom, as we shall see hereafter, of locating themselves upon the mountains. "Some of their monasteries (says Hamel) contain five or six hundred monks, whereof there are four thousand within the liberties of some towns." In fact, Korea swarms with monks. When a brother offends against the rules, his superiors punish him with strokes on the buttocks. From this we may infer, what Hamel says, that the private members who are thus subjected to the bastinado upon their seat of honor, are despised; while their superiors, who have the privilege of giving the bastinado, are respected.* There are also nunneries in Korea. Some of the monasteries on the mountains, and in other secluded places, are represented as being places of resort for purposes of debauchery. But enough of Korea and its monachism.

§ 6. *Monachism in Japan.*

Finally, we arrive at the empire of Japan, that singular country of islands in the farthest east. Here is the eastern frontier of Boodhism, and much that is worthy of observation. We shall endeavor, as heretofore, to present, in a concise form, the most important and the most curious facts relative to the religion and the monachism of the country under consideration.

Here again, far beyond the utmost range of early Christianity,*

* This is another feature of resemblance between heathenist and Christian monachism. Christian abbots formerly beat offending monks with whips and cudgels.

* Meylan, a president of the Dutch factory in Japan, relates a story, professedly from Japanese records, of a religion introduced into Japan in the year fifty, after the birth of Christ; which religion, in some points, resembled Christianity, and which some would be eager to take for Christianity, in order to account for the resemblance between the Japanese religions and Romanism. But, unfortunately, Meylan says, that this religion was Brahminical; and the date of its introduction into Japan, is entirely too early to admit of its having been Christianity. Then, too, the doctrines supposed

Boodhism exhibited its striking similarity to Roman Catholicism, when the country was first visited by the Jesuit missionaries.

They found, in Japan, two sovereigns—a spiritual sovereign, like the Pope, residing in the holy city of Meaco ; and a temporal sovereign, like an emperor, residing in his capital city of Jeddo. The former was the original sovereign, but had lost all civil power. Under this spiritual sovereign were religious dignitaries, priests and monks, with a system of worship, doctrines and practices, essentially identical with those which distinguish Romanism from Biblical Christianity. We shall notice the leading particulars as we proceed.

The spiritual sovereign just alluded to, was not a Boodhist, like the Grand Lama of Thibet. He was the head of the primitive religion of Japan. This religion is called Sint-yu. It is a system of idolatry, acknowledging one primitive, and many subordinate gods ; but founded, in a great measure, upon the deification of the ancient kings and heroes of the country. In Japan, as in Rome, the Supreme Pontiff assumes to himself the exclusive prerogative of canonization—that is, of declaring who among the departed is, and shall be, worshipped as a god, or divine saint. He founds his decision upon the same principles, and the same sort of evidence, as his holiness of Rome does ; to wit, *that* departed soul of saint or hero has become a worshipful divinity, who has appeared after death, or has wrought miracles. When a temple is built to one of these new gods, *his relics are carefully deposited in the sacred enclosure, and venerated by the faithful*, just as the Romanists do with the relics of their canonized saints—nay, the two religions have a still closer agreement in this matter; for both Sintoists and Romanists believe that *the relics have miraculous power in them*, because they are still animated, or, at least, haunted, by the souls that possessed them before death.

The Sintoists have also their monasteries of Cenobite monks,

to have been Christian, namely, those of a Divine Trinity and of a Redeemer born of a Virgin, are found also among the Braminical sects.

and their wild hermits, who live in the desert mountains, like the Christian hermits of the fourth and fifth centuries. These wild hermits are called Jammaboes. Properly speaking, they are of a mixed sect, called Rioboo-Synsyu. They have no settled abodes, nor any regular system of exercise, but practice much bodily mortification to purify their souls, and make pilgrimages to certain high mountain-tops in the desolate regions of the country.

Picard* relates a singular story of the manner in which these mountain hermits confess penitents; but where he found the story we cannot tell, as he cites no authority. His great work is, however, generally accurate. Hurd, in his universal history of religions, relates the same story, but cites no authority.

When a sinner wishes to get absolution from these holy wild men of the deserts, he must climb the mountains, and find some of them who live about the outskirts. These border hermits will conduct him to others more savage than themselves, in the wildest parts of the mountains. The latter then prescribe to the penitent certain preparations for his confession. He must endure excessive fasting, climb rugged mountains, and scale lofty precipices. If he goes through this stage of his preparation without flinching, he is then conducted through pathless wilds to a dreary solitude, where he must sit still upon the ground for a day and a night, with his arms crossed, and his head resting upon his knees. He must not budge, nor show uneasiness in that posture; for if he do, the fierce guards who watch him, are sure to beat him well with their clubs. During these twenty-four hours, he must take a deliberate review of all his sins. Being thus prepared, he is marched, by fatiguing ways, to the top of a high rock to make his confession. A great beam projects over the perpendicular side of this rock, and a pair of large scales is suspended from the outer extremity of the beam. The machinery is so contrived, that the beam can be drawn in and pushed out at pleasure. The penitent is placed in one of the scales, and an equal weight in the other. Then the hermits push out the beam and suspend their

* Ceremonies et Coutumes, &c., Tome 1, Des Japanois.

penitent, nicely balanced, over the frightful precipice below. In this ticklish situation, he must make his confession with a loud voice. If he falter in the confession of any sin, or give indication that he wishes to conceal anything, his savage examiners give the beam a sudden jerk, so as to throw him out and let him fall upon the rocks below. We can scarcely doubt, that, in such circvmstances, he would be careful and prompt—and loud also—in telling all that he could remember of his sins. If he satisfy his confessors that he has honestly discharged his conscience, he is relieved from his perilous situation, pays them a large fee, and is dismissed, with their absolution and a light heart, to render thanks to the gods, and to feast and make merry with his friends, in compensation for the labors and terrors of his confession.

We leave it to the judgment of our readers, whether or not this rough way of dealing with penitents be more likely to reform them, than the penances of the Roman Catholic priests, with their fish diet, (called fasting,) and their Pàternosters and Ave Marias counted upon a strand of beads.

Hempfer in his history of Japan* remarks, that in his time these hermits had much degenerated from the austerity of their predecessors; who, according to the rules of their founder, lived upon nothing but wild plants and roots, and exposed themselves to perpetual and very rude trials and mortifications, fasting, plunging into cold water, wandering through rocky solitudes, and wild forests, and the like.

The same author informs us, that there are many more religious orders established in the country; that the common people have a superstitious veneration for their ecclesiastics; that a religious life was easy and pleasant, according to the custom of the time when he wrote; that the convents possessed great wealth; and that consequently many, under the cloak of devotion and retirement, became monks that they might give themselves to uninterrupted luxury and wantonness. Such, we may add, appears to be in every country, and under every system of religion, the

* For an account of the Religion of Japan, see chapters xi., xvi.

natural, if not the necessary course of monastic institutions. Being founded on principles contrary to nature, (whose author is God,) insulted nature will resume her sway; having been forced out of the channel of virtuous enjoyment, she turns aside into the lawless courses of vice for gratification.

Boodhism, or Budsdo—as the Japanese call it—was propagated in Japan many ages ago, and in time gained a preponderance among the common people over the old Sintoism of the country; insomuch that many of the Sintoists adopted a sort of mixed religion, compounded of the two. The mixture was not very difficult, because the two systems agreed in several fundamental principles.

We may remark by the way, that religious persecution was scarcely known in China and Japan, and a perfect religious freedom reigned, until the Romish missionaries so managed as to excite, first the jealousy, and then the enmity of the government. Being Jesuits, they pursued the jesuitical policy of making their religion subservient to their ambition. Their sort of Christianity had so much in common with the heathenish systems of the country, that they found it no difficult matter to make converts. But no sooner had they gathered a strong party of adherents, than they began to pursue a policy which excited the suspicion of political designs. In Japan they took part in a civil war, that they might gain political power. Hence in both China and Japan they were expelled from the country; their followers were exterminated by persecution; and the very name of Christianity was made so odious, as to render the conversion of these populous nations a very difficult undertaking. Protestant missionaries, before they can gain even a hearing for their doctrines, have before them the hard task of removing a deeply-rooted prejudice against the Christian name, and of demonstrating to unwilling minds, that there is a true Christianity materially different from Jesuitism; one whose spirit is all purity, benevolence, peace, and submission to lawful authority; and whose end is not worldly power and wealth, but the salvation of the soul. But let us return to our subject.

As might be expected, Boodhism varies somewhat in different countries, retaining everywhere the material parts of the original system, but modified in some of its forms and circumstantials. The Boodhists of Japan have in their ancient books the five precepts of their founder, called by them the precepts Siaka—namely, first, kill not; second, steal not; third, whore not; fourth, lie not; fifth, drink no strong liquors.

These five commandments are expanded, first into ten Sikkai, which serve for the general conduct of life; and these again into five hundred rules called Gofiakkai, which are intended for those who aim at moral perfection in this life, and the highest felicity in the life to come. They are exceedingly strict, and prescribe an ascetic life of the rudest and austerest character; making the mortification of the bodily senses and appetites their chief end and aim. They show how deeply seated in the oriental mind, is that principle of the ancient heathen philosophy, which makes the chief part of human virtue consist in bodily mortifications. From this principle sprang the monachism of Eastern Asia; and with the introduction of this principle into the Christian Church in the second century, came asceticism; with its growth, in the third century, came monachism, with all its extravagancies.

The Boodhist Bible teaches doctrines very different from those taught in our Bible, but in some remarkable points identical with those of the Roman Catholic Church. For example, the doctrine of purgatory, or purification of the soul after death by torments for a limited time; and the doctrine of prayers and offerings—that is, of masses—for the souls in purgatory, who are supposed to be relieved in part or in whole by these masses, said by the priests and paid for by surviving friends.*

The priests also celebrate a yearly religious festival for the dead, very nearly in the same manner, and identically for the same purpose, as the Roman Catholics celebrate their Feast of

* Kempfer, ch. xvi.

All-Souls. "The priests perform the service every year on an appointed day, each in their rank, and in their own pagodas [or churches.] They go in a row, one after another in procession, round a covered grave, chanting litanies and a sort of service for the departed.*

In Japan, as elsewhere, the Boodhists have their monk-priests, their nuns, and their monasteries,—their shaven heads and their celibacy. Here they preach, read prayers in a dead language, bow to their idols, count their beads,—in short, do as the Roman Catholic priests do.

Here too they have stately temples with convents adjoining. The temples are full of gilded images,—"In the middle of the temple (says Kempfer)† stands a fine altar with some images upon it, and a beautiful candlestick with sweet-scented candles burning before it. The whole temple is so neatly and curiously adorned, that one would fancy himself transported into a Roman Catholic church, did not the *monstrous shape* of the idols evince the contrary."

From this description of Kempfer, who saw what he describes, it is evident, that the only circumstance which distinguishes a Boodhist temple in Japan from a Roman Catholic church, is *the shape of the idols.*

No wonder that the Jesuit missionaries who visited Japan were astonished, as their brethren were in Cochin China and Thibet, to find among these remote heathen a religion so much like their own. Their letters expressed their astonishment. Besides the particulars already mentioned, they noticed the close similarity between the monastic institutions of the two religions, and between their priests and ceremonies. The Bonzes—as the Boodhist priests of Japan were called—had large libraries in their convents; they summoned the monks together by ringing brass bells; the prior every evening prescribed to his monks a theme on which they were to meditate; at midnight certain choirs took it in turn to chant prayers at the altar, like the matins of the Romish

* Pinkerton's Collection, vol. vii. p. 629.

† Ch. xx.

monks; and at the dawn of day all the monks spent an hour in private meditation. They also had shaven heads and many festivals in the course of the year.

These things were good in themselves—in Roman Catholics very good; but in these heathenish Bonzes, the wondering missionaries took them to be the work of the devil.

In reading such accounts of the Japanese monk-priests, one can hardly divest himself of the impression that they belonged to the Mother and Mistress of all Churches—the Catholic, or Universal Church, as she claims to be. But supposing Boodhism and Romanism to be not the same, then we can hardly shake off the impression that they are sisters, the offspring of a very ancient mother, the primitive religious philosophy and superstition of Eastern Asia.

The Romish missionaries in Japan were excessively provoked by the discovery of such a likeness between themselves and those whom they had come to convert. They hated their brethren, the Bonzes, with superlative hatred. In their letters they blackened their characters to all intents and purposes. What was commonly practised among the Romish clergy, they imputed as a mark of extreme depravity in the Japanese clergy.

For one thing, the Bonzes drove a pretty lucrative traffic in the sale of Indulgences. They drew bills, containing a form of words, which they assured the purchasers would not only keep off evil spirits in this world, but would serve as passports to the felicity of the world to come. They were equivalent, therefore, to the Roman Catholic Bills of Indulgence, in which Holy Mother formerly traded so very profitably, and in which she has continued to deal in those countries in which the article is still in demand. Yet this is one of the grounds on which the Romish missionaries charged the Bonzes with being morally the impurest of mankind and the most avaricious.

Another sin of which they accused the Bonzes was, that they would borrow money on a pledge of repayment in a future state; and to secure the payment, they gave the lender a written bond, *which he was to carry with him into the other world.* If this priestly trick was not misrepresented by the Jesuitical enemies of the Bonzes, it was a piece of scurvy imposture which could deceive only the most ignorant.* Yet, in a moral point of view, it was not a whit worse than the Popish Bills of Indulgence. Is it any more fraudulent to sell a bond payable in money after death, than to sell a bill payable in merit to save a man's soul from purgatory? Few would be simple enough to buy the cash bonds, but many millions have been imposed on by the merit-bills of the Infallible Church.

They also charged the Bonzes with refusing to offer sacrifices and prayers for the dead, until they had received a fee; and this they must have (said the missionaries) even when the surviving relation who applied for the service, was the poorest of men. Oh, the wicked Bonzes! No wonder the good Jesuits were indignant

* Yet a Christian bishop of the fifth century is related to have played the same sort of trick. In the year 410, Synesius, a Platonic philosopher of Cyrene, was ordained Bishop of Ptolemais, though he was at the time as much a Platonist as he was a Christian. But he became zealous to convert pagans to Christianity.

He had a pagan friend, the philosopher Evagrius, who refused to turn Christian, unless convinced of the truth of the Scriptural proverb, He that giveth to the poor, lendeth to the Lord, who will repay him. Synesius at last overcame his doubts, and converted him. Then Evagrius put into his hand three hundred pieces of gold to distribute among the poor; for which the bishop gave him, in the name of the Lord, *a written bond for the money, payable after death.* Evagrius kept the bond carefully, and on his death-bed ordered his family to put it secretly into his hand when they buried him. They did so; and three nights afterwards he appeared in a dream to Synesius, and said, Come to my grave and take back your note; I have received all, and have written a full discharge on the note. Synesius had known nothing of the affair; but on inquiry of the family, he learned that the note had been buried with the corpse. On opening the grave, he found the note, with a receipt in full for the money, endorsed upon it in the handwriting of the dead philosopher, who declared that Jesus Christ had repaid the loan which he had given to the poor! The note was afterwards carefully preserved in the church of Cyrene. The story is found in the Pratum Spirituale of Moschus. The reader may find it also in Tillemont and in Jostin's Remarks, A. D. 410.

at their conduct. It is true, we admit, that the Roman Catholic priests have always made a great deal of money by saying or singing masses—that is, offering sacrifices and prayers—for the dead; and they have taken fees for this charitable service from even the poorest of men. But then, have they not a right? Are they not priests of the only true Church? And have they not power to pray souls out of purgatory? At least we can make bold to affirm that the Bonzes had no such power.

The famous missionary, Francis Xavier, a Jesuit, and the first who went to Japan, is still more severe on the Bonzes. In one of his epistles from Japan, he says:

"They are so shamefully given to all sorts of crimes, especially to sodomy, that they openly avow the practice; and instead of blushing, when reproved by Christians for using men as women, they answer them with scoffing and ridicule. They have in their monasteries many young and handsome sons of the nobility, sent there to be educated; these they abuse in the flower of their age. Some of the Bonzes resemble [Roman Catholic] monks, in keeping their heads shaved, and in wearing grey clothing. These are more lax than others in their discipline. They have nuns of the same order, with whom they live. All reports agree that when these women become pregnant, they procure abortion by the use of drugs."*

St. Francis Xavier, who told these things is almost divine authority; for, on account of the miracles which the Jesuits reported that he had wrought in the far East, the Pope of Rome canonized him, that is, made him a worshipful saint in heaven, to succor those on the earth who should pray to him.

It appears from the foregoing passage from his letters, that the Boodhist monks in Japan, as in other countries, conducted the education of youth. But we must intimate a little doubt, whether he is correct in saying that they generally abused the sons of the nobility in the shameful manner charged; for although a Dutch

* See Commentaries of the Jesuits on the affairs of India and Japan, quoted by Hospinian, De Origine Monachatus.

writer* charges the nobility themselves with the same crime, they would hardly allow their sons to be so abused. That some of the Bonzes kept catamites is, however, credible enough; for when men outrage nature in one way, by refusing a lawful indulgence to a constitutional appetite, they are very apt to outrage it also in some other abominable way, as these Bonzes were charged with doing, and as many a Roman Catholic priest and monk has done.

But enough: we will close this long chapter with the remark, which the reader has, no doubt, already made, that the facts detailed in it are very curious and interesting; and exhibit a resemblance between Boodhism and Romanism, which is too close to be accidental, and sufficiently important to deserve farther investigation.

CONCLUDING NOTE.

Since the time of Kempfer, little has been added to our knowledge of Japan. The best general account is by Von Siebold, a learned German. But all the late information, obtained through the Dutch traders, amounts to so little in respect to the religion of the country, that Kempfer, now about one hundred and fifty years old, is that from which we have drawn most of the preceding statements.

* Caron in his account of Japan.

CHAPTER IV.

MONACHISM AMONG THE MAHOMETANS.

As Mahomet arose about 600 years after Chirst, of course neither his doctrine nor his followers could have any thing to do with the origin of monachism among either heathens or Christians. On the contrary the Mahometans derived their ascetical notions and practices from the Christian and heathen nations amongst whom they found them.

Our motive for inserting a brief account of the monkish superstitions and fanatical penances of the Mahometans, is to show how these things operate upon mankind under every system of religious belief.

All the Mahometan nations have religious orders among them; that is, either monks, in the full sense of the term; or certain classes of devotees, who affect an ascetical austerity of manners, and claim on that account an extraordinary degree of sanctity, and often a divine gift of working miracles.

Niebuhr, the celebrated traveller, says that the Sunnites—the Mahometan sect to which the Turks belong, are known to have among them a great many religious orders; the members of which are distinguished by the name of Dervishes and Santons, and are discriminated from one another by a diversity of dress and manners.

"In Arabia the Dervishes are professors of the Occult Sciences, or Magic and Miracles. The highest of the sciences is called

Ism Allah. It enables its professors to discover what is passing in the most distant countries, to make themselves familiar with genii (a sort of spirits) ; to oblige them to obey their will ; to dispose of the winds and seasons according to their pleasure ; to cure the bites of serpents, and many other diseases. Persons who have gone far in the study of this science, have attained, as there are (pretended) instances to prove, to a facility of performing their prayers at noon in the Caaba of Mecca without going out of their houses at Bagdat or Aden."

"The art of procuring sublime visions is not unknown to these Arabians. They use the same means that are employed by certain societies in Europe. They shut themselves up for a long time in a dark place, without eating or drinking, and continue to repeat their prayers aloud till they faint away. After recovering from the swoon and leaving the cave, they relate what they have seen in their trance. The common pretences are, that they have seen God in his glory, angels and spirits of all sorts, heaven and hell."

"The second sort of these sciences, called Simmia, is not of so exalted a nature. Although the most sensible of the Mahometan clergy disapprove ofthis science, some orders of Dervishes, however apply themselves to it, and practice it, in order, they say, to prove the truth of their religion and the sanctity of the founder of their order. These pretended miracles are often performed at Bosra, where I have seen (says Niebuhr) a company of Dervishes of the order of Bedredden walk about all day in the streets, leaping and dancing, beating the drum, and making gesticulations with sharp-pointed irons, which they seemed to strike into their eyes."

"In the same city I was present at a festival, which the Dervishes of this order celebrate every year. The scene was in the open air and in the court of the mosque, which was illuminated with only three lamps. Several Mullahs and Dervishes began with singing some passages out of the Koran. They continued to sing with the accompaniment of some drums ; and during the music, the other Dervishes arose, took the sharp-pointed irons, and did as if they were piercing their bodies, and even driving the iron with mallets into their flesh. Next appeared the principal actor; who, assuming an air of inspiration, directed the music to proceed, and to be raised to higher animation, in order to assist his enthusiasm, or rather to stun the ears of the spectators. In his ecstacy he threw up his turban in the air, loosened his hair (for this order of Dervishes wear their hair) and pierced his body with five lances; then mounting a low building by which a pole sixteen feet long and pointed with iron had been set up, he impaled himself upon the pole, and was carried in this condition through the square."

"It was an affecting sight to see a lean man with a long beard and disheveled hair, wounded all over with spikes, and then carried about spitted on a pole. As I went away, I said to a Mullah of my acquaintance, that the Dervish performed his tricks by means of a wide belt which he carried in his drawers. The Mullah replied that he had suspected some such art, but avoided mentioning his suspicions, lest he should draw upon him the enmity of the order of Bedredden."

The science of Kurra teaches to compose billets which secure the wearer against the power of enchantment, and against evil accidents of all sorts. These billets are enclosed in small purses of skin and worn about the body. They are likewise bound upon the necks of horses and asses to give them an appetite for their food and to tame them when unmanageable. In the city of Diarbekar a billet of this sort put an end to a troublesome croaking of frogs. A man of eminence at Aleppo distributed every year, gratis, billets for freeing houses from flies. The efficacy of these billets depends upon the day, the hour, and the particular condition of the messenger sent to ask for them. Old women continue to use them, however after they fail; being simple enough to suppose always, that some of the conditions necessary to their efficacy have been wanting, when they were unsuccessful. These billets are at least no worse than those for making hens lay eggs, which were publicly sold by a Jesuit in the middle of the eighteenth century and among enlightened nations."*

These extracts from Niebuhr show what imposters the Dervishes of Arabia are.

But of all the Mahometans the Turks have among them the greatest number and variety of religious orders. They are little behind the Roman Catholics in this respect. Monkish saintship is in great credit among them.

Bartholomew Georgiwicz, a writer of the sixteenth century, says, as quoted by Hospinian, that among the Turks, the first order of their monk-saints have no property, go almost naked and torture themselves. Another sort wear their privy parts loaded with a ring of three pounds weight, to preserve their chastity. A third sort stay in the mosques, naked; fasting and praying for the revelation of future events.

John Cuspinian, a German, who died in the year 1529, wrote a history of the Turks, in which he describes their religious orders substantially as follows:

Some go naked, except a small covering over their privy parts. They seem to be insensible to suffering, exposing themselves alike to all weathers, and bear with indifference the laceration of their skins. Some profess absolute poverty, think nothing of earthly things, and lay up nothing for the morrow. Some live for days without food or drink. Others observe perpetual silence, refusing absolutely to speak on any occasion. Some profess to have visions and revelations; others to have supernatural raptures and trances.

The different orders of Dervishes are distinguished by marks and badges. Some wear feathers on their heads, to denote that they are given to meditations and revelations. Others wear earrings, in token of their obedience to the spirit, by which they are frequently ravished. Others signify the violence of their ecstacies by wearing chains about their necks. Others again represent

* Niebuhr's Travels, ch. cxxx.

their poverty by wearing garments composed of variously-colored rags and patches.

They have also different modes of living. Some mix with other men: some live separately in convents or villages of their own; but the greater number live in the woods and deserts as anchorites, or in the cemeteries, where they subsist on the alms of the people who visit these cities of the dead.*

The Dervishes do not observe all the rules and customs of their religion; for many of them reject marriage as unholy, use no ablutions, and observe not the stated hours of prayer. But these wifeless Mahometan saints are not always destitute of human comfort. Some female devotees secretly mix with them, and say that the children which they bear, were miraculously conceived, without human agency. These children of professed virgins are called Nefesogli. Two of these unbegotten men, in the city of Brusa, were reported to expel demons by means of their hair or their clothes; it being supposed—not without reason—that men supernaturally born must be supernaturally endowed.

All these votaries of an ascetic religion, are venerated as great saints, preservers of the kingdom, and special friends of God and Mahomet. They are of the opinion that the law is profitable; but that grace is sufficient for salvation without obedience to law. But they do not argue in support of their opinion; they prove their doctrine by working miracles. Precisely so did the ancient monks of Christendom prove the divine origin of monkery and monkish opinions.

But there is another sort of Turkish monks called Czofilar, because they devote themselves to meditation and other spiritual exercises. These are deemed successors of the prophet and fathers of the Sunnite sect, to which the Turks belong. They possess great authority, alleging in support of their opinion the tradition of the fathers. They assert that men are saved by merit

* The Turkish cemeteries are remarkable for their extent, and their large, costly monuments, some of which are roomy enough to serve as tenements for the living.

without grace or law, by giving themselves to certain forms of prayer, spiritual exercises, watchings, and beggings.* They pray continually. By night they assemble, and seating themselves in a circle, they repeat for some time the words, *La Illah Iillahah!* moving their heads in concert. Then they often repeat the word *Lahu!* and then *Huhu!* until they fall down from exhaustion and sleep. These are venerated chiefly by men who value themselves on the antiquity and nobility of their families. So far we follow Cuspinian.

Antonine Menavin, a writer of the same century on the religion of the Turks, says that their monks are chiefly of four orders. There were many others; but on account of their singular wickedness, they were all reduced to four. Those of the first order are clothed in a lion's skin, and generally carry a book in their hands. Those of the second order make a vow of chastity and keep it, though often with reluctance, says Menavin. The third order live by begging. The fourth go with a shaved head, and are utterly illiterate and rude. Menavin says that these are a sort of crafty impostors; that some of them are vagrants at large; some lay snares for women, and the rest devote themselves to gormandizing. It is evident that Menavin had a very bad opinion of the Turkish ascetics.

In the year 1503, a fanatical dervish attempted to assassinate the Turkish Sultan, Bajazet the Second; for which the whole order was for a time banished from the Turkish dominions. Knolles in his history of the Turks, gives, in his peculiar style, the following account of the affair.

"Bajazet departing thence, upon the way met with a dervisher, (which is a phantasticall and beggarly kind of Turkish monks, using no other apparell but two sheepskins, the one hanging before and the other behind,) a lustie, strong, fat fellow, attired after the manner of his order, with a great ring in each ear, who

* In these notions they agree with the ancient Christian monks. Monkery is founded chiefly on the supposed merit of such things.

drawing near unto Bajazet, as if he would of him have received an alms, desperately assailed him with a short scimitar, which he had closely concealed under his hypocriticall habit. But Bajazet, by the starting of the horse whereon he rid, (being afraid at the sudden approach of the hobgoblin,) partly avoided the deadly blow by that traitor intended."

This treacherous attack induced Bajazet to banish the whole order. The history of Christian monkery is not without examples of the same murderous fanaticism—as in the case of Ravaillac, the desperate monk, who, in the year 1610, under a supposed or pretended impulse of the Holy Spirit, assassinated the great and good King Henry IV., of France.

The fullest and most distinct account, that we have seen, of the religious orders of the Turks, is contained in an anonymous French work on the manners and usages of the Turks, published in Paris in the year 1747.*

The author justly supposes that the founders of monastic orders in Turkey imitated Christian models. He remarks, that the Turkish annals say nothing of monasteries before the year of our Lord 1325, when the Turkish dominions were still confined to Asia; and that at first the Turkish monks lived very austerely, like those of Christendom in the early ages. But fanaticism and extravagance corrupted their institution. Now (says he) they seem to think that the fur and white dress which they wear, is a sufficient mark of their sanctity. Some are married and keep shops; others practice celibacy.

The author describes eight distinct orders of Mahometan monks, the most of which are found in Turkey. We shall give from him the names and leading characteristics of these orders, inserting, as we proceed, some things from other writers.

1. *The Menelevis.*

These are so called from Meneleva, their founder. They affect

* Mœurs et Usages des Turcs; 3 vol., 4to. The account of the Religious Orders is in vol. 1, book ii., ch. vii.

to be patient, humble, modest, and charitable. Some of them benevolently carry water through the streets for the poor. Before their superiors and before strangers, they maintain a profound silence. They go with their heads bowed, eyes downcast, and backs bent. Their habit is generally a large brown cloth of camels' hair, with a leathern girdle. They keep their legs and breasts uncovered. They often burn their breasts with a hot iron. They fast every Thursday.

These are the famous dancing dervishes. Every Tuesday and Friday they have a sermon in their mosques on a text of the Koran; and after sermon, some of them whirl round like a top, to the sound of a flute. When the flute stops, they stop instantly stock still, as if they had been suddenly converted into statues. They practice this whirling dance, in imitation, they say, of their founder, Meneleva, who thus whirled incessantly for the space of fourteen days, while his companion Hamze played the flute. He then fell into an ecstacy, in which he received wonderful revelations, and directions for the establishment of his order of monks.*

Bell, who travelled in Asia about the year 1715, witnessed the worship of these dervishes.

"They are" (says he) "a religious order, who have a mosque in Pera [a suburb of Constantinople.] The mosque is built in a circular form, with a pulpit for the mullah and a gallery for the music. The sermon being ended, the musicians began to play on instruments like flutes and hautbois; upon which five of the dervishes stood up and danced round the mosque in a frantic manner, turning themselves round as they advanced with so quick a motion, that their faces were scarcely distinguishable from their heads. They followed each other at certain distances; but an old man of eighty years outdid all the rest in quickness of turning: yet, when he left off he did not seem to be at all discomposed by the violence of the motion. This extravagant sect make vows of poverty and chastity, and are held in great esteem by the devout."

This order of dervishes had formerly, and may still have, regu-

* Moreri, Grande Dictionnaire Historique. Article, Dervis.

larly organized monasteries, and a general superintendent, who resided in the monastery of Coigni, in Natolia. They had numerous monasteries in the several provinces of Turkey.

Whilst, like Christian monks, they profess poverty, chastity, and obedience, they have a very reasonable provision for weak brethren. If one finds himself unable to continue his vow of chastity, they permit him to return to the world and marry like an honest man. What an amount of impurities and disorders would have been avoided among the Roman Catholic monks and clergy, if they had adopted this salutary rule, inculcated by St. Paul, (1 Cor. vii. 9) and obeyed by the Menelevis!

There is a remarkable extravagance of the Egyptian dervishes. They have (says Moreri) assigned a place in Paradise to the horse of their Saint Chederlé, and to several other meritorious beasts; to wit, the camel of Mahomet, the ram which Abraham sacrificed instead of his son Isaac, the heifer of Moses, the ant of Solomon, the parrot of the Queen of Sheba, the ass of Ezra, and the dog of the Seven Sleepers. Some say also the ass of the Messiah; but others doubt this, seeing that Ezra's ass was already in Paradise. But the Roman Catholics of the Middle Ages did not forget this worthy Christian ass. They celebrated in France an annual festival to his honor. Among the worshippers in the church on the solemn occasion, was a living representative of his long-eared saintship. After mass, they sung a funny Latin hymn to his praise, and concluded the service by three rounds of hearty braying. Whether the four-footed ass joined in this act of devotion, we know not, but the priest led in this as in other parts of the service.* We take him to have been the chief ass among them.

The elegant Busbeque, in his Letters from Turkey, written about the year 1560,† relates some things of these monks that may amuse the reader. We have translated the following extract from his Letters:

* For an account of this Feast of Asses, see Du Fresne, Glossarium, Article Festa Afinorum; and Michelet's Hist. of France, B. 4, ch. 9.

† Busbequii Legationis Turcicae Epistolae.

"At Theke Thioi the Turkish monks, called dervishes, have a great house. We learned much from them concerning a certain hero named Chederlé, of great mental and corporeal fortitude; who, as they fable, was the same as our Saint George; and they ascribe to him the same actions, namely, that he saved a virgin from a huge dragon by killing the monster; to which they add many things of their own invention, as, that he was accustomed to travel to distant shores, and came at last to a river whose water conferred immortality on those who drank of it. But they do not say in what part of the world this river is to be found—unless, perchance, it be in Utopia. They affirm only that it is hidden by gloomy clouds and darkness, and that it was never revealed to any mortal's sight except Chederlé's; that Chederlé and his elegant horse, being here freed from the laws of death, wandered through the world, giving aid to the injured party engaged in war, or to the distressed who implored his help, of whatsoever religion they might be. What makes the story more ridiculous is, that they hold him to have been a companion and friend of Alexander the Great. For the Turks, disregarding chronology, confound and mix up everything in their stories." We may add to this remark of Busbeque's, that the Christian romancers of the Middle Ages were often quite as regardless of time and space, when they mixed up their stories of love and heroism, sorcerers and giants. But let us resume the narrative of Busbeque.

"The marble fountain of pure water which is in their mosque, they pretend to have originated from Chederlé's horse, that shed his urine there. They tell many stories also of Chederlé's companions, and of a niece of his. They show their sepulchres in the neighborhood; at these they pretend that great benefits are conferred on those who invoke their aid. They pretend that even the stones and gravel on which Chederlé stood, when he watched the dragon, were, if taken in one's drink, a remedy against fever, headache, and sore eyes."

Thus it appears from Busbeque that the Turkish monks imbibed from their Christian models the monkish spirit of romancing, and the practice of invoking the help of dead saints, as well as of ascribing miraculous cures to their relics.

Busbeque relates another story, which shows that they had also borrowed the art of imposing pretended miracles of living monks upon the credulous multitude.

Speaking of a certain monk, he says—"He walked with a coat and a white robe flowing down to his feet, his hair loose, and his whole person much like our pictures of the apostles. Under a fair face he concealed the soul of an impostor; but the Turks venerated him as a great wonder-worker. They got my interpreters to fetch him to me, that I might see him. He dined with me soberly and modestly. He then went out into the yard, and presently returned, carrying a large stone, with which he inflicted blows on his naked breast, sufficient to have felled an ox. He then took out of the fire a piece of iron prepared for the occasion, and now red hot. This he inserted into his mouth, and turned it about there for some time, making the saliva hiss with the heat. The piece of iron was oblong, and square at the thicker end, which he had put into his mouth, glowing like a live coal. When he had done, he put the iron back into the fire, saluted me and left the house, after having received a gift. One of my servants affirmed that it was all a trick; that the iron was not really hot; and, to confirm his opinion, he laid hold on it by the end which stuck out of the fire. But he was severely burnt, and then ridiculed by the others, who asked him whether the iron was hot."

"The same monk told me at dinner, that the abbot of his monastery, renowned for sanctity and miracles, used to spread his cloak upon the water of a lake by the monastery, and getting upon it, to sail pleasantly over the lake; and that he would dress a mutton, ready for roasting, and tying the fore legs to his arms, and the hind legs to his own legs, he would go with it into a hot furnace, and stay there until the mutton was roasted. These stories I believe were false; but the feat with the hot iron I saw; but I have no doubt that when he went into the yard, he fortified his mouth with a liquor that secured it from injury."

So far Busbeque. The feat with the hot iron does not exceed the power of jugglery; nor does that of the roast mutton transcend similar actions by some fire-kings of the nineteenth century. As to the real miracle of sailing upon a cloak, this was stolen by the Turkish monks—impostors as they are—from the Roman Catholic breviary or prayer-book. Some fifty or sixty years before Busbeque's embassy to Constantinople, the Italian monk, St. Francis of Paula, sailed over the boisterous strait of Sicily, where Charybdis whirled and Scylla howled—*upon his cloak.* There can be no doubt of the fact, or it would not have been inserted in the breviary. Many such miracles of the monk-saints are found in this great prayer-book, mixed with lessons of Holy Scripture,—all read to the faithful with equal solemnity, and all to be received by them with equal reverence, as the dictates of Holy Mother, whose word is infallible. But let us return to our Menelevis.

They sometimes procure ecstatic visions by intoxicating themselves with opium or spirits of wine. In this, however, they are not singular. Their cloisters are dispersed over the provinces, and serve as inns for their members, who travel a great deal as pilgrims and as spies. These sacred buildings sometimes also conceal ladies of pleasure. The Grand Vizier Kuprili had one torn down at Adrianople, because he discovered that it was no better than a baudy house. But we have said enough of the Menelevis, the most important and most regular of the Turkish monks. The other orders will be dismissed with brief notices.

2. *The Ebibuharis.*

These devote themselves to constant meditation and prayer, with fasting. They aim to abstract their souls from earth, and by holy devotion to participate in the glory of heaven. Being thus purified and abstracted in spirit, they deem the holy place of Mecca to exist in their cells, as much as elsewhere, to them. Still they are regarded as a sort of heretics, for not taking their bodies, as well as their spirits, on pilgrimage to Mecca, like other believers.

3. *The Nimetulahis*

These assemble at night to praise the divine Unity with songs. Candidates for membership in their order, pass forty days in a chamber, taking but three ounces of nourishment daily. During this retreat, they say that they see God face to face, and that all the glory of Paradise is revealed to them. When the period of their seclusion is expired, the other brethren take them into a meadow, and dance around them. If, during the dance, the novice has a vision, he casts back his cloak and falls upon his face, as if thunderstruck. Then the Superior comes and prays over him. When the visionary comes to himself, he raises his red, wandering eyes, and for a long time has the appearance of an idiot or a drunkard. Finally, he communicates his vision to the Superior, or to some other wise person, who understands the mysteries of religion. From these facts, the reader can perceive the spirit of the Nimetulahis.

4. *The Kadris.*

The Kadris place their religion in macerating their bodies, and in working themselves up to a divine fury. They go stark naked, except a clout about their loins. They join hands and dance in a ring for hours, or even a whole day; incessantly repeating vehemently one of the names of God, until, like men seized with a fit of madness, they fall to the ground with their mouths foaming and their bodies dripping with sweat. Enough of them.

5. *The Sejahs.*

Have monasteries, yet they are vagabonds. They go forth to collect money and provisions, like the Romish beggar-monks; and never return, until they have obtained the quantity required by the Superior, when he sends them out on a mission of beggary.

These monks have a peculiar way of begging. When one of them enters a city, he repairs to the market or some other place where multitudes usually collect. Choosing a conspicuous station, he bawls out with all his might—Oh, God, send me so many crowns, or so many gallons of rice! When a holy man begs so lustily of God, pious men are apt to think themselves called on to answer the prayer. Having received their contributions here, the devout beggar-monk goes in quest of another crowd.

Many of these vagrant beggars are found in Hindostan; but they wander over all Mahometan countries. They do not depend solely on the begging prayers just mentioned. They practice the art of story-telling, to amuse the people. Thus they often gain money where the other method would fail.

When Solyman the Magnificent was reigning over the Turkish Empire, the Great Mogul of India sent an embassy to offer him assistance in his wars. The Grand Vizier, Kuprili Mustapha, sent back for answer, that the greatest favor which the Great Mogul could do the Turks, would be to keep his Fakirs or beggar-monks, at home.

6. *The Edhemis*

Are so called after the name of their founder, Ibrahim Edhem, who spent his time in the mosques, humbly bent to the ground, reading the Koran and praying to God. His domestics and others so admired his piety, that they imitated his example, and thus an order of monks arose. They renounce the business and pleasures of the world, and live an austere life of fasting, prayer, and solitude. Most of their monasteries are in Persia.

7. *The Bektachis.*

Hadji (that is, Saint) Bektach, famous for miracles and prophecies, gave his name to this sect. They can scarcely be called monks, for they marry and live in towns among the other citizens. But they are bound to take long journeys to distribute to all whom they meet copies of the *Gazelle*, a pathetic song, allegorically applied, like Solomon's Canticles, to divine love,—and the *Elma*, that is, one of the names of God, of which they have one thousand and one.

Their worship consists mainly in crying Hu! hu! Let him live! Let him live. But as they do not observe the regular hours of prayer, they are considered to be a sort of heretics. In our opinion, Hadji Bektach founded a very silly and very fantastical sect.

8. *The Santons.*

Their maxim is, *To-day is ours—To-morrow his who shall enjoy it.* Hence, contrary to other sects, they abandon themselves, on principle, to licentiousness and debauchery. Their object is present pleasure. They will give anything to satisfy their appetites, and they consider the tavern as holy as the mosque. On the principle that God made us for enjoying the good that is before us, they pretend that they serve God as well by disorderly and sensual lives, as others do by fasting and bodily mortification. Yet they profess to be religious men! They pass their lives in pilgrimages to Jerusalem, Bagdat, Damascus, and other holy places. But these hypocritical pilgrimages are in reality expeditions of brigandage. They haunt the road-sides, watching for travellers, whom they will plunder when they can, either by sturdy begging or by sturdier violence.

The sanctity of some of them consists in acting the fool, that they may attract attention; gazing steadfastly at the moon; talking proudly, and quarelling with those whom they meet.

They generally go with head and legs naked, and the body covered with the rough, dirty skin of some wild beast, with a girdle of skin about the loins, and a pouch hanging by the side. Some, instead of a girdle of skin, wear a serpent-like coil of copper, which their doctors give them as a mark of knowledge. They carry a sort of club in their hands, which they flourish with an air as they go.

The Santons of India, who pass through Turkey on their pilgrimage to Mecca and Jerusalem, demand alms with a sort of contemptuous smile. They walk with measured steps. The little clothing that they have, is exceedingly ridiculous, being composed of rags of all colors, picked up on dunghills, and stitched one over another with coarse twine.

These monks are perfect charlatans. They make a business of selling relics to devotees, to wit, some hairs of Mahomet, and other like precious articles.

Nearly all are impudent hypocrites. They say their prayers aloud in the streets, and especially in the market places. There they are seen from morning till night. The market place may be considered as their oratory, their refectory, their cell, and their convent. If they tire of this mode of life, they have only to put on citizens' clothes, and forthwith they are Santons no more. But few ever quit their idle, vagrant life. Their feigning trade of beggary and saintship gives them certain advantages. They are deemed saints by many, and are secure againt taxes and military service. They never want simpletons who are ready to be imposed on by loud professions of sanctity; and then by practicing quackery, exorcism, charms, and other tricks of the craft, they can never fail of dupes, who will pay well for being cheated by almost any sort of religious impostor.

Concluding Remarks.

All the employments of the Turkish monks are sordid or ridiculous. The Menelevis are mercenary. Of the rest, some live in contemptible indolence: some pass all their days in the highways or at the corners of the streets, looking woefully upon the ground, and receiving whatever alms may be offered without their asking for them. Some walk the streets, clothed in a large sheet, their feet elevated on stilts, a sort of trident in their hands, and their mouths crying aloud, *There is no God but God, and Mahomet is his prophet.* Others run through the streets, carrying a large wallet full of musty bread and putrid mutton, to feed the cats and dogs which have no master:—Poor cats and dogs! There are many such in Turkey. Those who have a talent, amuse the people with buffoonery. Others go singing before every door, to the sound of a tambour. Some profess to be diviners and prophets. Others interpret dreams, exercise magical arts, and make certain conjurations, prayers, and exorcisms over the sick. Some affect dumbness and ask alms by signs. Others burn their flesh with a hot iron, or cut it with a razor. The people admire this sort of saints and give them plentiful alms.

The Turks have also their female saints, who generally imitate the Santons. They dance to the sound of the tambour in little mosques of their own. They tell fortunes, interpret dreams, and pray over the sick. The she-dervishes travel from city to city, to amuse the idle, and often to make a traffic of their charms.* Their obedience consists in running about to get money; their poverty, in taking with all their hands; and their chastity, in having none. Their slippers are violet, like those of the Jews; their veils are large, like those of our nuns—says the author of Moeurs des Turcs:—They profess to be saints; and many believe that they are, because they make many loud prayers in public, live unmarried, and follow no useful occupation! Poor human nature!

* Picard. Ceremonies, &c. Tome iii. des Musselmans.

CHAPTER V.

BRIEF NOTICE OF THE ANCIENT RELIGIOUS PHILOSOPHIES OF PERSIA, CHALDEA, AND EGYPT.

THE primary source of monachism was, as we have shown, the ancient religious philosophies of the Hindoos and Boodhists of Eastern Asia. The same fundamental principles of religion pervaded the ancient nations of Middle and Western Asia, and, to a great extent, formed the basis of the Egyptian religion. The origin and early spread of these principles date so far back in antiquity, that even the obscurest of historical traditions fail to reach them. Where, or among what people they originated, or how they came to be so extensively propagated, are questions which cannot be solved. The most ancient records of any heathen religion, are the Vedas of Hindostan. We may reasonably conjecture from these and other signs of remote antiquity, that Hindostan was one of the primitive seats of human civilization, and one of the original fountains of religious philosophy. The only other countries which may claim a rivalship in these respects with the Valleys of the Ganges and the Indus, are Egypt on the Nile, and Chaldea on the Euphrates. It may be, that they all derived the elements of their religious philosophy from their common ancestry, an aboriginal people, who branched off as they spread, and carried with them their patriarchal religion. On this common basis, each of these ancient nations may have built its peculiar mythology; and thus may have arisen that uniformity of leading principles, with diversity of doctrine and practice, which afterwards characterized their systems of religion. Commerce and missions may have, in later times, infused some doctrines and practices from the matured system of one nation into that of another, and thus produced a closer affinity between the two ;—such as existed between the Hindoo and the Egyptian systems.

It was from Egypt, Chaldea, and Persia, that the Jews and Greeks derived the principles of their ascetic philosophy, and it was through this philosophy, mainly, that the Church derived those principles of ascetism that led to all the extravagancies of Christian monkery. We purpose in this and some following chapters, to show, by a deduction of facts, that Christian monachism originated from the same principles of heathen philosophy, which had previously given rise to the oriental monachism described in the second and third chapters. Thus we shall account, in a great measure, for the striking similarity which was found to exist between institutions so remote from each other, and apparently so unconnected. If we succeed in this investigation, our Roman Catholic brethren will no longer need, as their missionaries did, to ascribe this similarity to the Devil ; nor shall it any longer seem, as it has seemed to many, to be an accidental coincidence between a heathenish and a Christian institution. It is unphilosophical, if not somewhat impious, to ascribe such coincidences to chance. The same moral causes operated to produce all the monachism in the world. Certain principles of oriental philosophy produced ascetism and monkery in Eastern Asia. The same principles spreading westward, and getting finally into the church, produced the same effects among Christians, which they had before produced among Brahminists and Boodhists.

As seeds of plants do not vegetate, unless circumstances are favorable, so neither do the principles of monkery always produce monkery,—at least not a fully-developed monkery. Sometimes they produce an abortive or stunted growth, where circumstances are mainly but not wholly unfavorable. Thus we shall see that among some ancient nations, among whom this religious philosophy did in some shape prevail, there was yet no regular or full-grown monachism. Still the operation of the ascetic principles was seen in the religious practices and institutions of the country, or of the sects who professed those principles.

Having thus explained the object of this and some following chapters, we proceed to give some account of the religious philosophy of several ancient nations.

§ 1. *The Religious Philosophy of the Persians.*

The Persians believed in one supreme God, whom they called Mithras. The sun was worshipped as his representative. From the supreme emanated two antagonistical Gods, Oromazd or Hormisdas, author of Good ; and Ahriman, author of Evil ; the former represented by light or fire, and the latter by darkness. Some held that these opposite principles were original and independent beings. Oromazd was spirit ; Ahriman was matter ; which is in itself dark and perverse, while spirit is light and benevolence. This doctrine of two principles is called *dualism.* When these principles are supposed to have originated from Mithras, the supreme God, the system has a trinitarian character, but very different from the Christian Trinity.

The Persians held that God pervades the world as its soul, and that fire or light being the most refined and vivifying element, and penetrating all things, is the representative or rather the element of the mundane soul. They believed in subordiate Gods of different ranks.

The human soul they believed to have pre-existed in a higher state, and to be sent into bodies, to keep up the harmony of nature. Of course they believed the soul to be immortal.

The priests of the Persian religion were the magi, who were of three ranks, the highest of which was the Archimagus or Chief Priest, who presided over the whole body. They rejected the use of images. Zoroaster, or Zerdusht, as the Persians called him, was the great reformer of the Persian religion. He taught a pure morality.

This very brief notice is all that we deem necessary concerning the ancient Persian religion, which is but obscurely and imperfectly known. A small remnant of its followers is yet found in India. They worship fire as the emblem of God.

From the little that is known of the principles of this ancient religion, we remark the following as belonging to the general system of the east.

1. One supreme God from whom other divine persons emanated. These divine emanations have the actual government of the world.

2. The pre-existence of human souls and the existence of demons.

3. The evil nature of matter, from which proceed sin and misery. Of course the body causes the pollution and suffering of the soul.

The distinguishing doctrine of the magian religion, was its *dualism*, or doctrine of two contending principles.

§ 2. *Sketch of the Chaldean Philosophy.*

The ancient Chaldean Philosophy, like that of Persia, is very imperfectly known. The following appear to have been its leading principles:

1. There is one Supreme God, Father of all, by whose providence the universe was arranged and adorned.

2. Below the Supreme Being are three ranks of spiritual beings superior to man: 1st. subordinate Gods; 2d. Demons, and 3d. Heroes.

3. Of the class of demons some are evil. These assume the deceitful appearance of gods, good angels, and souls. They are malignant and mischievous to mankind.

4. The inferior gods and good demons or angels, preside over the different provinces of nature, and the several nations of the earth. They govern in subordination to the Supreme God.

5. The Supreme God dwells in inaccessible light, and can' be approached only through the mediation of subordinate spirits. This was the universal doctrine of the East. Hence the worship of oriental nations was directed to these subordinate ministers or agents of the unapproachable Supreme. The heavenly bodies were popularly believed to be divine, and as such were worshipped.

6. Matter is the primary source of evil. Hence the Chaldeans, as well as the Persians and Egyptians, held that evil demons became such by being invested with a vehicle or light body, of coarser material than the element of fire or light that clothed the good spirits. Hence they, of course, believed that the human soul became impure and miserable by its imprisonment in a gross earthly tenement, like the human body.

The Chaldeans were famous for their magic and astronomy.

The Chaldean Magic, was at first, nothing but the secret worship of good spirits. It afterwards employed itself in discovering the virtues and effects of natural objects; and was then merely a natural science. It finally degenerated into what has been ever since understood by the term, to wit, conjuration and dealing with evil spirits.

The Chaldean Astronomy consisted at first in the study of the motions and laws of the heavenly bodies. Afterwards it degenerated into judicial astrology, and was closely connected with theurgy or black magic. The stars were supposed to influence the fortunes of men and all the affairs of the word, by their motions, aspects and conjunctions. Especially were the planets supposed to govern the course of human events. By pretended knowledge of these celestial influences, and the virtues of terrestial bodies, the Chaldean astrologers and magicians undertook to foretell the fortunes of men, and to prepare talismans by which men could ward off all sorts of evil accidents or evil influences.* These pretended arts continued in vogue, until two or three centuries ago.

* Brucker, Hist. Crit. Vol. i., L. ii., cap. ii.

Improvements in natural science have banished all such superstitions and impostures.

§ 3. *Religious Philosophy of Ancient Egypt.*

The philosophy of ancient Egypt agreed with the Hindoo in all its fundamental principles. The agreement is exact and so extensive as to indicate that there was, at some remote period of antiquity, a connection unexplained by history, between the Hindoos and the Egyptians. They both had that singular institution, the division of the people into casts, of which the sacerdotal cast was the highest. But whilst their religions had the same general principles, they differed in their mythology or fables of the Gods, which seem to have been invented long after the primeval dogmas in which they agree, originated.

The Egyptians, like the Hindoos, believed in a Supreme, Original God, whose attributes are unknown, and who exercises no direct agency in the affairs of the world. From this unknown God, emanated three divine persons, called, as Cudworth thinks, Phta, Ammon or Cneph, and Osiris; or, according to Plutarch, Osiris, Isis, and Horus, corresponding to mind, matter, and the world that is composed of these two.*

Among the general principles of the Hindoo and Egyptian philosophies, and adopted from them by some of the Greek philosophers, is the following as expressed by Creutzer.†

"In the Egyptian theology, as in all the oriental theologies, the predominating principle is that of emanation, which consists not only in distinguishing in thought, but in actually separating the divers attributes of the Great Being, the one universal God; so that each attribute becomes a distinct person, and the one God becomes a multitude of Gods. But at the same time, when referred to its source, each Attribute, itself God in God, is thereby alone the whole Godhead, is identical with God. Each divine Emanation, each Person, considered in his highest power, is himself

* Brucker, Hist. Crit. Phil. L. ii., cap. viii.

† Guignaut's Creutzer, Religion de l'Egypt. Chap. ii.

the Great Being from whom he emanated." The Supreme Original Godhead was considered as unknowable in himself to the human mind, and as revealing his existence and performing his works, only through the Divine Persons who emanated or proceeded from him,—continued in union with his Universal Being,—and constituted essentially but one God in that One Supreme. We shall see this fundamental idea of the Oriental Theology in the Platonic Philosophy of Greece.

Another of the common principles of orientalism was found in the Egyptian Philosophy,—namely, that God is the soul of the world, or that the Divinity resides in nature, so as to be its moving and animating and informing principle, as the human soul is of the body. All separate souls of animated beings were supposed to be emanations from the universal soul, and finally to return into it again. This was also an Egyptian principle.

Another common principle of the ancient theology of the East, is that of the incarnation and consequent suffering of celestial beings, from the highest Divine Person to the lowest of created spirits. Thus the Hindoo Vishnu and the Egyptian Osiris, both Divine Persons of the highest order, become incarnated on earth as men, labor and suffer for a time, die, ascend to heaven, and resume their celestial glory and dominion. Thus, too, inferior Gods are represented as occasionally becoming mortal men in the flesh.

On the same general principle is founded the oriental and Egyptian doctrine, that the souls of men did not begin to exist with the body, but pre-existed as demons or spiritual beings in the upper regions; to which they return, sooner or later, after experiencing the sins and sufferings of mortality, sometimes in one body only, but mostly through a succession of bodies, human or brute, before they ascend to their original abode.

The highest circles of the heavens—that is, the starry regions, are the proper abodes of the Gods. The old Sabean idolatry, which paid divine honors to the heavenly bodies, was incorporated with the more rational and refined theology, which represents the Gods as spiritual beings, by supposing the stars to be animated by divine spirits. The Egyptians identified their God Osiris with the sun, as the Persians did their God Mithras. So the Egyptian Isis was the moon. But the Egyptians conceived that their starry Gods descended and became incarnate on the earth,* it is evident that they considered them as being essentially spiritual substances, and separable from the heavenly bodies which they usually inhabited.

In the lower circles of the heavens beneath the moon, and in the atmosphere about the earth, dwell the demons or genii ; some of whom are evil, and those lower in station are inferior in nature as they inhabit less refined elements than the demons and gods above them. According to Diodorus Siculus, the Egyptians conceived the demons to be derived from the soul of the world.

When one of the demons in the higher and purer circles, so far apostatizes from God, as to desire a corporeal life on the earth, he is committed to the care of a guardian genius, or angel, who conducts him to this world, prepares him a body, watches over him during his trials and sufferings as a human soul ; and when these are over, he conducts him again to his native heaven, freed from his earthly predilections, and never more to wander from the seats of the blest.

Material bodies have an evil influence upon the spirits that occupy them. Every human soul contracts defilement from its connection with the flesh. This must be worked off by abstinence from carnal pleasures, and by elevating the mind to divine contemplations and enjoyments. They who in their earthly life become very sinful, are punished in hell for a time. Those who on earth are not sufficiently purified for heaven, but are exempt or released from purgatorial torments, transmigrate into other bodies, until their trials are over.† They may become brutes as well as men, of high or low degree. Those who do not sufficiently purify themselves in the probationary state of man, have to com-

* Brucker, as before cited. He found this doctrine in Diodorus Siculus. L. I. ch. xii.

† Guignaut's Creutzer. Religion de l' Egypt, ch. ii. and v.

plete a course of transmigrations during three thousand years before they are released.*

Matter is eternal and uncreated. Hence its evil nature is incurable ; and the only remedy for the spirits who are involved in it, is ascetic mortification of the flesh during life, and then a release from all connection with mortal bodies.

Ancient authors differ somewhat in their accounts of the Egyptian philosophy. Hence on some points it is difficult to come at the truth. We have followed the best authorities within our reach, and have given for the most part only the views which are least doubtful. Mosheim infers from the various accounts of ancient authors, that the Egyptians differed among themselves on some speculative questions. This is likely enough. Thus much however is certain, that the Egyptian and Hindoo philosophers agreed in all their fundamental principles, and that these principles are directly ascetic in their tendency. If they did not produce the same degree and kinds of fanatical austerities among the heathen Egyptians, before the Christian era, as they did in Eastern Asia, it was because their tendency was counteracted by circumstances into which we need not particularly enquire. We may remark, however, for one thing, that Egyptian fanaticism found sufficient meritorious employment in its brute worship. The sin which a Hindoo would work off by tormenting his body, an Egyptian devotee could atone for by feeding cats or crocodiles while they lived, and embalming them after they were dead. When, a long time afterwards, some of the same principles mixed themselves with Christianity in Egypt, they produced monkery, because there was nothing in Christianity, that could divert a superstitious mind from carrying them out to their legitimate consequences, and there was something in Christianity that would seem to a superstitious mind to lead to the same consequences.

Some of the principles of the oriental philosophy were found to have spread even to the western shores of Europe. The Keltic Druids of Gaul and Britain, believed that demons or spiritual be-

* Brucker. Hist. Crit., L II. cap. vii.

ings presided over the different parts of nature; that God was the soul of the world; that human souls were of divine origin, and transmigrated from one body to another.* Some however deny that they taught this doctrine, because they held that there was a Hades or infernal abode for departed souls. This, however, is not inconsistent with transmigration, for the Egyptians and Hindoos held that souls might go to Hell, and afterwards transmigrate.

We have gone somewhat largely into the religious philosophy of ancient Egypt for two reasons: first, because the Greeks derived from that source much of their ascetic philosophy, by which Christianity was afterwards corrupted; and secondly, because it was in Egypt where this corruption of Christianity began, and where the strange phenomenon of Christian monkery first appeared. Here too was Judaism corrupted by philosophy, and then contributed to the corruption of Christianity.

* Caesar (De Bello Gallico L. vi. c. 14) says the Druids held *non interire animos, sed aliis post mortem transire ad alios*,—which must mean transmigration from body to body.

CHAPTER VI.

THE ASCETIC PHILOSOPHY OF THE GREEKS.

Among the Eastern nations of whom we have been speaking, the religious philosophy of the learned might be called the essence, or rational part, of the popular religion of the country, the whole being connected and blended together. But in Greece the systems of the philosophers had little or no connection with the popular system of idolatry. The Grecian philosophers generally either imported their leading doctrines from the East, or formed theories of their own without regard to the old religion of the country.

There are traces of the oriental philosophy in the earliest systems of Greece. The reader will recollect that Egyptian colonies settled in the country at a very early period. It is easy to conceive, therefore, how the seeds of orientalism may have been planted in Greece, before the Grecian sages began to travel eastward for knowledge.

We shall give a sketch of the principal systems of Grecian philosophy, which were more or less imbued with the ascetic doctrines of the East, and served as channels through which oriental ascetism and monkery were communicated to the church.

§ 1. *Orpheus and his Philosophy.*

One of the earliest philosophers of Greece was Orpheus. The

6*

time when he lived is uncertain, but was it probably not less than seven or eight centuries before the Christian era. His history is wrapped in fable, and his doctrines are but obscurely and partially known. They were not transmitted to posterity in a written form, but by oral tradition through the Orphic mysteries or secret school of his followers. Therefore no full account of them was ever published to the world.

His doctrines, so far as known, had so much of the Boodhist character, that some learned men have thought him to have been a Hindoo disciple of Boodh, who had wandered into Greece, and there taught his master's system of religious philosophy. But Diodorus Siculus (b. iv., c. 25) represents him as a Greek who travelled in Egypt, and was there initiated into the religious mysteries. If so, we may easily conjecture that he got his oriental doctrines from the secret school of the Egyptian priests. He adopted in full the ascetic principles of the eastern philosophy.

He taught that all things had their origin in God, who contains and provides for all. Every being emanated from him and partakes of his essence. All souls, as they emanated from him, so they are finally absorbed into him again.

The Supreme God is unapproachable and unknown. Hence the inferior Gods, who emanated from him, are the proper objects of worship. Such is the Orphic doctrine concerning God, as reported by the ancients. It is entirely oriental,—the very same, so far as it goes, with the Hindoo and Egyptian theology.*

Plato says† that Orpheus considered the body as the prison of the soul; and that the general opinion in Greece during those of early times, represented the present life as "a life in the grave—a punishment for previous guilt; whence arises the universal necessity of *penance* and *purification:* while in the future life the just are to receive the rewards, and the unjust the punishment of their deeds." "Joined with these (says the cautious Ritter)‡

* Brucker. Pars ii., c. i. Orpheus. † In Phaedro.

‡ Not Carl Ritter, but the author of the History of Ancient Philosophy.

was probably the doctrine of the metempsychosis," or transmigration of souls.

The Platonists asserted that Orpheus also taught the oriental doctrine of demons and heroes; and the Egyptian doctrines afterwards adopted by Plato, that the stars are animated beings, bright Gods. Orpheus is said also to have introduced into Greece the poetical ideas of the Egyptians concerning Hades, the country of the dead,—its Elysian Fields of bliss for the good, and its hell of torments for the wicked. But Homer had taught these before.

He taught ascetical practices,—abstinence from animal food at all times, and bodily mortifications to purify the soul from sin and guilt;—also lustrations and ceremonies for cleansing and expiation. Those who were initiated into his mysteries, had to prepare themselves by a course of purifications, and by confession of their sins.

Such were the leading principles of the Orphic philosophy. They bear evident marks of their oriental origin, and are thoroughly ascetic in their character.

2. *Pythagoras.*

He was the greatest of the Grecian philosophers before Socrates and Plato arose. He lived between five and six centuries before Christ. He was reported to have travelled into Egypt and Chaldea, and some say also into India—to gather wisdom. Though born in the island of Samos, he finally settled among the Greek colonies of southern Italy, where he taught philosophy with great success. He founded the Italic sect of Grecian philosophers. His doctrines had great influence in Greece, until Plato and Aristotle arose; then the Italic sect declined. But a new Pythagoreanism, varying somewhat from the old, sprang up about the time of our Saviour, was embraced by a numerous school in the eastern provinces of the Roman empire, and contributed to spread ascetical notions and practices through the countries where monachism first appeared among Christians.

The Pythagorean philosophy was founded on oriental principles, and was decidedly ascetic in its character. Its theology was of the oriental stamp. The following are its leading principles :*

There is one Infinite God pervading nature as its soul, and the source of life to everything that lives.

Next to this supreme God are three ranks of spiritual beings, Gods, Demons and Heroes or Demigods. The last were men, exalted after death for their virtues.

The world is animated, intelligent, spherical : all without the boundaries of this universal system of nature is a void.

There are successive spheres from the centre to the circumference of the world. In the highest resides only the first cause, whatever is nearer to that, is better than the more remote. The sun, moon and stars are Gods. Mortals dwell in our gross atmosphere; immortals in the pure ether above. The ether is in perpetual motion.

The human soul is a particle of the mundane soul. It is composed of two parts, the one rational, the other irascible and concupiscible ; the former only is immortal, the latter comes from the soul of the world and finally returns to it. The mind or rational soul pre-existed as a spiritual being in the upper regions.

Souls transmigrate from body to body ; not always immediately after death (as Laertius represents the Pythagorean doctrine,) but often after a destined interval in Hades or in the celestial regions. When a soul migrates into the body of a brute, its rational faculties are cramped by a defective organization of its material body.

Pythagoras believed, with nearly all heathen antiquity, that innumerable demons float in the atmosphere and in the etherial circles above,—some of whom are good, and others evil. These airy beings exercise either a salutary or a noxious influence over human bodies, and cause our dreams. They enter into bodies

* Brucker, Hist. Crit. Pars ii. L. ii. c. x. In the huge and sometimes ill-digested mass of this work, we meet with apparently inconsistent doctrines ascribed to the same philosopher.

conceived in the womb, when they find such as suit them, and thus become souls.

Pythagoras adopted the opinion, that the incarnation of souls is a punishment for sins committed in a prior state. Therefore he regarded the body as a penitentiary house of the immortal soul, and as the source of its sufferings on the earth. By its conjunction with that base associate, the animal soul, it is agitated by impure passions, and its intellectual vision is obscured.

Hence the necessity of adopting a strict ascetic mode of life for the purpose of dispelling the clouds from the intellect, and purging the immortal soul from the stains of sin. Carnal desires must be subdued by abstinence, the pleasures of sense must be avoided, and the soul must be elevated by the contemplation of pure entities. By pure entities are meant abstract ideas, which exist independent of matter, and are apprehended by the understanding without the aid of the senses.

The *Moral Rules* of Pythagoras conformed to his philosophical theories. He taught his disciples to abstain from animal food like the Hindoos, and to practice an austere self-denying temperance. He deemed it salutary to inure the body to hardships by adding voluntary sufferings to those which nature imposes.

"The Pythagoreans (says Stanley*) exhorted those who came into their society, to shun pleasure,—for nothing so deceives us and draws into sin as this passion. In general, it seems, they endeavored not to do anything that might tend to pleasure;—this scope or aim of action being, for the most part, indecent and hurtful."

Pythagoras did not enjoin celibacy upon his followers; but whilst he tolerated marriage as a necessary institution, he endeavored, like the Christian Fathers long afterwards, to reconcile it to his principles by restricting matrimonial indulgence to a point not far from total abstinence. He allowed it only at a certain season of the year, and then rarely.

The spirit of Pythagoreanism is best seen in the establishment

* History of Philosophy, part ix. ch. 2.

and regulations of his *Esoteric School*, or *Secret Association*. To the *Exoteric* or outward disciples Pythagoras taught only plain, simple precepts, suitable to men aiming at only imperfect attainments—and certain mysterious emblems which he did not explain. But the Esoteric, or inner disciples, were instructed in the mysteries of philosophy, and trained to the perfection of virtue. The members of this Secret Association were bound by an oath, never to divulge what they were taught behind the veil; for Pythagoras concealed himself behind a veil when he lectured to the uninitiated; to the initiated he spoke face to face.

Candidates for membership had to go through a trial of five years. During a part, or the whole of this time, they had to keep an unbroken silence.

All the members lived in common, like Cenobite monks. They might have families with them in the cloister, but no private property or separate table. Their behavior, employments, dress, food, &c., were prescribed by the rules. Their daily exercises were not essentially different from those of a Cenobite monastery. They consisted of worship, study, meditation, and business—partly in society, partly in solitude. Their diet was vegetable, selected and prepared for nutriment, not for pleasure. All stimulating food and drink were avoided. Their dress was plain, white, and clean. In everything they were to exercise temperance and sobriety, to avoid the pleasures of sense, to quell the tumults of passion, and to cleanse the soul from earthly defilements, that it might soar, unencumbered and undisturbed, to the region of pure entities, and of intellectual truth.

It concerns us not at present to mention the scientific studies of Pythagoras, his mystical emblems, or his affectation of mystery and miracle, to gain respect and excite curiosity. We shall only add, that long after his death, his disciples pretended that he had wrought supernatural wonders during his life-time. Such pretences have been too common to excite our surprise. We do not find, however, that any of these reporters, like the apostles, professed to be eye-witnesses of what they related, and sealed their testimony with their blood.

The Pythagorean philosophy flourished among the Greeks and exerted a powerful influence, until it was superseded in a great measure by later systems, especially those of Plato and Aristotle. It was revived with some modifications about the time of our Saviour, and flourished again in Western Asia during two or three centuries. Before its first decline, several eminent followers of the great founder taught the system with distinguished success, but with some unessential variations and additions. The greatest of these early teachers of Pythagoreanism was

Empedocles.

He taught that there are two eternal principles, God and Matter,—that God pervades nature as a soul, giving to all life and motion;—that the human soul is twofold;—the superior rational part derived from the Divine Soul of the world,—the inferior sensitive part from the physical elements, combining under the natural laws of love and contention—or, in modern phrase, attraction and repulsion He had the notion, we presume, that the sensitive desires and aversions of the human constitution were but individual actings of this general law of physical love and contention.

He taught, like his great master, that the rational soul is sent into the body for punishment. It assumes bodies of all sorts, animal and vegetable, migrating from one another, until purified at last, it returns to God and becomes itself divine.

Plutarch (De Exilio) has preserved some verses of Empedocles, in which he expresses this oriental doctrine. We give a translation.

The Fates ordained, the gods of old decreed,
If long-aged demons sin, they wander far;
Each suffers pains, an exile from high heaven;
Through earth he strays, full thirty thousand years.
So now I wander by divine command.

In other verses he represents the demons as being hurled from heaven by the angry Gods, and as driven and tortured by the elements, until purged and expiated by punishment, they are restored to their former nature and place in heaven.

We shall mention the later Pythagoreans hereafter.

§ 3. *The Stoical Philosophy.*

We shall notice this system briefly. It was austere and tended to ascetism in its morality; but its principles differed in some material points from those that were most influential in producing Christian monachism.

Zeno, the founder of Stoicism taught that there were two eternal principles,—Matter, passive,—and the Divinity, active; —that God is a living fire, unlike common fire; he is also spirit; he produces, fashions and permeates all things. He animates the world, as its soul. The human soul is a particle of this mundane soul, but like other individual beings, liable to perish.

All nature is bound fast by the decrees of Fate, and the course of events is unalterably fixed.

The wise man will live conformably to nature. He alone is free. All true happiness consists in virtue. Hence, as man strives in vain against his destiny, and virtue is the only good, pain is no evil, and all external things,—riches and poverty—honor and infamy—health and sickness—are in themselves indifferent.

On these principles the Stoics professed to despise all that the world in general pursues as good or shuns as evil; and wrapping themselves up in the pride of their virtue, to bid a stern defiance even to Fate. Such in brief was Stoicism.

§ 4. *Plato and his Philosophy.*

The philosophy of Plato was that which ultimately gained the strongest and most extensive influence over the minds of men in the Roman empire,—especially during the first centuries of the

* Tenneman's Hist. of Philosophy, Stoicks.

Christian era. Being full of entertaining fancies, and giving sublimer conceptions of the Godhead than other philosophies of the time, it suited the imaginative minds of the East, and did more than all other systems to corrupt the doctrines of the gospel, and mislead the practice of Christians, in the second and third centuries. It had from the beginning a large infusion of Pythagorean and oriental doctrines. By the time that Christianity began to prevail in the eastern provinces of the Roman empire, it had in those countries received an additional dose of orientalism, and in its form of Eclecticism and New Platonism, it mixed itself with the Christianity of the age, and aided no little in producing that religious monster— a Christian monk.

Plato lived about 400 years before Christ. He was first a disciple of the admirable Socrates at Athens. He then travelled after knowledge into foreign countries,—particularly into Egypt, where he cultivated acquaintance with the priests, and studied their philosophy. After some years he returned to Athens, and there taught philosophy during the remainder of his days. His lectures were delivered in a public school called the Academy ; hence his followers were long called Academics.

His system of doctrines is very extensive and in great part very abstruse. We shall endeavor to give an intelligible sketch of his theological and moral philosophy,—these being the only parts of his system that have an important bearing upon the subject of our present investigation.

According to Plato there are three uncreated principles or substances,—God, Ideas, and Matter. These constitute the primordial Trinity of Plato. It is not a Trinity of divine persons, but of essentially different substances.

The original supreme God, according to Plato and the orientals, is utterly beyond human knowledge, in respect to his nature and his attributes. All that we know of him is, that he is an immaterial being, and the primary source of all that has life, action and intelligence.

In the Infinite mind of the supreme Being exist the eternal Ideas or Forms, after which, as patterns, all created things were made. They are neither material nor spiritual, but nevertheless substantial beings. They exist forever unchanged. They are perfect. They cannot be apprehended by the senses, which perceive only material objects, which are imperfect representations of ideas; as a gold-ring imperfectly represents the abstract idea of a circle. The ideas can be apprehended only by intellect or pure reason; hence they are called *Intelligible Things*, to distinguish them from the *sensible*.

Matter in its primary state was without form, and void of all sensible properties: it was an obscure, indistinct, elementary material; out of which God created the world, by impressing upon it the forms that compose the system of material nature, after the pattern of his eternal ideas.

But as in the oriental theology, so in the Platonic; the supreme unknown God was not the immediate agent in the creation of the world. He employed in this work a divine emanation and image of himself, who is the second God, called by Plato *Demiurge* or Creator,—sometimes *Logos*, meaning word or reason of God, and sometimes simply *The God*. Through his agency also subordinate Gods and Demons were created.

All these intelligent beings were originally pure; but by some means many of the demons became vitiated and malignant.

The more exalted of the Divine Intelligences are invested with the actual government of the world in subordination to the Creator. Their residence is in the fixed stars of the highest heavens. Indeed Plato speaks of the stars as animated beings and gods of fiery splendor. This was the Egyptian doctrine. How far he intended here to speak poetically, and to be understood with allowance, we cannot tell. His rich imagination often led him to invest his doctrines with poetical imagery, so as to make it doubtful to his readers, whether he meant to express facts or fancies, to state his doctrines or merely to embellish them. However, he seems to have seriously taught that every globe of the universe was an animated being, and that each of the bright orbs which shed so benign a light upon this dull earth, was at least the residence if not the substance of a God.

The good demons who inhabit the space between the starry heavens and the earth, preside over the different parts of nature. They heed the several tribes of terrestial animals, guard the cities of men, and conduct the operations of nature—all under the authority of the higher powers. They act as mediators between Gods and men. They convey our prayers up to heaven, and bring down messages and blessings from above. This doctrine of mediating demons or angels, between poor mortals here below and the Supreme Powers of heaven, was almost universal in the Eastern world.

According to Plato, therefore, three ranks of beings separate the human species from the Infinite Supreme. 1. The Divine Creator, Father of Gods and men, wholly incorporeal, and so sublime in his nature—though he is but the Image of the Supreme—that he can be but obscurely and partially known by man. 2. The celestial Gods of the starry regions,—the subordinate rulers of the world—of a bright and fiery nature. 3. The demons, who are of an aerial nature, and therefore inferior to the Gods, whose essence is of the finest element in nature. The higher demons about the orbit of the moon, are of a more etherial substance than those who dwell in the grosser atmosphere of the earth. Yet they are all of a finer composition than terrestial animals, whose spirits are invested with the coarse element of water and earth. Every created spirit, not excepting the human soul, when divested of its earthly covering, is clothed with a vehicle.* The more refined and pure the element out of which this *instrument* of action was made, the more perfect is the spiritual being. This was a common opinion among the ancients.

* Οχημα as the Greeks call it. Every finite spirit was supposed to need such a vehicle or body, to give it place and locomotion.

The Demiurge, or Creator—according to Plato's philosophy—endowed this world with a soul, by virtue of which it became an animated being. The mundane soul is diffused through all the elements, and is the source of life, and feeling, and action to all the animated beings of the earth. They derive their corporeal organization and animal souls from this mundane soul.

Thus is completed the second Trinity of Plato : the Supreme, the Demiurge or Logos, and the soul of the world,—all Divine Persons; but unequal, and derived successively, one from another.

The mundane soul is of a middle nature between Mind and Matter. It is superior to Matter, because it possesses Life, Sensation, and Action or Power ; but it is inferior to mind in not possessing Intellect or Reason.

The lower animals have naturally no souls but those which they derive from the soul of the world. But man has also a rational soul or mind, which pre-existed as a demon in the upper regions. The animal and the rational souls are united by a third principle or soul, which Plato calls *The Irascible.** The soul of man is therefore threefold. It consists of the Rational Soul, which possesses Reason ; the Animal Soul which possesses Appetite ; and the Irascible Soul which possesses Wrath or Excitable Energy, and serves as a connecting principle between the other two. The Rational Soul or Mind is immortal ; the others perish with the body.

Matter is essentially imperfect and refractory, so that everything formed of it or connected with it, partakes of the natural and insuperable imperfection of the material. Hence the origin of evil. Hence the imperfect nature of the Mundane Soul, and all animal souls ; and hence the defilement of the immortal soul, when it inhabits a material body.

Our animal sensations and desires belong only to the animal soul. Being of an earthly nature, and having relation to the body,

* So the Greek word θυμος, is commonly translated. But we agree with Ritter in thinking that the German word *muth*, Spirit or Energy, more nearly expresses Plato's meaning.

they darken and corrupt the rational soul. In its pre-existent state as an incorporeal being, the Mind enjoyed a pure happiness in the contemplation of the divine ideas, which it could then clearly perceive. But when it became immersed in the gross elements of the body, and associated with the animal soul, it became infected with low sensual desires, forgot its former state, ceased to perceive those ennobling ideas, and became a dim-sighted carnal thing of the earth.

The only way in which the immortal mind can recover from the darkness and defilement of its fallen state, is by the enlightening influence of philosophy. It must strenuously resist the debasing influence of carnal desires and evil passions, and devote itself to the pure contemplation of intelligible things. By subduing the sensual propensities, quieting the turbulence of the passions, and abstracting its attention from sensible objects, the soul is able, even in its corporeal prison-house, to disenthral itself in a great measure from the gloom and oblivion of its fallen state, and to recover a portion of those intellectual visions of truth and beauty, which it had enjoyed in its etherial birth-place.

Those who during their mortal life have thus subdued their earth-born affections, and purified the mind by divine contemplation, are exalted after death to the celestial abodes, where a bright star becomes their happy dwelling-place. But those who live immersed in the sensuous desires of the flesh and spirit, are punished after death in the infernal regions, for a period of time proportioned to their degree of sensuality and wickedness: or if their defilement be comparatively small, their immortal souls are condemned to transmigration into bodies of a degraded cast; they become *women* (says Plato), or slaves, or even brutes. Nor shall any who sink, after one life in the flesh, ever rise to their star of glory, until they have, on a new trial, purified themselves from the vices of their carnal state.

Plato was consistent, when he asserted that none of the vulgar class of mankind could attain true happiness in a future state. Their condition and habits subjected them to the dominion of animal affections; and being destitute of "divine philosophy," they had no remedy. Alas for the poor working men of the world, if Plato's philosophy had been really "divine." But a sublimer character than the Grecian sage, has taught a far simpler and far diviner philosophy, by which the laboring poor can be saved without dreaming away their lives in abstract contemplation. Faith, hope, and charity will serve them better, than would a Platonic knowledge of "the intelligible."

Plato taught that the *rational* soul has its seat in the head; the *irascible*, in the breast; and the *animal*, in the lower parts of the body;—and that this arrangement indicated the comparative dignity of the several parts of the soul. Virtue he made to consist in the subjection of the inferior parts to the government of reason. Of the four cardinal virtues, he assigned prudence to the *rational* soul in the head; fortitude to the *irascible* in the breast; and temperance to the *animal*, below: Justice he considered as the result of a proper union and subordination of all the parts of our nature.

In his moral precepts, Plato did not enjoin any definite system of ascetic discipline. He did not prescribe any specific rules of fasting, continence, poverty, or devotional exercises in seclusion from the world. Such an application of his principles would not have suited his age and country. But it is obvious to remark that his philosophy contains all those principles, which in Eastern Asia brought forth the extravagancies of ascetism and monkery. So, when Platonism became rooted in the congenial soil of Egypt and Western Asia, it gathered to itself more and more of the oriental dogmas, and tended more and more towards the ascetic form in the practice of its professors.*

The foregoing sketch of Plato's philosophy, shows how much

* The foregoing account of Plato's philosophy has been digested from Brucker's and Ritter's Histories of Philosophy, and Apuleïus on the Demon of Socrates and on the Philosophy of Plato. For a sketch, taken chiefly from Enfield, see Anthon's Classical Dictionary, article Plato.

he was indebted to Pythagoras and the orientals for the elements of his system. He merely digested, improved, and adorned what others had already taught. What we are chiefly concerned to remark, however, is that by his elegant manner of combining and treating the elements of the oriental philosophy, he made it popular among the Greeks, and gave it prevalence in Egypt and Western Asia, at the time when Christianity began in those countries, to be embraced by learned men and philosophers. Thus his philosophy came to be the chief medium through which the principles of the oriental philosophy were introduced into the Church. Before this came to pass, however, new schools of both Pythagorean and Platonic philosophers had begun to arise in those eastern provinces of the Roman Empire, where the Christian doctrine was first corrupted by philosophy, and Christian monachism originated. It is important, therefore, to give some account of these new schools of Pythagoreans and Platonists, especially of the latter, by whose doctrines the Church was so much influenced in the second and third centuries. This we shall do after we have noticed the earlier philosophy and monachism of the Jews.

CHAPTER VII.

PLATONISM OF PHILO THE JEW.

It was in the great city of Alexandria in Egypt, that the Platonic Philosophy found its most distinguished disciples and teachers after the commencement of the Christian era.

Alexandria had been before, and continued long to be afterwards, the greatest commercial emporium in the world. Here were congregated men of half a dozen nations and religions—Hindoos, Egyptians, Arabians, Syrians, Jews, and Greeks. It was the chief point of contact between the eastern and the western nations: the focus into which their doctrines were collected, and the centre from which they radiated in all directions. Here arose a great university, the greatest in the world after Athens began to decline. In this celebrated school of learning, philosophy, science and literature, were taught by distinguished men. Its founders and early patrons were the Grecian Ptolemies, who, after the death of Alexander, the founder of the city, reigned over Egypt. These enlightened rulers furnished their university with the greatest library of ancient times. It was this great storehouse of knowledge thas made Alexandria the chief seat of learning for the space of eight hundred years; until that fanatical disciple of Mahomet, the Caliph Omar, made fuel of seven hundred thousand volumes—on the principle, that if they agreed with the Koran they were superfluous; but if not, they were pernicious. This was like the water-trial of supposed witches in after times. If they sank and were drowned, they perished as innocent persons; but if they floated on the water, they were burnt as witches.

The Jews constituted, from they foundation of the city, a numerous and wealthy part of the Alexandrian population. Josephus quotes from Strabo the statement, that their quarter constituted a large portion of the city;—that they had a special governor of their own entitled Ethnarch—and that they were a numerous and powerful people in Egypt.* The Ethnarch had also the title of Alabarch. He administered justice among the Egyptian Jews, and had the oversight of both civil and religious affairs.

Here many of the Jews learned the Greek language, and, for the first time in the history of their nation, some of them studied the Grecian philosophy. We should remark that the conquests of Alexander the Great had diffused the language, and in some measure the population of Greece, over Western Asia and Egypt. Greek was thenceforth during many years the language of science, and to a considerable extent also the language of the people, in all those countries.

It was for the numerous body of Jews in Egypt, that the Hebrew books of the Old Testament were translated into Greek, more than a century before the birth of Christ. Many of these Jews had been already, for so long a time, denizens of a foreign country, that they had forgotten, not only the ancient Hebrew, but even the Syro-Chaldaic dialect, spoken in Judea after the Babylonish captivity.

As to this Greek translation of the Old Testament, it was undoubtedly made in Egypt during the reign of the Ptolemies; but the story which Josephus took from Aristaeus concerning the seventy interpreters, is unquestionably fabulous. It obtained from him such currency, however, as to give the translation the title of the Septuagint, or Seventy.

* Josephus. Antiquities. Book xiv. chap. 7

It is evident from the style and manner in which the different parts were translated, that the work was done by different hands, and probably at different periods of time.

The most distinguished man among the Alexandrian Jews, in the time of the Apostles, was Philo, surnamed Judæus, the Jew. He was brother to Alexander, the Alabarch, and was sent once, by his countrymen, on an important mission to the emperor, at Rome.

He was deeply imbued with the philosophy of Plato; yet, also, a zealous disciple of Moses. What a conjunction! Plato and Moses! There was no affinity between them. How then could the philosophical oil be combined with the water smitten out of Sinai's rock? As Plato united the rational soul with the animal, through the medium of the irascible, so the philosophizing Jews united Greek Platonism with Mosaic Judaism, through the medium of the allegorical. The ceremonial worldly system of the law, (designed only for a temporary purpose,) would appear to the mind of a Jew, imbued with Plato's idealism, exceedingly dry and uninstructive. He would, therefore, endeavor to find under the hard shell of the literal sense, a nutritious kernel of divine philosophy. In this attempt he could not fail, for he had only to exercise his imagination. He could then find Platonism in the books of Moses, quite as easily as Shakspeare's Jacques could find "Sermons in stones, and good in everything."

Philo was not the first Jew who resorted to the allegorizing and spiritualizing method of expounding the Holy Scriptures. Jewish doctors had adopted it to some extent, ages before, chiefly at Alexandria, where the Gentile philosophy began to allure the Jewish mind with its ingenious theories. Of course Judaism then began to be corrupted with Oriental and Platonic fancies, just as Christianity suffered afterwards from the same cause. Whenever religious doctors begin to dive beneath the proper sense of the sacred writings in search of mystical and allegorical senses, they soon lose sight of the firm land, and bring up from the wide abyss of human thought whatsoever may please their fancies, be it the elegant philosophy of Plato, or the puerile day-dream of Swedenborg.

Philo's works consist chiefly of tracts on certain passages in the books of Moses, and some on other subjects, mostly philosophical. In all these he teaches Platonic doctrines, but not the pure system of Plato. Pythagorean and Egyptian sentiments corrupt his Platonism. The doctrines of Moses constrained him also, in spite of allegory, to deviate, in some things, from the track of the Grecian philosopher. This syncretism, or mixture of doctrinal systems, led Philo into frequent inconsistencies, which have puzzled his commentators in their attempts to reconcile himself with himself, and to make out a clear statement of his doctrines. It would be unimportant to determine what they were, if his fame and his writings had not contributed to infuse heathenish philosophy into apostolical Christianity, and thus to produce errors of doctrine and practice, which Romanism retains in full, and Protestantism in part, and probably will retain for ages yet to come. Especially did his writings serve as a medium, through which ascetical and monkish sentiments passed from heathenism into the Church. We shall, therefore, give a sketch of his doctrines, so far as they relate to our subject, and conclude with a specimen of his allegorical method of interpreting the writings of Moses. We give the result of our own examination of his writings.

1. *Of God and his Chief Powers.*

Philo conceived that there was a substantial, but not a formal agreement between the Platonic and Mosaic doctrines concerning the Godhead. According to both, as he conceived, there is one Supreme God, who creates and governs through the agency of his divine powers. These powers are personal agents, divine emanations from the Infinite Supreme, existing in him, and one with himself, yet, exercising each his distinct agency. They are, in short, the divine attributes personified, not figuratively, but really. They are the powers of God, acting distinctly, yet in union with the Supreme Father.

This is the old Oriental doctrine, the general theory of which is given in our account of the Egyptian philosophy.

In respect to the number and relation of these Divine Powers, Philo differs from Plato, and is inconsistent with himself. He represents them differently in different places. He adopts Plato's doctrine of the Divine Logos or Word, speaks often of this Divine Agent, but so variously and obscurely, that his commentators differ in their explications of his doctrine on this interesting point. One thing is certain, however, that he ascribed Personal Agency to the Divine Logos, though Mosheim thought that he meant by it the "Intelligible world," or Divine Ideas collectively—according to Plato's theology. He adopted Plato's doctrine of a Mundane Soul, from which animal souls proceed; but he does not make this soul of the world one of his Divine Powers, though sometimes he apparently confounds it with the Logos.

We shall confirm our statement by translated extracts from his works; in which the reader will see what his doctrine is, and how inconsistently he presents it at different times.

In his tract *On Abraham*, speaking of the three angels who appeared to the patriarch, he says:

"The middle one is the Father of All, properly-named in the Scriptures, He-that-is (Jehovah.) Those next to him, on either side, are called *The Maker* and *The Governor*. The former of these is called *God*, by whom all things were made and disposed. The other is called Lord;* for it is fit that the creation be governed by the Creator. That Middle One, with his Powers on either side, exhibits to the discerning mind the appearance, sometimes of *one*, sometimes of *three*; of *one*, when the mind is most

* Philo here translates into Greek, and we into English, the meaning of the three Hebrew names of the Supreme Being. (יְהוָה) Jehovah, He-that-is, commonly rendered Lord in our English Bible; (אֱלֹהִים) Elohim, God; and (אֲדֹנָי) Adonai. Lord or Ruler. These are often used interchangeably in the Old Testament.

accurately cleansed; of *three*, when the spectator is not initiated in the Greater Mysteries, but labors in the Lesser, and cannot yet comprehend Him, as existing alone and of himself—but as existing in his works as Creator and Sovereign."

In this passage Philo attributes to the three angels the three Hebrew names of the Supreme Being: the first representing Jehovah, the Father; the other two, the Divine Creator and Divine Ruler of the world. These three appear to the imperfectly-instructed, as three different Gods; but to those who fully understand the Mosaic doctrine, as one and the same God, or Supreme Being. The Heathen Mysteries of the Gods—or Secret Schools—to which he here alludes, were of two degrees; the Lesser, into which the candidate was first initiated, are supposed to have corrected the grosser errors of Polytheism; but the Greater, to have taught the true doctrine of the Divine Unity—namely, that all the Divine Beings who emanated from the Supreme, were united in him, and made with him but one God. This doctrine of Divine Emanations, constituting distinct agents, yet altogether one God in the Supreme, was so prevalent among the ancients in Asia, Egypt, and Greece, that we cannot hesitate to construe the language of Philo in this sense. It is the easiest and most obvious meaning of his expressions.

In his tract *on the Cherubim* (Gen. iii. 24) Philo speaks of the divine Persons or Powers somewhat differently. His text is,—"He (God) placed at the east end of the garden of Eden Cherubims, and a flaming sword which turned every way to keep the way of the tree of life."

"Next to the one only true God (says Philo) are two supreme and first Powers, *Goodness* and *Authority:* the universe was made by *Goodness;* the creation is governed by *Authority*. A third that unites the two is *Logos*—*Word* or *Reason*,—in the middle. The Cherubim were the symbols of the two Powers,—the flaming sword, of the *Logos*."

In the former passage Philo made a divine Trinity; here, he makes a quaternion, by adding the Logos to the primary Power of the Father; thus constituting a *Trinity of Powers* in the Supreme God, according to the Hindoo and Egyptian theology. If in any way the former statement can be reconciled with the latter, we must suppose that three angels represented the three Powers, and that the Supreme God did not appear in either of them. But this is scarcely feasible: so that we must give up Philo as inconsistent in his theology.

As to the Logos mentioned in the latter passage, our learned Jew often speaks of him as a Divine Person in the Supreme God. In his tract *On the Confusion of Tongues*, he calls the Logos, "The First-born of God," "The oldest Angel," "The Archangel of Many Names, who is called The Beginning," "The Name of God," and "The Man after his Image." Elsewhere he calls him "The Image of God," The Vicar or Vicegerent of God" and his "Minister." He says that the Logos is the seal from whose impression created beings received their forms (which is the Platonic doctrine), and that he is clothed with the world as with a garment, and that by him the creation is held together and sustained;—which seems to identify him with the soul of the world, though possibly Philo meant not so.

In his tract *On Migration*, he says that the high-priest under the Law of Moses, represented the Divine Logos, whose father is God the Father of All, and whose mother is Wisdom, through whom all things were generated. He seems here to allude to the description of wisdom in the Book of Proverbs, chap. viii. 22—31.

We shall quote but one thing more under this head. In the tract *On Dreams*, speaking of the visible appearances of God, he says it was the Logos who appeared to the Patriarchs; for, says he,—"as they who cannot look at the sun, may see the reflection of his rays; so we are to understand that it was the Image of God, his word (Logos) and Angel, whom they saw as himself." Again he says, "God is the primary light; his Image, the Logos, is also most perfect light, and *similar to no creature*."

From these various expressions concerning the Divine Logos, our readers may judge for themselves what conception Philo had of this divine being. In the specimen of Philo's allegorical interpretations, near the end of the chapter, the reader will see that the Logos is represented as God's agent or instrument in the creation and government of the world.

2. *Of Angels and Demons.*

Philo, like Plato and all the orientals, taught that our atmosphere and the ethereal regions above it are full of spiritual beings, some of whom enter into human bodies and become men.

In his tract *On the Giants*, he comments on the text in Genesis vi. 2—4, " The sons of God saw the daughters of men that they were fair," &c. The Septuagint translation, used by Philo and all the Greek Fathers of the Church, reads *angels* of God instead of *sons* of God, as it is in the Hebrew. On this ground they all held that these lovers of fair women and fathers of Giants were Angels, not men. But according to Philo, the only difference is, that angels have no flesh and blood. For in this tract he says as follows:

" Those whom other philosophers call demons, Moses usually calls angels; but they are spirits flying through the air. The whole world must in all parts have animated beings; the other elements, earth, water, air and fire* have theirs; so must the stars of heaven. These spirits are wholly immortal and divine. The air is full of living creatures that are invisible to us as the air itself. Some of these souls descend into bodies; the others disdain to be connected with the earth, and are employed as ministers and servants by the Father, the Creator, in administrating the affairs of mortals. But the former, descending into the body as into a river, are overwhelmed as in a whirlpool. But some of them by struggling emerge and [after death] fly back to their home in the upper regions. These souls have, in the body, been taught a sublime philosophy. But those who sink, are the souls of men that neglect the wisdom that pertains to the mind, and

* The ancients believed that salamanders lived in fire, as their proper element. Some imagined that they had seen them.

give themselves to carnal things. Now, if you consider souls, demons, and angels to differ only in name, you will relieve the subject of much superstition."

He teaches the same doctrine in other tracts, particularly that *On Dreams ;* in which he adds that some souls, after they have once tried the experiment of a corporeal life, become weary of its vanity, and consider the body as a sepulchre; and, therefore, when dismissed at death, they fly up into the ethereal regions and never return; but that others are so pleased with mortal life, that they transmigrate into new bodies after death. It is the spirits who inhabit the grosser parts of our atmosphere, that usually enter into bodies; but the more refined spirits of the celestial regions, prefer to serve God as mediators between him and his sons on the earth; conveying divine messages down and the prayers of the devout up to God.

3. *Of the Human Soul.*

Philo fully adopted the Patonic doctrine that the human soul consists of three parts, the rational, the irascible, and the animal or appetitive. The first is *breathed into us by God* and is immortal. The others, he says, sometimes are made by inferior creative powers—" nature's journeymen," as Shakspeare expresses a similar idea. He says also that the *Nous* or Rational soul generates some of the subordinate faculties, such as sense, voice, and generative power.

In his account, as given above, of God's breathing into us the rational soul, he seems in following Moses to have forgotten Plato. How do the demons get in to be souls—and that too of their own choice,—if the rational soul be an immediate emanation from God's spirit or breath ?

4. *The Human Body.*

He always speaks of the body as a burden and a prison of the immortal soul, which enters it as a sojourner from a foreign land; and that it is an act of Divine mercy which releases it from the gloom and the miseries of its fleshly tenement, and restores it to its native country in the heavens.

5. *Of Virtue.*

He is perfectly Platonic in saying, that virtue is the union of the three parts of the soul under the government of reason.

"The lovers of virtue," he says in the tract *On Dreams*, "have a hard task to perform in resisting the body and its pleasures, and a hard struggle, besides, against the temptation of external goods, such as riches, honor," &c.—"The true disciples of Moses exercise continence, frugality, and patience; they disregard wealth, pleasure, and glory; use only sufficient necessary food to keep off famine; are ready to bear all hardships for virtue's sake; are content with mean clothing, and esteem luxury a disgrace and a reproach. To them the grassy sod is a precious bed, with boughs and leaves for a covering, and a stone for a pillow. The luxurious esteem this a hard life, but the followers of virtue think it delightful."

6. *Of Ascetism.*

The last quotation is from a commentary on Jacob's dream, when the patriarch slept in the open air. It is a picture of the ascetic life when not carried to excess. He is fond of calling Jacob the Ascetic. The following extract from the same tract, is expressly to the point:

"Virtue is acquired in three ways—by doctrine (or instruction), by nature, and by exercise (or the ascetic life.) Of these three, the first and last are most easily united; for that by exercise springs from that by instruction. The faculty of hearing is most prompt for instruction; the ascetic power fits a man for striving (against evil influences.)

7. *The Contemplative Life.*

This he considers, as Plato did, the necessary means of purifying the soul. In the same treatise *On Dreams*, he says:

"The good man, loving a quiet life, delights in *solitude*, shunning vulgar eyes; not because he hates society, but that he may fly from vice. Wherefore he usually shuts himself up at home, and seldom goes out. To avoid frequent visitors, he prefers a rural solitude, where he may live more sweetly, conversing with the writings of the virtuous dead."

Again, in the tract *On the Migration of Abraham*, he says:

"The senses are an impediment to the contemplation of intelligible things. We should therefore close the senses by seeking darkness and solitude."—"God gave the mind the power of knowing the intelligible world by itself, but the visible world by the senses."

Putting all these things together, we find that Philo was an advocate of ascetic discipline and solitary contemplation, and these two things constitute monachism. He was an ardent admirer of the monachism of his countrymen, the Essenes and the Therapeutes, and he wrote laudatory accounts of these monastic sects. He has the credit, therefore, if credit be due, of uniting Platonism, Judaism, and Monachism into a Triad, sacred to all who should be influenced by his writings, among both Jews and Gentiles.

But Philo did not approve of a merely ceremonial and superstitious ascetism. "If you see one (says he) taking his food and drink at a late hour, refusing to wash and anoint himself, neglecting to clothe his body, lying on the ground without covering, and then priding himself on his temperance, he is not to be admired; for his exercises thus far are useless vexations. Nor will costly sacrifices, ablutions, rearing of temples, &c., entitle one to be reckoned among the pious. He has erred from the way of piety in placing his sanctity in ceremonies and rich offerings to Him who will not accept them, and in attempts to flatter Him whom no flattery can reach. The truly pious offer sincere sacrifices, but are averse from ostentatious services."—Excellent observations, and a graphic sketch of monkish ascetism, as some individuals seem to have practiced it in his day; though some Christian monks, three hundred years after his time, went far beyond his description, in affecting dirt, destitution, and devotion, in order to rid their souls of all corporeal incumbrances and influences.

Finally, we shall give, as we have promised

8. *A Specimen of Philo's Allegorical Interpretation.*

In the treatise *of the Migration of Abraham*, he is commenting on Genesis xii. 1. "*Now the Lord said unto Abraham, get thee out of thy country, and from thy kindred, and from the house of thy father, &c.*"

"God wishing to amend the soul of man (says Philo) first gives him, as an incitement to salvation, migration from three things, the body, the senses, and uttered speech ; for you must understand the *country* as a symbol of the body—the *kindred* as a symbol of the senses—and the *father's house*, of speech. Wherefore ? Because the body received its substance from the earth,* and will at dissolution again return to the ground from which it was taken, as Moses testifies, *Dust thou art, and unto dust shalt thou return.* For he says that it was formed of clay, and when dissolved, it must return to what it was at first. But sense is a *kinsman* and brother of the mind,—the irrational, of the rational, —since both are parts of one soul. But speech is the *father's house;* because our father, the intelligent mind, sows into the other parts its own powers, and bestowing its energies upon them, assumes the care and management of them all. But its dwelling-house is speech, separate from the other buildings. Wonder not then, that he calls the mind's utterance or speech, a house ; for God, the mind of the universe, says that the word (Logos) is his house. For Jacob the Ascetic, when he had a vision of him—that is, of the Logos—openly confesses, *This is none other than the house of God and the gate of heaven ;* as if he had said, The house of God is not any of these visible things, nor can be perceived by sense, but is invisible, obscure, and can be appre-

* The Hebrew *Aretz*, and the Greek *Ge*, both have the double signification of *earth* and *country*.

hended only by the soul as a spiritual being. Who can it be then, except the Logos, older than created things, by whom, as a helm, the pilot of the world steers all things, and whom he employed as an instrument in effecting a faultless creation."

And so this Platonizing interpreter of Moses goes on with his fantastical allegories, through many and many a page, conjuring out of the single-minded old Hebrew prophet many a doctrine which he never "dreamed of in his philosophy."

Such were the philosophical opinions current among Jews and Gentiles, and such the Scripture interpretations, by which they were incorporated with revealed religion, during the early ages of Christianity. How then could Christianity escape corruption, as soon as inspired men ceased to be its teachers?

CHAPTER VIII.

THE PHILOSOPHY AND MONACHISM OF THE JEWS.

Before the Babylonish captivity, the Jews had no philosophy of their own, and were too little acquainted with foreign nations to learn the philosophy of others. They had no speculative opinions; they formed no theories concerning the origin and nature of things; that is, they did not philosophize—they did not reason on the things in heaven or the things on the earth. King Solomon, who married an Egyptian wife, showed some turn for philosophical pursuits. But in general the only question that divided their religious sentiments was, whether they should serve God according to the precepts of Moses, or Baal, according to the custom of the Canaanites.

Their residence in Babylonia gave them some knowledge of the Chaldean philosophy. The conquest of Babylon by the great Cyrus, brought many of them into contact with the Magian religion. When they had again filled their own country after their restoration, the settlement of many of them in Egypt, Asia Minor, and Europe, softened their prejudices against everything foreign, taught them the languages of the Gentiles, and opened their minds to the admission of new ideas and opinions.

The effect of these circumstances became visible in some of their subsequent writings, and in the rise of religious sects—indicating freedom of thought and a disposition to form opinions.

Some of the Apocryphal Books of the Old Testament bear

evidence of an incipient intermixture of the Gentile philosophy with Scriptural Judaism.

Thus the Apocryphal book called The Wisdom of Solomon, written in Greek, probably by an Alexandrian Jew, exhibits evident traces of Pythagorean and Platonic doctrines. In chap. i. 7, the author says, that "*The Spirit of the Lord filleth the world, and containeth all things* [συνεχει ταπαντα];" which are Platonic phrases concerning the soul of the world. Again, in chap. vii. 22—29, the author gives a description of wisdom, in which he utters several Platonic notions, making her a personal emanation from God. He says she is "The worker of all things;"—that in her is "An understanding spirit, holy, only-begotten, subtle, lively, clear, &c., —having all power, overseeing all things, going through all understanding, pure and most subtle spirits." She is "*the breathing of the Divine power, a pure emanation* (απορροια) *from the glory of the Omnipotent;—the brightness* (*or effulgence,* απαυγασμα,) *of the everlasting* (*or invisible,* αιδιου) *light,*—the unspotted mirror of God's power, and the image of his goodness." All these expressions are conformable to the oriental doctrine, that Divine Wisdom (εννοιαν) was a certain substantial power, eternal and immutable, which they called Aeon (αιων), and which flowed or emanated like a ray of light from the fulness (πληρωμα) of the Omnipotent God.* Again in chap. ix. 15, the author speaks of the body "pressing down the soul, and the earthly tabernacle weighing down the mind that museth upon many things," which is the oriental and Pythagoreo-Platonic notion of the body's being the prison of the soul and darkening the intellect. In the preceding chap. viii. 20, the author says, "I was a witty child and had a good spirit; yea rather, *being good, I came into a body undefiled*:" which is the oriental doctrine of the pre-existence of the soul as a demon or spirit, before it came into the body.

This book was written, it is supposed, in the time of the earlier Ptolemies, long before the Christian era.

* Brucker. Hist, Crit. Period. II. Part. i. L. ii. c. i.

The Jewish Sects were chiefly three, the Sadducees, Pharisees and Essenes.

The fundamental difference between the Sadducees and Pharisees, was, that the former professed to take the written Law of Moses, literally interpreted, as the rule of their faith and practices, while the latter followed the Tradition of the Elders, or in other words, the authority of the Doctors of former times, as the true expounders of the Law. The Sadducees would not admit anything to be Law or Doctrine, which was not expressly taught in the Books of Moses. Hence they denied the immortality of the soul, and—strangely, we think—the existence of angels or incorporeal spirits. The Pharisees—like our Roman Catholics—took the Scriptures in the sense of the Fathers, and received as of Divine authority, whatsoever doctrines and practices, the ancient Rabbis or Doctors delivered as such. If they were not contained in the Sacred Records, they were considered as transmitted from Moses and the Prophets through *Oral Tradition*, and therefore of the same authority as if they had been written by inspired men.

With the Sadducees our subject has nothing to do; as they ran to the opposite extreme, from everything tending to ascetism and monkery. But the Pharisees inclined much towards an austere and flesh-mortifying system of doctrine and practice. Their fundamental rule of following the Tradition of the Elders, admitted of many admixtures of foreign notions and practices with the pure system of the written law.

Transmigration of souls was believed among the Jews, and especially among the Pharisees, as Brucker says. We have a sign of that belief in the Book of Wisdom before quoted.

A leading doctrine of the Pharisees was, that to attain righteousness, a man must make satisfaction for his sins by fasting, ablutions, alms and sacrifices; or by confession of his sins, prayer for pardon, and purification by suffering after death—as the Talmud teaches.

They taught works of supererogation—that is, meritorious performances more that the law requires, and therefore efficacious to remove guilt.

They macerated their bodies by fasting, watching, lying on rough narrow boards, and wearing around the border of their garments a fringe of thorns, with the points projecting inwards, so as to strike upon their flesh when they moved. They made long prayers. Some walked the streets with mortar-like hoods over their heads and faces, to aid their meditations; but as they could see only the ground at their feet, they often ran their heads against walls and posts,—which, we fear, disturbed their meditations;—others walked without this covering, but so absorbed in contemplation, that they forgot to lift their feet as they walked, and thereby stumbled over everything in their way,—which tended, we may conceive, to break the thread of their divine contemplations. If any one would know whether the common people admired them for their sanctity, we can tell him that they did: and if he does not know that they were hypocritical, self-righteous pretenders to sanctity—let him read the Gospels and learn their true character.

The Pharisees were ascetics, but not monks. But the Jews had among them two monkish sects, who arose some four or five hundred years before monachism appeared in the Church; but long after the Babylonish captivity and the cessation of Jewish prophecy. The one of these sects resided in Judea, the other in Egypt. Josephus gives an account of the former—Philo, of both. The Roman philosopher Pliny, also mentions the Essenes.

The Essenes, a Sect of Jewish Monks.

We have digested, under distinct heads, the materials facts given by Josephus, Philo, and Pliny, respecting this remarkable sect of Jewish monks, whose principles and practices agreed essentially with those of the Cenobite Christian monks of the fourth and fifth centuries.

1. The Essenes formed a *Separate Society*, and had little intercourse with other men. Some of them occupied houses in the

smaller towns, but the greater number lived in the wilderness of Judea in the vicinity of the Dead Sea.

They did not beg; but, like honest men, supported themselves by regular industry. In towns or villages, they carried on innocent trades, but avoided merchandise and navigation, probably because these occupations would cause them to mix too much with other men, and might also tempt them to indulge an avaricious desire of gain. In the wilderness they were husbandmen, shepherds, and keepers of bees. They produced only necessaries, being opposed to all sorts of luxury, and leading a simple and frugal manner of life.

Their number in the time of Josephus—some fifty or sixty years after Christ—was about four thousand.

2. They had a community of goods, like the Cenobite monks of later ages. What each one had when he entered the society, and what he procured afterwards by his labor, was put into the common stock from which all drew their supplies.

The general body was divided into particular associations, who labored, ate, and lodged together, like the inmates of a Christian monastery, under the government of officers.

3. They admitted no women into their society, abstained from marriage, and practiced a rigid continence. Yet (says Josephus,) they did not condemn marriage in others, considering it necessary for the propagation of mankind.

There was an order of Essenes, who differed from the more rigid sort, in permitting their members to marry; with the austere restriction, however, that in the marriage state, they should confine sexual intercourse to the single end of procreating children, allowing the constitutional appetite no indulgence but what was necessary to this end. We shall, however, show that this austere rule was prescribed to married people by some Christian Fathers, as early as the second century, and was one of the signs of forthcoming monkery.

The stricter sort of Essenes appear to have had an ill opinion of the female sex. Josephus says that by abstaining from marriage, they guarded against the lacivious behavior of women, being persuaded that none of them retain their fidelity to one man. Brucker tries in vain to make this signify only, that they could not keep a secret. For Philo goes even further, saying that the Essenes had the acuteness to perceive the incompatibility of marriage with the existence of their association. "For (says he) woman loves herself too much, is devoured by excessive jealousy, and can easily corrupt the morals of her husband by artifice and enticement. And, if she bear children to her husband, then she who before used artful blandishments, now comes out boldly and undertakes to rule her husband by main force. Wherefore, wives were considered most inimical to this society; for the man who is overcome by voluptuousness, or is ruled by his wife, can neither be pure in himself, nor honest towards mankind."

This atrocious opinion of the female sex,—which we apprehend to have been Philo's own,—is truly monkish, and outrageously unjust to the amiable sex, who are in general far more virtuous than the male,—not excepting even the monks, with all their vows upon them.

4. They supplied their society with new members by training up boys or young men;—or as Philo, quoted by Eusebius, says—men of mature age,—who are given by their parents, or who offer themselves, for that purpose. They were to pass through a noviciate of three years, before they were admitted to membership. The first year was a trial chiefly of their continence. If approved on this point, they were then purified by baptism, and subjected for two years longer to the full rigor of the society's discipline, as a final trial for membership. If they willingly submitted so long to their rules of temperance and modes of life, they were then received into full communion, on their taking a solemn vow, or as Josephus calls it, "a tremendous oath" of fidelity and obedience to the rules;—one of which was that they should never conceal anything from their fellow-members, nor reveal any of the society's secrets to others,—not even to save their lives.

5. The Essenes, while all, in theory at least, fared alike, had nevertheless a system of strict subordination among them. They had curators or directors, who governed all the movements and operations of the society. The curators belonged to the oldest class of members. Below them were three other classes divided according to age. The younger were bound to reverence and serve the elder,—a good rule, if it had not been carried too far. "The juniors are so far inferior to the elders, (says Josephus), that if an elder be touched by a junior, he must wash himself,—as if he had been defiled by the contact." Their government was therefore a despotism, like that of the Roman Catholic monasteries.

6. If a member committed a heinous offence, they expelled him from the society. This was almost equivalent to a sentence of death:—for being bound by his "tremendous oath" not to associate with other persons, nor to partake of their food, the excommunicated member was obliged (says Josephus) to eat grass, until he was famished with hunger. They sometimes restored the offender, when they found that he was ready to perish rather than violate his oath.

7. Their *System of Morals* was pure even to austerity. Their vow bound them to be temperate in all things; to deny themselves all corporeal enjoyments beyond what life and health required; to be scrupulously faithful, just, and true; to be pious towards God, just and charitable towards men; to reverence their superiors in age and office, and to obey the rulers of their country. They also exercised themselves in fortitude to such a degree, as to despise death, and to bear any kind of privations and tortures, rather than violate their rules. They also "swore not at all," except their solemn oath of admission at membership. Their system of morals was founded on the Pythagorean and oriental principle, that *Pleasure is morally evil*, and therefore to be avoided as incompatible with virtue. It is the principle of monachism.

8. Their *Doctrines* were in the main Jewish, but considerably adulterated with Pythagorean and oriental notions.

They had a profound reverence for their lawgiver, Moses, and for the writings of the prophets. They neglected the sacrifices and worship at the temple, just as the Christian hermits afterwards neglected all social worship; but to make up for this defect, they not only practiced a rigid ascetism, but kept the Sabbath with more than Pharisaical strictness. They would not, on that day, kindle a fire, nor move a vessel, wherein they were no better than the Pharisees; but then, neither would they *go to stool*, which was a ceremonial constipation, we think, somewhat *superpharisaical.*

They believed the *Body* to be temporary, and therefore rejected the Pharisaical doctrine of its resurrection; but the *Soul* they believed to be immortal. They held that the soul is composed of a subtle air, and that the body is its prison. They considered mortal life in the flesh, to be a state of bondage, and death a deliverance. Here we find Oriental and Pythagorean doctrines mixed in their system with Biblical Judaism, and laying a foundation for their monkish ascetism. The body, with its senses and appetites, is essentially evil, all material things, and all the pleasures of sense are evil. Therefore, the soul must be saved from their polluting influence, by mortifying the senses and subjecting the animal body and soul to a strict regimen. All the pleasant things of the world were to be shunned as evil. What do such monkish philosophers think of the Creator, who made our bodies, and our senses, and so many pleasant objects to gratify them?

The Essenes disregarded all purely speculative philosophy. With a few principles, such as we have mentioned, they regarded only what was practical, and taught them to despise all riches, elegancies, pleasures and amusements.

They were rigid predestinarians—more so than even the Pharisees. Josephus says, "The Essenes affirm that Fate (or God's decree) governs all things; and that nothing befals man but what is according to its determination."*

* Josephus Antiq., B. xiii., Ch. v. Sect. 9.

Superstition is of the essence of monkery, and is therefore always found in connection with it. The following particulars show that the Essenes were a superstitious sect. They would not spit between themselves and another. This might have passed for a rule of decency, if they had not been equally scrupulous *not to spit upon the right side.* They imagined too, that by studying the Holy Books—especially by poring constantly over the discourses of the prophets, and using sundry sorts of ceremonial purification—they could acquire prophetic skill, interpret dreams and foretell future events. Their admirer, Josephus, says, that they *seldom* failed in their predictions. By the same means they also expected to acquire medical skill, and to find out what minerals and herbs would cure their diseases. These superstitions seem to have been a modification of the Chaldean magic and astrology.

10. Their daily course of life is thus described. The hour of morning twilight they consecrated to prayer, using the forms received from their ancestors. Then their curators sent them to their labors till eleven o'clock, when they assembled in one place, bathed themselves in cold water, put on their white garments, and went silently to their seats at the dinner-table. The dinner consisted only of bread and one other kind of food. The priest said grace before and after their meals. After dinner they laid aside their white garments, and went to their labors again until the evening. Then they returned to the house and took a silent supper. When they eased nature, they dug a hole in the ground, then filled it again, and afterwards washed themselves. These Jewish monks, like the Pharisees, did not conceive—as the Christian hermits afterwards did—that corporeal filthiness contributed to their spiritual sanctification. But, perhaps, it was not the love of cleanliness that made the Essenes wash themselves so, but an opinion that ceremonial ablutions purified the soul; for they wore their garment to rags before they changed them, and they would not, like other Jews, anoint themselves, but thought it a

good thing to be sweaty with labor. Oiling the body was a comfort to the Jews; therefore the Essenes would not indulge their vile bodies with an oiling. For the same reason they would not recline at table, according to the general custom of the age, but sat upright, as we do in modern times. Stolberg remarks that they adopted this position as an austerity.*

These are the chief particulars mentioned by our authorities, in their account of the Essenes. A few remarks will conclude what we have to say of them.

First, it does not appear that the Essenes practiced any fasting, except the daily abstemiousness of their diet; or that they inflicted any tortures upon their bodies, by whipping, burning, thorny garments, &c. In this respect they displayed less fanaticism than even the Pharisees. Their views of bodily mortification were therefore more sober and rational, than those of most fanatics of other times and nations. They do not appear to have held the Pharisaical and Roman Catholic dogma concerning meritorious works of supererogation.

Secondly, the quiet, temperate, and regular lives of the Essenes made them healthy and long lived. Many of them lived to be a hundred or more years old. We shall see hereafter, that in spite of their filthiness and excessive abstemiousness, many of the Christian hermits of after ages lived to be very old. From these facts, we may draw a useful lesson in favor of temperate eating as well as temperate drinking. The gluttonous voracity and luxurious viands of this sensual age and this plentiful country, fill its inhabitants with diseases, poison their enjoyments, stupify their intellects, and, we verily believe, deduct on the average some fifteen or twenty years from the duration of their lives. We would not be thought, in expressing our disapprobation of monkish austerity, to sanction the gluttony, drunkenness, and debauchery, so common among all ranks of society.

* Religionsgeschichte, vol. iv., p. 646.

Stulti dum vitant vitia in contraria currunt.—Fools snun vices of one sort by running into the contrary.

In matters of this sort all extremes are vicious. According to the true saying just quoted from the Roman poet, monks and sensualists are at the opposite extremes of intemperance. Both are guilty of folly. The one party refuse, the other party abuse, the gifts of a wise and good Providence.

Thirdly, we shall here take from Stolberg a notice of the ancient opinion concerning the Elysian Fields. We mentioned this as an Egyptian dogma adopted by Orpheus. Stolberg remarks that the Essenes held this doctrine of the Elysian Fields, as the happy abode of good souls after this life; but he is wrong, for Josephus says that their idea of future happiness *resembled* this, not that it was identical. Our German author quotes Pindar's and Homer's descriptions of Elysium.

Pindar (Olymp. II. Antist. IV.) thus describes it.

There ocean breezes gently blow
Around the island of the blest:
There flame the flowers of golden hue,
Mantling the sod, while others wreathe
The spreading boughs; the waters bloom
With many more: the blest encircle
Their heads with chaplets, and their arms
With flowery wreaths that never fade.

Homer (Od. IV. 56, &c.) had before described the Elysian Fields as the abode of heroes, after this manner:

'Tis not ordained for thee, O God-like Menelaus,
In Argive fields where horses feed, to die.
But thee sometime to the Elysian Fields
At earth's remotest bound, the blest shall guide;
Where Rhadamanth, the swarthy hero dwells.
There free from care shalt thou abide in peace.
No wintry snows, no thundering rainstorms fall
Upon that blissful shore; but ocean sends
Soft, cooling zephyrs to refresh the soul.

From these passages it is evident that the beautiful idea of the Elysian Fields was conveyed into Greece from Egypt, before the time of Orpheus.

Finally, respecting the time, place and circumstances of their origin, nothing is certainly known. They must have originated more than 200 years before Christ. Josephus names them with the Sadducees and Pharisees, as one of the established sects among the Jews, at a period about 160 years before Christ.* Brucker thinks that they arose in Egypt between 300 and 250 years before Christ, after Alexander the Great had planted Greeks in that country, and the Pythagorean philosophy had become known to the Jews in that country. Mosheim's hypothesis is that they originated from the persecution of the Jews by Antiochus Epiphones, when many fled to deserts and there learned to lead solitary lives. But after all, we do not know their origin, so that it would be of little use to discuss opinions on the subject.

The Therapeutes.

These were a sect of Egyptian Jews, resembling the Essenes, yet distinct from them. The only original account of them that has come down to modern times, is given by Philo, who considered them to be a branch of the Essenes; and perhaps they were originally; but Philo's own account shows, that they were different sects at the time when he wrote.

They were called *Therapeutes*, or *Healers* by those who wrote in Greek,—from the verb *Therapeuein* to *heal*, to *serve*. Philo doubts whether they got this name from their professing to *heal* the mind, or to *serve* God, in a superior manner.

They were, like the Essenes, a sort of Cenobite monks. They retired from the society and business of the world, gave their property to their relations and friends, and betook themselves to solitary places, where without distraction they might exercise them-

* Joseph. Antiq. B. xv. ch. v.

selves in subduing the body and purifying the soul, by prayer, reading and contemplation.

The most of them lived on the border of Lake Moeris, about 120 miles south of Alexandria. Here societies of them occupied cloisters, or enclosed gardens, apart from the other inhabitants of the country. Each one had within the walls his separate cell, or little house, in which he could be solitary, yet conveniently meet his brethren in their synagogue for social exercises. The first monasteries of the Christian Cenobites, 300 years afterwards, were formed on a similar plan.

The cells of these Therapeutes were of the simplest and plainest sort, and were furnished with nothing but what was necessary for shelter and subsistence.

They ate only at night, which they considered to be the proper time for attending to the body; but the day was consecrated wholly to spiritual exercises. Some of them ate only once in three—or even sometimes in six,—days;—so intensely were their souls occupied with divine contemplations. Their food consisted of bread only,—or if anything was added, it was salt and hyssop. Their only drink was water. Their clothing consisted of one plain garment of linen in the summer;—in the winter they added a large mantle. They shunned all ornament of dress as the emblem of falsehood.

They prayed every morning and evening, and employed the interval in studying the Scriptures, in which they endeavored to discover an allegorical or spiritual sense. They considered the literal sense as the body, within which the allegorical sense lay hidden as the soul—the principle of life—which the devout student must draw forth for his spiritual nourishment. They read also the books of the Fathers of their sect, in which the Scriptures were so allegorized. They also composed psalms and hymns in praise of God, and in every variety of metre. They meditated so constantly on Divine things, that in their sleep they often dreamed of them.

They practiced celibacy and continence; but contrary to the

custom of the Essenes, they had among them female votaries—virgins generally advanced in life, who out of religious zeal devoted themselves to the same pious exercises.

On the Sabbath day they assembled in the Synagogue; which was divided into two parts by a wall five or six feet high. The women occupied the one side and the men the other. They seated themselves in order, according to age, with their hands concealed under their clothes, the right upon the breast, the left, below. Then one of their best instructed elders addressed them with a mild countenance and voice, aiming at instruction without the embellishments of speech. All listened in profound silence, and expressed their approbation only by looks and nods.

Their principal festival was that of Pentecost. He whose turn it was to conduct their public worship, gave them notice, and they assembled, clothed in white, to pray, eat, and sing together, with joy. When they were ranged in order, they lifted up their hands in prayer for a blessing on their feast. After prayer they reclined on rush mats, leaning on their elbows; and kept the profoundest silence, not daring even to breathe audibly. Then one proposed a question out of the Scriptures, and resolved it himself, slowly and distinctly, that he might be well understood. The others listened attentively, and signified by mute signs, whether they understood, or had some doubt. The interpretations of Scripture, as before mentioned, were allegorical.

After the discourse was finished, they applauded it; and then the speaker rose and began to sing a hymn, either one of their ancient ones, or a new one composed by himself. All the others listened silently to the main part, but joined, both men and women, in repeating the chorus.

When the hymn was finished, young men chosen for the purpose, brought in the tables, and furnished them with leavened bread, salt, hyssop, and water. Only the more delicate among the old men, had warm bread.

When they had partaken of this repast, they cleared a space in the middle of the hall, and formed two choirs, the one of men, other of women, each conducted by the one who was considered as the most honorable and the best singer. They sang several hymns in honor of God, sometimes in concert, sometimes by responses. Meanwhile they gesticulated with their hands, danced, and expressed the transport of their souls conformably to the tenor and spirit of their song.

Then they all united in a general dance, intended to represent the passage of the Israelites through the Red Sea. This was intended to represent Miriam's choral dance upon that occasion (Exodus xv.) The grave voices of the men (says Philo) and the shrill voices of the women, formed an agreeable concert.

Thus they passed the night, and found themselves more lively at the end of it than they were when they first assembled. At sunrise they lifted their hands and prayed to God for a happy day, and for a mind capable of understanding the truth. Then they retired, each one to his cell, and resumed their ordinary course of life.*

Such were the Therapeutes, according to Philo. Whilst they agreed with the Essenes of Judea in being Jews, monks, ascetics, allegorists, enthusiasts, and so forth, the two sects differed in their manner of life, so much as to make it evident, that they composed independent associations, and had lived for ages apart from one another. They differed in their government and discipline—the Therapeutes allowing much more individual liberty than the Essenes. They fasted more: they sang and danced, and had women amongst them to animate their devotions, so that their manner of life was much more spirited and impulsive, than that of the grave, silent, mechanical Essenes, who moved day by day like clock-work, under the regulating power of a mainspring.

About two hundred and fifty years after Philo, Eusebius the

* See Philo's Tracts *On the Contemplative Life*, *On the Practical Life of the Essenes*, and *Every Virtuous Man is Free.*

Church historian copied the foregoing account of the Therapeutes,* and had the absurd presumption to say, that these Therapeutes were Christian converts of St. Mark, the Evangelist, who, according to an oral tradition, was founder of the Church in Alexandria. Mark, the Evangelist, may have founded the Alexandrian Church; but to suppose that he founded the monastic association described by Philo, or that they were Christian converts of St Mark, or any other saint, is exceedingly ridiculous. Philo was an aged man, when the Alexandrian Church was founded. How then could the monastic establishments, which he describes as existing about the shores of Lake Moeris, far up the country, have been founded by the Evangelist? Or how could those Jewish monks have been converted so soon to Christianity? Philo describes them as a sect of long standing, without one particle of Christianity in their doctrines or practices—mere Jews, who had imbibed some ascetical notions from the Oriental philosophy, and had long pursued, as Philo did after them, an allegorical method of interpreting the Scriptures. In fact, Philo never once alludes to Christ or Christians in all his works.

But no sooner had Eusebius, who wrote after monkery arose in the Church, started the idea that they were Christian converts of St. Mark, than Sozomen the Church historian, and other monkery-loving Fathers of the Church, seized upon the idea, in order to give this new institution of Christian monachism the appearance of an apostolical origin. This shows what the professed opinions of these Fathers were worth, when they had an end to serve by propagating an error. So manifestly absurd is Eusebius' opinion of the Therapeutes, that the less credulous writers among the modern Roman Catholics have given it up. Valesius, in his notes on Eusebius, refutes it. Even Fleury, a strong believer in the miraculous stories of the Fathers, hints his dissent: but Tillemont, whose capacious faith could swallow the Fathers whole,

† Eccles. Hist. B., II., ch. 17. See also Sozomen's Eccl. History, B. I, ch. 12.

endeavors to sustain Eusebius by a feeble argument.* Father Helyot, the monk, in his great History of the Religious Orders, makes an elaborate attempt, on the authority of this passage of Eusebius, to trace Christian monachism back to the apostolical age. His argument is too feeble to require a particular refutation.

* Tillemont. Ecclesiastical Memoirs, (English folio edition.) Vol. I. Fol. 74 and 399.

CHAPTER IX.

THE LATER JEWISH AND GENTILE PHILOSOPHY.

Christian ascetism began in the second, Christian monachism, in the third century after the birth of Christ. The earlier philosophy of the Jews and Gentiles prepared the way; their later philosophy hastened the progress of monastic principles and practices in the Church. We have before remarked, that the Pythagorean and Platonic philosophies did, after the Christian era, imbibe more and more of the Orientalism with which they had been strongly dosed from the beginning. The same is true of the Jewish philosophy. Both contributed—but the Grecian more than the Jewish—to fill the Christian mind with ascetic notions, and to lead the enthusiasts of the Church into all the extravagancies of monachism.

We shall now give a concise account of the later systems of philosophy prevalent among Jews and Gentiles in the eastern parts of the Roman empire, where monachism arose.

1. *The Jewish Cabbalistic Philosophy.*

A short notice of this will suffice to show how deeply the principles of the oriental philosophy had worked themselves into the minds of the Jewish doctors in the early ages of Christianity.

But before we touch the Cabbala, we must give the learned among our readers a taste of Jewish Rabbinism in the first century of our era. We copy from Brucker, who took it from the Talmud, that huge collection of the wise, and the foolish, sayings of the Rabbis. We regret that decency forbids us to expose it to common readers in our vernacular English,—it is so exquisitely philosophical in its way.

"Rabbi Akibha dixit:—Ingressus sum aliquando post Rabbi Josuam in *sedis secretae locum;* et tunc ab eo didici, Prime, quod non versus orientem et occidentem, sed versus septentrionem nos debemus convertere [quando alveum deoneremus]:—Secundo, quod non in pedes erectum, sed jam considentem, se retegere liceat:—Tertio, didici, quod *podex* non dextro sed sinistra manu, abstergendus est:—Ad haec objecit ibi Ben Hazar,—Usque adeo vero perfricuisti frontem erga magistrum tuum, ut *cacantem observares?* Respondit, *Legi haec arcana sunt*, ad quae discenda id necessario mihi agendum fuit."

What refinement of moral teaching was this, when the most unsavory of human actions was to be so regulated as to give a mystical signification to the whole process! We did not know, until we met with this passage, that there could be so much philosophical wisdom in *cacando*, when it was done by rule.

The Hebrew word *Cabbala* signifies *Traditions.* In a general sense, it means that system of oral Law, which the Pharisees pretended to have come down from Moses, and to be of equal authority with the written Law. The Cabbala comprehended at first only a system of traditional doctrines and mystical interpretations of the written Law, founded on the number, forms &c., of the letters, and on other equally insignificant circumstances. With this early part of the Cabbala our subject has nothing to do. But after the time of our Saviour, the Cabbalistic doctrine was greatly enlarged. It then embraced a system of philosophical speculations and magical superstitions, some of which were of an ascetic tendency. We shall give an outline of this part of the Cabbala.

The Cabbalistic Philosophy contained the following principles:

1. Of nothing, nothing can proceed or be made.
2. God is the primary source of all beings.
3. All things proceed from God by emanation or outflowing,

as light proceeds from the sun. But one being only emanated immediately from God. This primary emanation is called Adam Kadmon. He is the image of God, the First-Born ; from whom all other beings derived their existence. Like the Demiurge of Plato and the Logos of Philo, he is the Divine Agent by whom creation was made. He is the Divine *Man* after whose image our first parents were made.

4. From Adam Kadmon emanated ten luminous fountains or spirits of purest light, called Sephiroth ; from whom, as their immediate source, all celestial beings emanated, and in whom they yet dwell in their state of emanation, that is, they are not separated from their source, though existing as distinct personal agents.

5. These heavenly beings are of two ranks ; the higher being pure spirits, not formed of any pre-existent material ; the second are angelic, composed of a fine substance or material previously existing.

6. Four worlds proceeded from these celestial sources.

7. The matter of this world is the last of a series of ten emanations ; one thing proceeding from another, and each successive emanation being inferior to the preceding. The tenth and lowest is matter. It is therefore the most imperfect of all substances, containing the last dregs of existence, and so near to nonentity, that nothing can emanate from it. The possible degrees and extent of being are therefore complete, beginning with the absolutely perfect God, and ending with the almost non-existing matter of the earth.

8. The universe is composed of ten concentric spheres, corresponding with the ten Sephiroth and the ten degrees of existence. This earth is the central and lowest sphere ; the outermost and uppermost is the highest heaven, around which infinite space is filled with Divine light, called in the Greek language, the *Pleroma* or fullness. In this the highest order of celestial beings have their habitation. The term *Pleroma* is several times used by St. Paul, but never in this peculiar sense. But the Gnostics

of the second century made great use of the notion of a supercelestial Pleroma, which they, as well as the Jews, borrowed of the Persian philosophy.

9. As the spheres are all composed of solid substance with large spaces between them, there was need of some channel by which beings could pass through from one sphere to another. Such a channel of communication was therefore cut through all the upper spheres, a sort of hatchways one perpendicularly above another, like those made in the floors of five story warehouses, for hoisting up and letting down goods.

10. The Cabbalistic doctrine concerning demons, good and evil,—that is, the different orders of spiritual beings between God and man,—is similar to that of all the orientals.

11. The human soul is not a demon incarnate. All souls pre-existed in Adam, and not as demons of the upper regions. The Cabbalists here varied from the heathen philosophy, as they were constrained to do by the Mosaic account of the creation of man.

12. They, however, adopted the Platonic notion of the compound nature of the human soul, but with some modifications, partly conformable to the doctrine of the New Platonic school of Alexandria.

First, there is a sensitive soul, called Nephesch in Hebrew, and corresponding to the animal soul of Plato's philosophy. It gives the body its vitality, action, and sensibility. This soul is common to animals, and perishes with the body.

Secondly, there is a self-subsisting mind or spirit, called Ruach, endowed with reason and diffused through the body. It is proper to the body, being necessary to complete the constitution of man, if not of all animals who possess any degree of intelligence. It seems to have been considered as the animal intellect.

Thirdly, there is a superior intellectual soul called the Neschamah, corresponding to the rational soul of Plato's philosophy: but instead of being, as Plato taught, a pre-existing demon, it is derived by special communication from the Divine Intellect, and as an emanation continues in union with its Divine source. By virtue of this union it has an intuitive perception of intelligible things. The notion seems to have been, that it is the high intellect or reason of man by which he is distinguished from all other animals. It might be called the scientific soul, possessing the faculty of discerning abstract ideas, and of discovering the laws of nature and the existence of invisible beings.

One soul invests another as its vehicle. *Nephesch* is the vehicle or coat of *Ruach*, and this of *Neschamah;* so that one soul envelopes another, like the coats of an onion, or like the above-described spheres of the universe, only, we suppose, the successive souls are more closely wrapped about one another than the spheres. This notion of spiritual envelopes was borrowed of the New Platonists.

Such is, in sum and substance, the Cabbalistic system of philosophy. Mixed with it was a belief in the Chaldean magic. The reader will discern in the system a compound of Pythagorean, Persian, Chaldean and Egyptian doctrines, modified by a few ingredients from Moses.* Tenneman remarks that many of the Jews embraced also the Persian and Gnostic doctrine of two eternal principles, contending for the mastery of the world, as well as the doctrines of a primitive uncreated light, and of demons inhabiting the upper regions.†

At what time this philosophical Cabbalism was matured, is uncertain. The earlier books on the subject are very obscure, and the later ones, which develope it more clearly, were written after the rise of monachism in the Church. We can hardly doubt, however, that as early as the first half of the third century, when Christian monachism was as yet unhatched in the shell, many of the oriental notions embraced in the Cabbala, had already gotten possession of the Jewish mind, and some of them a century or two earlier.

* See Brucker, Hist. Crit. Phil., vol. ii. Jewish Phil. y.

† Tenneman's Hist. of Phil. (Compend.) § 209.

There is considerable affinity between this Jewish philosophy and that of the Gnostics, who so troubled the churches in the second and third centuries. The Jewish Cabbalists did not all adopt the Persian doctrine of two eternal principles, as the Gnostics did. But the doctrines about concentric spheres and a *Pleroma* of Divine light above the heavens, of the descent of supernal beings from the pleroma to the earth, the base nature of matter, and its evil influence upon the soul, were common to both systems.

---

2. *The later Pythagoreans.*

A few words must suffice for these; just enough to show that Pythagoreanism lost nothing of its oriental and ascetic character in the hands of its later professors.

Ocellus, one of these, taught that every part of the universe has its distinct sort of beings; the heavens have the Gods, the air has the demons, and the earth has the human race. This characterizes his theory of nature. His austere system of morality is marked by the following principle: "The act of generation is for children only, not at all for pleasure."

Archytas, another Pythagorean, has left us a maxim, which indicates the spirit of his moral philosophy. "There is no greater pest of mankind than pleasure.

Between these and the latest Pythagoreans appeared *Heraclitus*, a distinguished philosopher, but not of the same school. He taught a system, which, in some points, was strongly oriental. We therefore insert here a brief notice of some of his doctrines.

The *soul of the world* is from humid evaporation. This mundane soul surrounding a man, passes into him through the channel of the senses; that is, if we understand him aright, the soul of the world animates the human body at the time of its conception.

All things are full of souls and demons. Souls after death return to the soul of the world, which is of a kindred nature.

The body is to be despised as viler than dung. The soul loses much of its fiery nature, while it is compressed in the body, but regains it when it is released by death and joins the soul of the world.

Those who were more particularly distinguished as New Pythagoreans, flourished in the Eastern provinces of the Roman empire after the Christian era. The most famous of these was Appollonius of Tyana, a man of austere life, and a reputed miracle-worker. He lived in the second century. Among his doctrines we select the following as characteristic of his moral system:

"The body is a prison of the soul, and this life is a state of punishment."

"No bloody sacrifice should be offered, because of the relationship between the souls of men and of brutes."

"Riches bring trouble and anxiety. Why then should a man desire to be rich?"

"Loquacity is dangerous; but silence is safe."

The two last maxims have nothing in them decidedly ascetic, unless they be taken in a Pythagorean sense, as they should be. Suffice it to say in general, that the later Pythagoreans, instead of relaxing the ascetic austerity of the original system of their great master, rather increased its severity, and showed a constant tendency, like the new Platonists, towards a monkish hatred of the body, and an ill usage of it, for the purification of the soul.

---

3. *The Eclectics and New Platonists.*

The city of Alexandria, as we have mentioned before, was no less famous for its schools of learning, than it was for its wealth and commerce. The Grecian philosophy coming here into contact with the Oriental systems, could hardly fail to receive some mixture and modification from the constant collision and agitation of opinions. This might be expected to take place especially in the Pythagorean and Platonic systems, which were originally derived in part from the philosophies of the East.

Besides the circumstances just mentioned, another tended greatly, in the second century, and afterwards, to give a gloomy and ascetic cast to the opinions of mankind in the Roman empire. The empire was then in its decline; bloody civil war often raged; fierce barbarians often ravaged the frontiers; taxation to the utmost consumed much of the fruits of industry; and slavery, while it increased the vicious luxury of the rich, diminished the population, and almost ruined the agriculture of many provinces, but mostly of Italy, the heart of the empire.* The distresses of the times and discouraging views of the future, gave a souring tendency to men's feelings, and disposed them to gloomy views of mortal life, and to dissatisfaction with the constitution of nature in this world. Hence the prevailing system of philosophy would bend towards a conformity with the general tendency to melancholy in the minds of the age. The Oriental philosophies presented those gloomy views of life in the body which suited this state of mind, and therefore influenced the views of those who studied and taught the Greek philosophy.

About the year 200, arose at Alexandria a new sect of philosophers called Eclectics, because they selected principles from different systems and endeavored to combine them together into a new system. They were also called New Platonists, because they took the old philosophy of Plato as the basis of their new system, and modified it by incorporating with some of his leading doctrines those which they selected from other systems. Modern writers sometimes speak of the Eclectics as distinct from the New Platonists. As different professors made different combinations in selecting, or eclecticising, from different sources, so there was a distinction among the new schools; but that which prevailed and had most influence was properly New Platonism. We shall therefore confine our attention to that. The reader will see how directly this system tended to all the enthusiasm and extravagance of monkery.

The first distinguished teacher of New Platonism was Am-

* Pliny Hist. Nat. l. xviii., c. 1—7. Livy, l. vi., c. 12.

monius Saccas of Alexandria, who had been educated as a Christian, but became merely a philosopher with little or no Christianity in him. He was followedby Platinus and Porphyry of the third century, and Jamblichus of the fourth. These were the most distinguished teachers of the sect. Writings remain of the three latter, but none of Ammonius.

Their doctrines, so far as they concern our subject, are summarily comprehended under the following heads:

1. *Of God.*

There is one infinite Supreme God, from whom three chief Gods emanated, who created and rule the world with supreme power.

Theodoret, a Christian Father, thought, that the trinity of the New Platonists resembled the Christian trinity; but as Brucker well remarks, it was more like the Hindoo Trimunti, three sovereign Gods, sprung from an original infinite quiescent Brahm. The later Egyptian theology contained a similar doctrine, as we have stated in our account of the Egyptian philosophy in Chapter V. Some of the Eclectics, however, taught the doctrine of three eternal principles, which brought their trinity nigher to that of the Christians, as defined by the council of Nice. That abovementioned was the doctrine of the Alexandrian Eclectics, who mixed the old Egyptian theology with the Platonic.

The reader perceives in this new Platonic theology the oriental doctrine of emanation, more distinctly developed than it was in original Platonism.

2. *Celestial Beings.*

There are various orders of beings between the highest Gods and men;—subordinate Gods, angels, demons and heroes. The notion of Angels was borrowed from the Jews, Christians or Chaldeans.

The Gods exercise the government of the several departments of nature. Angels and demons have charge over subordinate affairs. All the celestial beings act as mediators between the supreme Gods and men. This notion of the mediatorial agency of inferior Gods and demons, is of oriental origin, and was adopted by Plato.

The Gods are void of passions; but the demons, of a nature inferior to them, have passions, and thus partake of both the divine and the human natures, being eternal like the Gods, but subject to passions like men. The heroes are the lowest order of celestial beings, and are but one degree above men.

Demons are invested with a body or vehicle—as all created spirits are,—but this body is not material and corruptible, like the human body. It is composed of a refined substance, different from the substances with which we are acquainted. These celestial bodies are incapable of suffering and of change; but they derive nourishment or refreshment from the sacrifices that men offer to them; hence these demons—who were the Gods of the heathen world—are pleased with sacrifices. They do not, however, derive nourishment from those material parts of the sacrifice, which are suitable to the human body, but from the immaterial part, or refined essence, purged of everything gross enough to be apprehended by the senses. This notion of spiritual beings feeding on immaterial substance existed also among the Boodhists of Eastern Asia, as we have shown in our extracts from Borri, in Chapter III. of this work.

Jamblichus following the old Egyptian Theology, taught the doctrine of guardian angels, or demons. The office of the guardian angel of every man was to unite the soul to the body, and to attend upon it, until it was restored to its original blissful abode in the heavens. The monks adopted the same notion, that every man had a guardian angel who attended him through life.

3. *Apparitions.*

We come now to those doctrines, in which the new Platonists departed most widely from Plato himself, and which gave a particularly enthusiastic and ascetic character to their religious philosophy.

Whilst they taught that the Gods and demons—indeed all spiritual beings—could not be perceived by our senses; they nevertheless believed in spectres and apparitions of Gods, of demons both good and evil, and of the departed souls of men. They held, therefore, that these spiritual beings were able to invest themselves with visible forms, and thus to become objects of sense.

Visions of the Gods (says Jamblichus) are salutary, they bring health, virtue and intellectual elevation, restoring the faculties and cheering the heart. These salutary visions are also uniform and immutable.

Apparitions of good demons, called archangels and angels, are of the same character, but in a less degree. As angels are charged with attendance on individuals, or with special services and messages, so, when they appear, it is to bring some special benefit.

Apparitions of evil demons are variable; but always frightful in appearance, as well as hurtful in their effects. They oppress the body, inflict diseases, hurry the soul into some passionate excitement, and prevent its aspirings after heavenly things by chaining it to earthly and sensual things.

Spectres of departed souls, if pure and enrolled among the angels, call us upwards and fill us with good hopes. But impure souls, on the contrary, turn our desires and hopes to sensual pleasures, excite evil passions and corrupt the mind.

As apparitions differ in their effects, so they do in their attendants and phenomena. Gods are attended by angels surrounding them. Archangels—that is, the highest order of good demons,—have a train of angels after them. All good demons appear with tokens of their good works. Avenging demons exhibit the various sorts of punishment which they inflict. Evil demons bring with them noxious beasts with bloody mouths. Departed souls exhibit a fire of no certain character, representing the soul of the world A purified soul shines with a pure fire, but a sinking soul is accompanied by the appearance of chains and tortures. In short, all exhibit the sort of appearance which is congenial to their nature and condition. Aerial spirits exhibit a bright aerial fire; those of earth, one that is gross and dusky; but the heavenly Gods shine with a pure and brilliant light.

Such was the demonology of the New Platonists. Psellus truly remarked, that the same fancies were adopted by the Christians, who related numberless fables of apparitions. The reader will see in the following life of St. Antony, by St. Athanasius, a demonology so much resembling this, as to show that they were both derived from the same source.

4. *Theurgy.*

The New Platonists believed that apparitions of superior beings could be produced by human agency, according to the rules of magic or Theurgy. They derived this as well as some of their other notions from the Chaldeans.

The theurgist must, in the first place, purify himself by fasting and other bodily mortifications, and by devotional exercises, so as to release the soul from its fleshly incumbrances and qualify it for communion, with the Gods.

He was then, by intense meditation, accompanied by certain ceremonies to work himself into a state of Divine Enthusiasm, the signs of which are thus described by Porphyry and Jamblichus, especially the latter.

The subject of this Divine Enthusiasm was not in his proper senses, which were in a sleeping state. He had no command of his mental faculties, nor consciousness of what he said or did. He was insensible to fire or to any bodily injury. Carried off by a Divine impulse, he passed through impassable places, through fire and water, without knowing where he was. He lived not an animal life, nor that of a human being—but a life more divine.

The cause of this peculiar condition was the divine illumination, which took full possession of the man, absorbed all his faculties, motions, and senses, making him speak what he did not understand—or rather seem to speak it ; for he was, in fact, merely the minister or instrument of the God who possessed him.

We need scarcely remind the reader of the striking resemblance between the state here described, and that of mesmeric somnambulism, which has caused so much wonder during some years past; and we cannot help believing that this Divine Enthusiasm of the ancients, as here described, was the same thing.

By such means, the theurgist could produce visions and apparitions of both good and evil spirits. He performed certain rites and sacrifices, and thus brought upon himself the enthusiastic state, and produced apparitions. If all was purely and rightly done, the good Gods or angels appeared. Then evil demons fled, and nothing could disturb the pious theurgist. But if he was not duly purified, or if he impiously invaded the sacred rites; he failed to reach the Gods, but was filled with evil and impious spirits, and became wicked and lascivious like the spirits who possessed him.

5. *Of the Human Soul and Body.*

The New Platonists retained the oriental and Platonic doctrine of the pre-existence of the human soul as a demon in the upper regions. Porphyry endeavored to explain how these spiritual beings came to descend into gross matter, and assume terrestrial bodies: but his theory is not worth repeating.

They also held the doctrine of transmigration of souls.

They not only considered matter as the source of evil, and the body as a prison of the soul; but they went so far as *to hate the body, and to feel ashamed of it.* So long as the soul is enveloped in matter, they believed that it could never enjoy true happiness, unless it delivered itself from the malign influence of the body by a severe course of ascetic purification.

6. *Ascetical Purification of the Soul.*

The New Platonists carried out their principles by observing *the severest rules of bodily mortification.* They acknowledged and lamented *the depravity of human nature, resulting from the influence of material things upon the soul*, through the appetites and passions. They laid the blame upon the body in which the soul is confined, and therefore declared war against the body and all the pleasures of sense. Porphyry wrote a special treatise in commendation of fasting, and especially of abstinence from animal food. This sect also *considered marriage as a less holy state than philosophical chastity*. Some of them, like the Christian Father Origen, went so far as to cut off their genitals, that they might never again defile the soul by venereal gratifications.

Ammonius, the founder of the school, taught, about the year 200, that *the soul should cast off the shackles of the body, by resisting its motions and desires, and breaking off all commerce with it, and reducing its strength by severe fasting*;—that the mind should ascend to its source by prayer and divine contemplations, night and day, mixing hymns of praise to the Gods, with other pious exercises; that it should by all means cultivate pure affections, and devote itself to spiritual exercises, taking care *not to indulge in any pleasure of sense.*

In short, the New Platonists, while they differed from the Christians in their theology, agreed with the Christian ascetics in warring against the body and all the pleasures connected with it. Thus it appears that the oriental doctrines that led to monachism had thoroughly penetrated the mind of society in the countries where Christian monachism arose.

The chief end of this New Platonic philosophy—as Brucker observes—was enthusiasm. Considering the mind as debased by the body, it aimed to purify and to elevate it by bodily mortifications and divine exercises, by which they hoped to attain to an intuitive perception of God and a spiritual communion and intercourse with celestial beings. By a course of purifying exercises, and by prayer and sacrifice according to the rules of theurgy, they expected to be so filled with divine illumination, as to have visions of God and holy beings, thus to prepare themselves for ascending at death to the celestial abodes, where they would enjoy etern.l felicity with God and the angels of light.

The same enthusiasm characterized the Christian ascetics, and especially the primitive monks. Essentially the same notions of the body, and of the means by which the soul was to be purified and delivered from its evil influences, actuated their conduct. They had essentially the same system of demonology, the same visions of good and of evil spirits.

So close an affinity between the two systems, shows that they had the same origin. Brucker supposed that the New Platonists borrowed of the Christians of their time, and, to some small extent this may be true. But on the other hand, we cannot doubt, that the Oriental philosophy was the primary source of all those notions and practices, in which this system differed from the teachings of the Gospel. We have now concluded our investigation of this subject. We have fully shown the influence of the Oriental philosophy upon the religious opinions of mankind, in the countries where Christianity was infected with ascetism and monkery; and thus we have traced Christian monachism to the common source of all monachism—the religious philosophy of the Hindoos and Boodhists of Eastern Asia.

CHAPTER X.

IS MONACHISM A SCRIPTURAL INSTITUTION?

In the year 1626, the Capuchin Friar, Jacob Boulduc, published at Paris a book on the state of the Church in all ages. In this work he gave a history of monachism among the patriarchs before the flood. It began—that is, monachism began—he said, with Enos the son of Seth. When Enos heard his grandfather Adam describe the lost felicity of Paradise, he determined to renew this happy life by turning monk. He and his brothers and sisters, therefore, betook themselves to a solitary life in the desert, where they lived like angels, praying, singing psalms and working.*

And whence did Boulduc learn all this? Why, from Genesis, chapter iv. ver. 26, where it is said, that when Enos was born, "men began to call upon the Lord." That is all. Now, when a monk can find monkery in a text like that, he can be at no loss to find it anywhere in the Bible.

But this poor Capuchin Boulduc, was not the first, nor by a long way the greatest advocate of monkery, who imagined that there was some authority for it in that text. Cardinal Bellarmine, the ablest defender of popery before Bossuet, had previously cited the same text, though rather timidly, as evidence that monachism existed before the flood.

Now every man who reads the Bible without having his head previously stuffed with monkish prejudices, must perceive that no such institution as the monachism existing in the Roman Catholic

* See Weber's "Moncherei, oder Geschichtliche Darstellung der Klasterwelt," at the beginning.

Church, is in any way recognized, taught or suggested, either in the Old Testament or in the New. The advocates of monachism, rely mainly on the Old Testament, as affording examples, which justify the institution.

Now, we might, properly, in this case, foreclose all argument from the Old Testament, by alleging these three unquestionable facts:

1st. That no monastic institution is recognized by Christ or his Apostles as existing, or as authorized to exist, among the Jews, in their time. The Essenes did exist, we know; but they are never once alluded to in the New Testament.

2d. That neither Christ nor his Apostles established, authorized or suggested anything like monachism, solitary or Cenobite: and

3d. That the Christians of the two first centuries never understood, either from Scripture or from oral tradition, that such an institution or manner of life was either necessary or proper for a Christian man.

Of what avail would it be then, if examples of monachism could be found in the Old Testament? They could never reach us through such a triple wall of separation. We are Christians, not Jews; we are under the Gospel, not under the law; we are not bound, nor even authorized, to do everything or anything that may have been done under the old dispensation, even by inspired men and holy patriarchs. Jacob had four wives. May we have four? Samuel hewed Agag in pieces. May we do such a thing? David, as an inspired poet, cursed his enemies. May we curse, therefore? The prophet Elisha by his solemn curse brought two she-bears out of a wood to destroy the children who mocked him. May we therefore have wicked children torn in pieces by bull-dogs? Yet Elisha is the main example of Old Testament monachism. Why take one act of his as an example for our imitation, and reject another which was sanctioned by a divine m racle? Elijah, the prophet, and King Jehu slew the prophets of Baal. This was an example of religious persecution; and well has the Church of Rome followed it, to the utmost of her power. But does this example, though divinely approved, authorize Christian persecutions? We say that it does not; because the Gospel authorizes no such thing. Neither could Old Testament examples of monachism, if such existed, authorize Christian monachism, without the sanction of Christ and his Apostles.

But let us see what the mighty Bellarmine alleges from the Bible in favor of monachism.

1. He cites the text before mentioned in the fourth chapter of Genesis, as evidence of antediluvian monachism. We have not another word to say on that text.

2. He alleges the vow of the Nazarite, in Numbers, chapter vi. as an example of legal monachism.

The material part of this provision of the Mosaic Law is contained in the following verses:

V. 2. When either a man or a woman shall separate themselves to vow the vow of a Nazarite, to separate themselves unto the Lord;—v. 3, he shall separate himself from wine and strong drink,—neither shall he drink any liquor of grapes, nor eat moist grapes nor dried;—v. 5. All the days of the vow of his separation, there shall no razor come upon his head; until the days be fulfilled in which he separateth himself, he shall be holy, and shall let the locks of the hair of his head grow.—v. 6. All the days that he separateth himself unto the Lord, he shall come at no dead body. —v. 8. All the days of his separation he shall be holy unto the Lord.

The rest of the law of the Nazarite only prescribed the sacrifices that he was to offer, when he happened to touch a dead body, and when the days of his separation were fulfilled, and he might cut his hair.

This law neither enjoins nor recommends the making of a vow of separation; it merely regulates a custom which some Israelites had followed, in imitation probably of the Egyptians, who like the Hindoos were much given to ascetic superstitions. Indeed we may safely infer from the form and provisions of the law, that it wae intended not to encourage but to restrain excesses of this sort. The customary vow of Nazar or separation was so regulated, that it came essentially short of monachism. The vow of the Nazarite did not separate him from his usual business, nor from the society of his family or of mankind in general. When Saint Paul, on one of his missionary tours, took such a vow in his character of Jew, he still pursued his ordinary course of action. (See Acts xviii. 18). The Nazarite limited his vow to such time as he chose. Two extraordinary cases are mentioned—those of Sampson and of John the Baptist, in which the parents by divine admonition made their unborn sons Nazarites for life. In such cases only was the obligation perpetual. The Nazarite was bound to three observations only. 1st. abstinence from wine and grapes: 2d. avoidance of ceremonial defilement by touching a dead body: and 3d. to let the hair grow uncut. The vow embraced not a single particular comprehended in the vows and practices of monkery;—neither poverty, nor obedience to a superior, nor chastity;—neither prayer, nor fasting, nor watching, nor solitude, nor anything else that characterizes the monastic life.

3. We next take up his argument from the Rechabites. He cites their customs as an approved example of monachism. (Jerem. xxxv.)

These people were not Israelites, though they lived among them and professed their religion. They were of the Kenites, who descended from Jethro, Moses' father-in-law. Jonadab, ancestor of these Rechabites, enjoined it upon his family, not to drink wine, nor live in houses, nor till the ground; but to live in tents as shepherds and herdsmen, like their fore-fathers in the desert. And so they lived with their families from age to age, as the pastoral tribes of Asia have continued to live until this day. And their mode of life is solemnly quoted by a learned divine of the church of Rome, as an example of monkery!—A tribe of monks keeping cattle *with their wives and children.* Oh! but the Rechabites drank no wine!—No; nor do the tribes of the Mahometan

Arabs, who now pasture their flocks upon the same ground. Are they monks, therefore?

4. "We have (says Bellarmine) in the same Old Testament Elijah and Elisha, and the sons of the prophets, living without wives and worldly riches: of whom St. Jerome says in an epistle to Rusticus;—"The sons of the prophets whom we read of as monks in the Old Testament, built themselves cells by the Jordan, away from the crowds of cities, and lived upon barley bread and herbs." And in another epistle to Paulinus, speaking of monks, he says,—"Our founder Elijah, our Elisha, and our leaders, the sons of the prophets, lived in the fields and deserts, and made themselves tabernacles by the flowings of the Jordan." Such is Bellarmine's, or rather St. Jerome's, argument from the case of these prophets.

Now supposing that Elijah, Elisha, and their disciples had been monks, and that their example could break through the triple wall which separates Old Testament facts from Christian obligation,—still this example would fail to sustain the Roman Catholic system of monachism; because it is example, not of an established or permanent institution, but of a temporary expedient adopted by a few individuals under pressing and peculiar circumstances, and which was laid aside and never resumed, after those individuals and those circumstances had passed away.

But what are the facts of the case? Jerome with his head and heart full of monkish prejudices, did not state the facts either fully or fairly.

In a time of general apostacy in Israel, when both king and people had forsaken the law and worshipped Baal; God raised up Elijah and Elisha, who at the continual hazard of their lives should testify against the prevailing idolatry, and preserve the knowledge of the law among such disciples as they could gather around them. These prophets, like some of the apostles and primitive Christians, were obliged for their own safety, to live without wives, and without the care of worldly goods, and to keep themselves much of the time in solitary places, and often to flee from place to place, that they might avoid the persecuting rage of their enemies. "Lord, (said Elijah once, when he took refuge in the desert,) the children of Israel have forsaken thy covenant, thrown down thine altars and slain thy prophets ; and I only am left, and they seek to take away my life."

These two prophets gathered their sons,—that is, their disciples,—into schools at several places, after the example of former schools of the prophets. Bethel and Jericho were the chief seats of these schools, (2 Kings, ch. ii.) These cities were within the kingdom of Judah, and less exposed to persecution, than the more idolatrous country of the ten tribes of Israel.

The school at Jerico, a few miles from the Jordan, had increased so much in number during Elisha's time, that they needed more house-room, and as no timber grew about Jericho, they proposed to their master Elisha, that they should go to the river where trees grew, and cut beams suitable for the enlargement of their accommodations. (2 Kings, ch. vi.)

As the circumstances of their living on barley bread and herbs, and their building themselves cells by the flowings of the Jordan—that is, in an uninhabited place—these existed nowhere, that we have seen, but in the monkish imaginations of Jerome and Bellarmine. As the circumstances on which the argument is founded, vanish upon inspection, so does the monkery of Elijah, Elisha, and the sons of the prophets, who could never have been dreamed of as founders of monachism, had not the want of Scriptural authority driven the advocates of the system to build upon such a slight and unstable foundation.

5. Finally, Bellarmine says, that nearly all the Fathers consider John the Baptist as the first hermit.

It is true that John lived in the wilderness, ate locusts and wild honey, and wore a coarse garment of camel's hair, girded about him with a leathern girdle. We may certainly infer that he was also unmarried, and that having been a Nazarite from his birth, he had never been either shaven or shorn, and probably not often either combed or washed ; and that he looked exceedingly shaggy and wild. He was therefore very like a hermit.

But it is a very questionable point whether he did not after all lack one essential quality of a hermit—that of being a recluse, or solitary devotee. In Luke, (ch. i., 80,) we are told that John "was in the deserts until the day of his showing unto Israel." The country in which he and his parents lived, is elsewhere (in verse 39) called the Hill Country. Though comparatively wild and mountainous, it was not uninhabited. It is the region that extends from Jericho southwards along the Jordan and the Dead Sea. Being generally too rocky for cultivation, the inhabitants depended for subsistence mainly on pasturage and fruit-trees. Here the Essenes led their austere monastic life. Here was the city—doubtless a small one—in which the Baptizer was born. (Luke, i. 39, 40.) Here he led his private austere life, until he came forth as a prophet and preacher of repentance. Whether he lived as an anchorite in some mountain cave, or like an ascetic of the second century, with his relations in the city, neither Bellarmine, nor any other man of later ages, could determine. His food and dress, as described by the Evangelists, would not appear so strange to the rude shepherds of his native wilderness, as they did to the more polished citizens of Jerusalem. No man, therefore, not even a monkish Father of the fourth century, had authority to affirm that John Baptist was the first hermit—or a hermit at all in the sense meant by Bellarmine and the Fathers. He came in the spirit and power of Elijah, and like his prototype, he was an extraordinary man, raised up for an extraordinary occasion. His austere manners became him as the preacher of repentance to an evil and adulterous generation.

But his manner of life is not exhibited as a model for our imitation. Jesus is our pattern, and he was no monk. He came eating and drinking like other men, and associated freely with all classes of society. Had Elijah and John been monks to all intents and purposes, what would Christ's disciples have to do with their example, unless Christ had instructed his disciples to imitate their peculiar mode of life? The only case in which a Christian could imitate their uncouth austerity, with any appearance of reason, would be when like them he was divinely commissioned to rebuke the sins of a generation of vipers. Then a wild, shaggy exterior, and a body gaunt with famine, may attract public attention and enforce the lessons of a harsh but salutary wisdom.

We have mentioned that the Baptist was brought up in the same wilderness, in which the Essenes practiced their monastic austerities, virtues, and follies. Here then was a most apt occasion for the evangelists and for the Saviour to take some notice of those Jewish monks. Had they deemed monachism a good thing, here were monks, ready made, severely virtuous, and needing but the Christian doctrine to make them pattern-monks for all future ages: Yet were Christ and his apostles as mute concerning them, as if they had been Gymnosophists of India.

We have now reviewed all the examples which the defenders of monachism imagine to exist in the Bible tending to justify the monastic system. The reader is convinced, we trust, that they are of no force whatever.

When a learned monk, who argues in defence of monachism, rejects the whole mass of these Biblical examples,—St. Jerome and all the Fathers, and Bellarmine being in this matter set at naught,—we may presume that the examples are futile. Yet this was done by no less a writer than Father Helyot, in his great History of the Religious Orders.

"It is useless," says he, in his Introductory Treatise, "to go back to Elijah and Elisha; for all that we read of these prophets and their disciples,—of the Nazarenes, the Rechabites, and of St. John the Baptist, whom St. Jerome calls the first of the anchorites, and St. John Chrysostom calls the prince of the monks, were only the shadow and form of monachism:"—which means that they contained nothing of the substance or reality of monachism in them.

As it is not pretended that either Christ or his apostles established or recommended any form of monastic institution, our argument is complete, and the conclusion is, that *Monachism is not a Scriptural Institution.*

CHAPTER XI.

ASCETISM AMONG CHRISTIANS OF THE EARLY AGES.

We have now presented a sketch of the prevailing systems of religious philosophy among Gentiles and Jews before monachism arose in the church. We have shown how certain dogmas concerning the soul, the body, the material world, and the spiritual beings supposed to inhabit the atmosphere and regions above it, led to ascetism and monkery before our Saviour's advent. We have shown how these same dogmas spread among Greeks and Jews, and then mixed themselves with the doctrines of Christianity in the minds of its early professors. We propose now to trace the growing influence of these heathenish notions in the church from the age of the apostles, until they gave rise to Christian monachism and other extravagances in the third and fourth centuries.

When the reader considers how thickly the countries where the gospel was first preached, were sown with the seeds of ascetism and monkery, he will not be surprised to find that these tares began to spring up with the wheat, even in the apostolic age.

We find in several passages of St. Paul's epistles, evident signs of an ascetic spirit (not approved of by the apostle) among the first converts to Christianity. The obstinate attachment of the Jewish converts to the "beggarly elements" of the ceremonial law and the pharisaical additions to it, was not all that the apostle discerned of a tendency to excess in religious observances among the primitive Christians. There was a disposition to repudiate marriage as unholy, to abstain from pleasant meats, to practice an affected humility and a system of bodily mortifications. These principles and practices he pointedly condemned, as the offspring of a vain and deceptive philosophy.* He foresaw that they would in after times grow up into a complex system of error and superstition. He therefore, in addressing Timothy,† uttered a solemn warning against them, and against the doctrine concerning demons, taught by the heathen philosophers, afterwards adopted by Christians, and introductory, not only to the extravagances of monkery, but also to the worship of human spirits in the character of saints. He also condemned the worship of angelic beings,‡ called demons by the heathen philosophers, thus intimating, that both Jews and Gentiles entertained some false notions respecting celestial beings.

But these warnings were in a great measure unheeded. The tendency to ascetic austerity and superstitious devotion was too strong to be counteracted. The one-sided views of the devotees, made them look only at those principles and those phrases of the Divine Word, which seemed to favor their preconceived notions. In reference to marriage, they caught at what our Saviour said about those who made themselves eunuchs for the kingdom of heaven's sake, and at St. Paul's qualified recommendation of celibacy.§ They construed these expressions as laying down a rule for Christians at all times and under all circumstances; when in fact, they had reference exclusively to the poverty, distress and persecutions to which the primitive disciples of Christ were exposed, and were merely counsels of prudence to those who were unmarried and had the gift of continence.

It was argued, however, with some plausibility, that St. Paul expressed an absolute preference to celibacy, as a holier state than marriage, though he justified the latter as free from sin.¶ Yet a

* Colossians ii. 8, 18, 23. See M'Knight, Rosenmuller and Loesneri Observationes, on the place.

† 1 Tim. iv. 1—3.

‡ Col. ii. 18.

§ Mat. xix. 12. and 1 Corinth. vii. 7—9, 27, 28.

¶ 1 Cor. vii. 32—34, 36, 38.

careful examination of the whole passage will show conclusively, that he founded his advice upon expediency alone, and that he limited it to cases in which a man could exercise continence, while his circumstances would render family cares burdensome and distressing. He expressly referred to the distress of the times and the trouble in the flesh which the married were then liable to,* as the reason why those who innocently could, had better remain unmarried at the time when he wrote. His advice is just such as a prudent man would at any time give to a friend, under like circumstances. St. Paul seeking especially the spiritual good of those whom he addressed, enforces his advice by the consideration, that the unmarried could attend to their religious duties without distraction, whereas they who had the care of families, in circumstances of worldly trouble and distress, would be too much harassed by cares to serve the Lord with a free and cheerful mind.†

But the reader should observe how attentive the apostle is, in giving this advice, to guard against the inference, that there is anything unholy in the matrimonial state or in the enjoyments connected with it, and how he abstains from even suggesting, that a Christian should macerate his body with fasting, or adopt any other monkish austerities, to destroy the appetites which the Creator implanted in our constitution. On the contrary, he takes occasion more than once to condemn ascetic austerities.‡ Especially in writing to Timothy, he disparages "bodily exercise"—that is, ascetic mortifications of the flesh—as unprofitable. He declares marriage to be honorable *in all* and the marriage-bed to be pure.§ No where does any inspired writer intimate, that there is any superior purity or merit in virginity, or that any kind of ascetic practice entitles man or woman to higher rewards in heaven, than those can attain who live piously and virtuously in the world.

But even in the first century the contrary opinion got posses-

* 1 Cor. vii. 26, 28, 40.

† 1 Cor. vii. 32—34.

‡ Colos. ii. 23. 1 Tim. iv. 3, 8.

§ Heb. xiii. 4.

sion of some Christian minds. Influenced by a preconceived opinion to construe St. Paul's language erroneously, some primitive Christians lived unmarried, not merely from considerations of expediency, but from a notion that celibacy was a holier state than matrimony. Others no doubt had correct views on the subject, and abstained from marriage in consequence of "the present distress," either of the Church or of their private circumstances. They feared that if they had families, they would be distracted with worldly cares, and be tempted in the days of persecution to apostatize for the preservation of those whom they loved.

As to the first class, who conceived that virginity was more meritorious than matrimony, many of them, even before the end of the first century, took it into their heads to esteem themselves holier than others, and were puffed up no little with spiritual pride and arrogance, so that they had to be reproved by the bishops. As yet bishops had not generally conceived so exalted an opinion of the merits of virginity, as those of after ages; yet even by the close of the first century, some of them appear to have taken up the notion that religious celibacy was in itself better than matrimony.

The notion seems to have been founded on the fact that perpetual virginity is a perpetual mortification of a constitutional appetite, and this requiring no little self-denial, it seemed to indicate great strength of religious principle, and therefore, great merit in the devotee, especially as the sexual appetite is naturally one of the strongest in the human constitution.

There is a natural connection between this and the appetite for food and drink. If the one was to be mortified as an enemy, so should the other be. They were both members of that grand enemy, the body, against whom the war could be most effectually prosecuted by attacking him in his stronghold, the stomach, where all the materials were stored up from which every appetite and carnal pleasure derived their supplies. By the end of the first century, a regular system of fasting, or keeping stations, as they called it, was adopted by many Christians. The principle gained ground, that all pleasures connected with the body were dangerous to the soul, and should be regarded with jealousy. The figurative language of St. Paul respecting the flesh and spirit, seemed to confirm the notion of the heathen ascetics respecting the evil nature of the body and its senses. The Apostle justly cautioned Christians against excessive indulgence of the pleasures of sense, and admonished them to keep the passions in subjection to the moral law. But whilst he taught the dangerous nature of carnal temptations, he never dreamed of teaching, that the temperate and lawful enjoyment of the divine blessings with which the world is full, could be evil in itself, or dangerous in its consequences.

But the devotees laid hold on the literal sense of his metaphorical expressions respecting the flesh and spirit, overlooking the proper sense and general tenor of his language. The oriental dogma respecting the evil nature of the body, was now fixed in the general mind of both Jews and Greeks. Therefore, a one-sided view was taken of the Apostle's doctrine, and the body condemned as a nuisance. No food or drink was allowed, but such as life and health might require; and no clothing or furniture, but such as might afford a moderate degree of physical comfort.

During our Saviour's ministry his disciples did not fast,* and he severely censured the useless austerities of the Pharisees.† He himself freely partook of whatsoever food and drink were set before him.‡ He condemned long and oft-repeated prayers.§ In short, whilst he enjoined a spiritual service of God, and a reasonable attention to all the duties of religion, he expressed a pointed disapprobation of the ascetic practices of the age, and all excessive devotion, to the neglect of the duties and enjoyments of the world in which we live. The Gospel inculcates temperance, not abstinence, in regard to the pleasures of sense. But to proceed with our historical sketch.

* Matt. ix. 14. † Luke, xviii. 12; Matt. xxiii. 14. Do. vi. 5—18.

‡ Matt. xi. 19, and ix. 11. Luke, xiv. 1, 7, 12, 15.

§ Matt. xxiii. 14, and vi. 7.

We are not to suppose that the germ of ascetism, which we have mentioned as having appeared in the first century, was then much developed, or received a rapid development afterwards. With the exception of some cases of celibacy, founded on the opinion of its superior sanctity, and probably more cases of stated fasting, and many more of a voluntary renunciation of all luxury and all fashionable amusements, it does not appear that Christians adopted a very austere mode of life in the first century. Generally they set apart some days, as they found it convenient, every year, during which they devoted themselves to private fasting, prayer, and meditation on their spiritual concerns. This practice was entirely consonant to the principles of their religion, and might well be imitated more generally than it is by Christian professors in these times of luxurious ease and busy fortune-hunting. But it grew by degrees, among those who aimed at high attainments in sanctity, until it became a habitual exercise of bodily mortification and austere devotion. This was especially the case after the middle of the second century, when the ascetic philosophy of the Gentiles began to have a strong influence upon the sentiments and teachings of the clergy. We see the first manifestations of this influence in the writings of Justin Martyr, who had studied the Greek philosophy before he became a Christian, and whose theology was strongly tinctured with Platonic notions. He flourished about the year one hundred and forty.

When the stricter sort of Christians had once made a perpetual war against their bodily appetites and senses, the next step was to renounce the means by which the appetites and senses might be gratified. For this, too, the aspirants after spiritual perfection imagined that they had scriptural authority. Our Saviour's command to the young ruler, "Go sell that thou hast and give to the poor,"* they understood to be a rule for every one who aimed at Christian perfection; though it was in reality nothing more than a test which our Saviour applied, in order to discover to that young man a secret vice in his character.

* Matt. xiv. 21.

Afterwards, when the oriental doctrines got a deeper hold, some went so far as to make a general rule of our Lord's declaration, that a man must "forsake all that he hath," before he can be Christ's disciple.* Yet they were absurd enough to admit, that a man could be a disciple, though not a perfect one, without giving up all his goods. All such declarations of our Saviour evidently related to the time and circumstances of his personal ministry. He was a persecuted teacher, moving from place to place ; and they who would attend upon his instructions,—that is, become his disciples,—must forsake all that they had.

Neander remarks in his Church History, that some converts, when they were baptized, felt such a glow of gratitude and love to the Saviour, that they wished to give him all that they had, and thought that they were doing so when they gave their worldly goods to the poor, or put them into the treasury of the Church. But this was not the only motive which led Christian devotees to renounce their property. After the second century, the notion began to prevail in the Church, that everything adapted to give pleasure to the senses was not only worthless in itself, but injurious to the soul, by withdrawing its affections from heavenly things, and attaching them to the present evil world. Hence the soul must detach itself as much as possible from material things by renouncing earthly possessions. It was imagined, also, that the more earthly good the soul renounced, and sacrificed for heaven's sake, the more of heaven's felicity would God bestow upon it. Like the poet Horace, the Christian ascetic thought,

> Quanto quisque sibi plura negaverit,
> A Diis plura feret. Nil cupientium
> Nudus castra peto.

The more a man denies to himself, the more will he receive of the Gods. Naked (therefore) I fly to the camp of those who desire nothing.

So, at last, did the Christian ascetics. For a time, they thought it sufficient to lead a retired life, with their friends and Christian

* Luke xiv. 33.

brethren, avoiding the common business and turmoil of the world, spending much of their time alone, in the exercises of fasting and prayer. Many of them, after they had given away their property, gained a frugal subsistence by some kind of simple labor. What they earned above a present supply for their few wants, they gave to the poor. They needed little ; for they had no families ;—ate only the plainest food, and not much of that ;—clothed themselves scantily with a coarse garment or two,—and shuned all soft and pleasant accommodations. They could therefore employ the most of their time in the purgation of their souls, by prayer, meditations and bodily mortifications.

We have already intimated that from the time of Justin Martyr in the year 140, professors of the ascetic philosophy of the Greeks began to enter the Church, and corrupt the Christian doctrine by foreign admixtures. Had they been content to elucidate the religion of Christ by the aid of sound reason and philosophy, they would have done good service ; but instead of this, they incorporated much of their " vain and deceptive philosophy," as St. Paul characterized it, with the doctrines of the gospel, as part and parcel of the same. Alexandria was the chief radiating point of this Platonic Christianity. Here the Christians had,—as the Jews had had before them,—a celebrated theological school, as the Greeks had also long before had a great university. The Christian school was taught by men of learning and sent forth continually both books and theologians, that spread these corrupt views of Christian doctrine over nearly all the Christian world. Hence the heathen "doctrine of demons," or evil spirits infesting the human mind, was fully incorporated with what the gospel taught upon the subject, and filled Christian souls with superstitious fancies and fears. The Christian no longer considered himself exposed merely to the evil suggestions of an invisible tempter : he now imagined himself to be perpetually beset by legions of foul fiends, who could at pleasure assume any visible shape, and assault him in a thousand ways. The Pythagorean doctrine of " abstinence from meats," was by degrees carried to the extreme of a constant famine, out of hatred to the body as the worst enemy of the soul. The doctrine "forbidding to marry," became the fixed idea, that virginity was second only to angelic purity of nature, and that marriage would be an abominable pollution, if it had not the redeeming merit (as some of the fathers said) of "producing virgins."

But we must not impute all these extravagant notions to the intermixture of the Greek philosophy with the Christian doctrine, although, as we have seen, the Eclectic philosophy had imbibed at Alexandria an additional dose of ascetic principles from the oriental systems. Other influences were at work. Gnosticism, Montanism, and other heresies founded on ascetic principles, although they were condemned by the Church, had extensive influence upon the sentiments of the age, and were both the sign and the effect of a strong tendency in religious minds towards an ascetic austerity of manners. The excessive luxury and other vices of the irreligious, tended also to drive those who feared God into the opposite extreme of a fanatical hatred of the body and of the world.

Whatever causes may have combined with the influence of the Gentile philosophy in producing the effect, the effect itself was wonderful. Before the middle of the third century, the principles of a gloomy ascetism became so powerful, that some Christian devotees began to withdraw themselves from the dwellings and society of men into lonely hiding places about the cities and villages where they had lived. Some of the Gnostic enthusiasts had in the second century adopted a wild sort of monastic life in the mountains, as we learn from a passage in St. Irenaeus; but there is not a shadow of evidence that any Catholic Christian had fallen into this sort of extravagance until near the middle of the third century, when a few began to retire from the haunts of men into solitary places. This sort of life had scarcely begun, before the Decian persecution arose and drove multitudes of Christians into the deserts for safety. When in a few years this necessity ceased, some of the refugees returned to their homes; but others, who were inclined to ascetism, remained in the deserts. It seems not to have been the intention of these incipent monks, whether they became such of choice or of necessity, to continue all their lives in solitude. But many of them never did return to the cheerful haunts of men. Habit made this sort of life pleasant to melancholy minds; and nothing is so productive of melancholy, as the sort of life which they lived in the hot and dreary solitudes of Egypt and Syria, combined with their gloomy notions of religion. Still, many of them would have returned to the society of their friends, if they could, like many of their Hindoo predecessors, have completed the undertaking for which they had fled from the face of human society. They had undertaken the hard task of conquering the demons who infested them, and the harder task of eradicating the appetites and passions of their nature,—all by dint of fasting, prayer, and meditation in solitary places. But the more they hungered and pined away, the more did gloomy fancies—that is, the demons—haunt and worry them; and the more they resisted nature in their dreamy solitude, the more powerfully did nature resist their opposition to her laws, and fill their imaginations with forbidden pleasures. Thus was the war against their physical constitution, like that of Dryden's Alexander against the nations of the earth; it was "never ending, still beginning,—fighting still and still destroying,"—until death ended the strife.

We have arrived at the consummation of Christian monachism About the time that the great St. Anthony retired into the deserts of Egypt, the primitive seat of Platonic Christianity and Christian monachism, the principles had gotten firm hold of the Christian mind, that the desire of earthly pleasure was evil, that the corporeal senses, and the pleasures derived from them, were evil; that the body itself was a machine for producing sin, and a loathsome prison of the spirit; that as the body was of earthy materials, and derived its pleasures, through the senses, from earthly objects, therefore all the things of the earth that could afford pleasure to the senses, are evil, and consequently to be avoided as a snare to the soul. Therefore cities are evil; human society is evil; green fields, verdant woods, refreshing streams, balmy breezes, gay and fragrant flowers, the music of voices and the music of nature, all that was sweet to human senses, was poison to the soul. Impressed with this abominable notion of his Maker's works, the superstitious votary at last fled from all that is "beauty to the eye and music to the ear," into the dreariest deserts, where arid sands, and naked rocks, and noisome beasts and reptiles, only presented themselves to view. There, confined in some miserable den, or roaming naked over burning sands, beneath a fiery sun, he determined to spend his days in punishing his body, fighting with demons, praying to God and dreaming of heaven.

Thus was Christian monkery brought to maturity, about three hundred years after the birth of that Redeemer through whom men are saved by grace, justified by faith, and guided by the law of love, under the government of the God of love. Compared with the law of Moses, the Saviour's yoke is easy, and his burden is light. But through the influence of a vain and deceitful philosophy, a yoke and a burden were laid upon the Christians of a superstitious age, so oppressive, that the Mosaic law was light and easy in comparison.

CHAPTER XII.

SCATTERED NOTICES CONCERNING VIRGINITY, ASCETISM, &C., COLLECTED FROM THE EARLY FATHERS OF THE CHURCH.

To confirm the preceding statement respecting the growth of ascetical principles and practices in the Church during the early ages, we shall now give the reader some extracts from the Fathers, expressive of the opinions and practices of their times.

Few Christian writings of the first century have come down to us, except those of the Apostles and Evangelists. Few others were written, and they were generally very short. The longest piece that has any evidence of genuineness, is a work entitled, "The Shepherd," by Hermas, supposed by many to be the Hermas that St. Paul mentions in Romans, xvi., 14. But this is very doubtful. The book was originally written in Greek, but we have it only in a Latin translation, made in ancient times by some unknown author. We cannot judge whether or not the translation was faithfully made. Frauds and forgeries became so common in the Church after the middle of the second century, that one is often at a loss what to think of such writings as this Latin translation of Hermas. There is reason to suspect that some phrases, at least, were foisted in, to give an air of authority to certain practices which began in the Church after the time of Hermas. But we are willing to suppose that the translation is in substance correct.

In the passage from which we are about to quote,* Hermas re-

* Book iii., Similitude v.

presents himself as sitting alone on a mountain, fasting and meditating, when the angel whom he calls the Shepherd appeared, and asked him what he was doing. "I answered, (says Hermas,) 'To-day I keep a station.' He answered—What is a station?' I replied—'It is a fast.'* He said—'What is that fast?' I answered,—'I fast as I have been wont to do.' 'Ye know not,' said he, 'what it is to fast unto God.' 'Hearken,' said he, 'the Lord does not desire such a needless fast; for fasting in this manner, thou advancest nothing in righteousness. But the true fast is this:—Do nothing wickedly in thy life, but serve God with a pure mind, and keep his commandments, and walk according to his precepts; nor suffer any wicked desire to enter thy mind. Keep the commandments of the Lord, and thou shalt be approved. *But, if besides those things which the Lord hath commanded, thou shalt add some good thing, thou shalt purchase to thyself a greater dignity, and be in more favor with the Lord, than thou shouldst otherwise have been. If, therefore, thou shalt keep the commandments of the Lord, and shalt add to them these stations, thou shalt rejoice.*'"

The first part of this extract we consider to be conformable to sound doctrine, but the latter part teaches unscriptural sentiments. It attributes direct merit to ascetic exercises, such as fasting, and broaches the idea of meritorious works of supererogation—of gaining favor with God by doing more than his law requires. This is the principle upon which the Romish doctrines of Justification by works, satisfaction for sin, Purgatory, Virginity, Monachism, &c., are founded. The passage admits, however, of an explanation less repuguant to sound doctrine, though still in part at variance with it. Hermas may have meant that fasting is a duty additional to those prescribed in the Ten Commandments, and, if duly observed is a good thing, and will purchase for us a higher reward from God.

* For an explanation of the Stations of the early Christians, see Du Fresne's Glossary, article *Statio:* and Hornbeck's Miscellanea Sacra, p. 606. See also on this passage, Osborne on the Errors of the Early Fathers, p. 148.

We can heartily recommend the following rule which the Shepherd of Hermas gives for fasting:

"*Having performed what is before written*—(that is, kept the commandments,) *the day on which thou fastest thou shalt taste nothing but bread and water; and computing the quantity of food which thou dost usually eat upon other days, thou shalt lay aside the value thereof and give it unto the widow, the fatherless and the poor.*"

It was customary in early times for Christians to keep two weekly stations or fastdays, Wednesdays and Fridays. When this rule began to be observed cannot be exactly determined: but certainly not in the first century,—probably not until the latter part of the second. Hermas wrote about the close of the first century.

Besides the merit which he ascribed to fasting, we discover in him a tendency to ascetism in other particulars. Not only does he inveigh against luxurious living, which he might do by apostolical authority; but he goes farther, and censures the possession of wealth, as incompatible with a good Christian life. "They who are rich in this world (says he) *unless their riches be pared off*, cannot be made profitable unto the Lord:"—And he exhorts Christians "to procure no more than what is necessary and sufficient for them," and not "to buy houses and lands with their money, because all such things shall perish with this present time," but to spend their wealth in works of benevolence.* So far as he enjoins moderation in our desires for worldly possessions and a spirit of benevolence in the use of them, he is scriptural; but there is in his principles an evident leaning towards an austere mode of life, and a renunciation of earthly goods as unprofitable because they are temporal, and even injurious because they are pleasant.

He does not condemn marriage, but he expressly attributes superior merit to celibacy. "I said unto the angel, If a husband

* For these passages see Book I. Vision 3. and Book. II. Commands 4 and 12.

or wife die, and the surviving party marry again, does he sin in so doing? He that marries (said the angel) sins not; howbeit if he remain single, he shall thereby gain to himself great honor before the Lord."* Here is no reference, as in St. Paul's advice in 1 Corinthians, to any distress as making celibacy expedient. Abstinence from marriage without regard to circumstances is considered as meritorious before the Lord—no doubt for the reason that it is an austerity, a mortification of the flesh. This is the vital principle of ascetism and monkery.

The book of Hermas was in great repute for a century or two; it was publicly read in many churches, and was thought by some in those times to have been written by divine inspiration. Yet it is, on the whole, a tedious and insipid production. In some parts it is downright silly and utterly unworthy to be ranked among the inspired writings.

In an epistle ascribed to Clement, the first bishop of Rome, who is named by St. Paul (in Philippians iv. 3), we find the following admonitions:—"*Let not him that is pure in the flesh grow proud of it, knowing that it is from another he received the gift of continence.*"

Ignatius, another of the earliest Christian Fathers, in his epistle to Polycarp, bluntly rebukes these self-conceited professors of chastity, male and female:—"*If any man* (said he) *can remain in a virgin state, to the honor of Christ, let him remain so without boasting; but if he boast he is undone; and if he desire to be more taken notice of than the bishop, he is corrupted.*"

These allusions show very plainly that virginity among Christians, as before among certain heathen devotees, had by the end of the first century begun to be considered by many as meritorious in the sight of God, and that the professors of virginity had begun already to assume airs of superiority over the married working Christians of the time. We shall see the spiritual pride of these celibates swelling higher in after times, and leading to its natural consequences.

* Book III. Similitude 1.

Second Century.

In this century we begin to meet with Christian writers who had studied the Greek philosophy, and we discover at once a mixture of Platonic notions in their Christian theology. The heathen demonology begins to appear. Justin Martyr, who flourished about the year 140, adopted the notion of Philo the Jew, or rather of the Septuagint Greek translation of the Old Testament, that the giants mentioned in the sixth chapter of Genesis were the offspring of angelic beings, called demons by the Greeks. In his First Apology for the Christians, he says :—" Evil demons in ancient times, when they showed themselves to mankind, *debauched women*, *corrupted boys*, and *exhibited fearful appearances to men*, who being filled with awe, and not knowing that they were evil demons, called them Gods." Here we find ideas of evil demons such as neither prophets nor apostles taught, but such as were familiar to the heathen mind in the current fables of the Gods.

In the same apology, speaking of the chastity of the Christians in reference to the saying of Christ, that "*some make themselves eunuchs for the kingdom of heaven's sake*," he says, " There are among us many men and women sixty or seventy years old, who became disciples of Christ in their childhood, and have ever since continued pure [that is, virgins], and I can show such persons among all classes and conditions of people.

Next comes Tatian, a disciple of Justin's. In his oration against the Greeks, he contrasts the temperance and chastity of the Christians with the impurity of the heathen Greeks.—" You Greeks say that we play the fool among wives and boys, virgins and old women. But your poetess Sappho was an impudent courtesan, and sang her own wantonness. But all our women are chaste, and our virgins at the distaff utter divine oracles, much more clearly than that girl of yours." He seems to intimate here that the Christian virgins had a sort of prophetic inspiration Their virginity was supposed to produce in them such a degree of spiritual purity, that they were filled with a divine illumination.

We need not wonder that Tatian should have entertained such a notion; for after he had written this oration, he set up a sect called Encratites, or Temperate people, who condemned marriage as an impurity, and adopted a strictly ascetic rule of life. This fact, and the prevalence of Gnosticism in the second and third centuries, show the strong bias of religious minds in those days towards an ascetic and flesh-mortifying austerity of manners. We have already seen in chapter ninth how this bias operated to infuse into the Greek philosophy of those times more and more of the ascetic principles and practices of the oriental nations.

For a long time the struggle between the Catholic Christians and the various branches of the Gnostic heresy was severe and doubtful in its issue, especially in Egypt and Syria, where the oriental systems of philosophy had taken deeper root than in Europe.

The foundation of Gnosticism was the ancient Persian and Egyptian philosophy, whose first principles was what is called Dualism, or the doctrine that there are two primary causes of things, the one good and reigning supreme in the highest heavens, the other evil, and contending for the mastery in this lower world.

The Gnostics all held the principle common to the oriental philosophies, that matter is essentially evil, and that the body is the prison of the immortal soul. Hence their hatred of the body and their professed aversion to all earthly pleasures. They held also that the universe is full of various orders of spiritual beings both good and evil; and that Christ was one of the highest Aeons or good angels of the celestial world, and descended to the earth for the purpose of delivering mankind from the evil influences of material things and from the power of the evil demons who ruled the world.

To these general principles each leader of a Gnostic sect added a number of details according to his fancy, and from them he deduced such practical rules as suited his particular principles or peculiar taste. The most of these leaders adopted a severe system of ascetical mortification, because they held that the body and its pleasures are evil: several of them rejected marriage altogether, as a pollution of the soul; but a few gave a loose to sensuality, on the principle that as the soul is of heavenly origin, it cannot be polluted by so vile and foreign a substance as matter, no more than a diamond can lose its purity by the accidental contact of mud.

One is at some loss to conceive how the Gnostic doctrines, many of which were glaringly inconsistent with the teaching of of the apostles, could find acceptance with well-meaning, intelligent, and reflecting people, such as many of the Gnostics certainly were. We cannot easily make due allowance for the influence of prevalent notions of philosophy, and of circumstances, all differing so greatly from what we see and feel in our time. But equally strange must it appear to us Protestants in these days, that monkish fanaticism should have taken such strong and lasting hold upon the minds of Catholic Christians, in that branch of the Church which retained in early times the largest portion of true Christianity.

Neander in his Church History* thus philosophizes upon the character of the age during which Gnosticism prevailed. He remarks that although Gnosticism was a combination of elements drawn from old religious systems; yet these elements were but the corporeal form; the peculiar sentiment of the age was its animating principle. Every age has its peculiar stamp of feeling, and this, in times of mental commotion, gives rise to a variety of systems and sects, which have no external connection, yet are all to be traced to the same radical principle. The reigning principle of this age was that of Dualism, or the contest between the divine powers of good and evil.

" The key-note (says Neander) which governed the sentiments

* Kirchengeschichte, vol. I. p. 639. For want of an English translation, we refer to the Second German Edition. For a charitable account of the Gnostic leaders and their doctrines, we refer the reader to Lardner's Credibility.

of many a serious mind, was a consciousness of the power of evil, —a feeling that two parties were contending,—dissatisfaction with the present state of being,—a desire to pass the narrow bounds of the earth, and a longing after a higher and better order of things."

To this profound remark of Neander we will venture to add, that the feeling of which he speaks was caused in a great measure by the declining state of the Roman empire, which—although it maintained its external grandeur,—was decaying in the roots of its prosperity. There was a deep corruption of morals, an oppressive weight of taxation, a failing energy and success in business, and a consequent sinking of the hearts and hopes of the people.

But to return from this digression;—from a passage in Irenaeus, it would appear that by the year 170, the Marcionites, a Gnostic sect who condemned marriage, practised a sort of monachism.

They had charged the Israelites with having robbed the Egyptians, when they left Egypt under Moses,—and the orthodox Christians of their own times with defiling themselves by commerce with their heathen neighbors.

"If (says Irenaeus in reply) he who makes these charges glories in his science or [Gnosticism*], separates himself from the company of the unbelievers, and gets nothing from other men, but is simply naked and barefooted, and lives houseless in the mountains, like the animals that eat grass,—shall he be excused, because he does not know the necessity that we are under of dealing with other men."†

This is a lively description of an anchorite. It clearly indicates what is probable in itself, that these flesh-hating Marcionites, if not other Gnostics also, had among them the same sort of savage monks that afterwards appeared among the Catholic Christians. Hence it is evident that Christian monkery began among the here-

* The Gnostics professed to have the true *Gnosis*, that is, Science or Knowledge of Divine things. Hence the name.

† Irenaeius Contra Hereseis. Lib. iv. C. 30. Epiphanius says that Marcian, founder of the sect, was an anchorite. This confirms the fact that the Marcionites practiced monachism.

tics more than a century before the orthodox portion of the Church adopted the institution. The style of contempt with which Father Irenaeus, in the year 175, speaks of this manner of life, shows that monkery was not as yet recognized among the Catholics as existing, or as worthy to exist among Christians.

But the principles which led to monkery were gaining ground in the second century. Athenagoras, contemporary with Irenaeus, says in his Apology for the Christians (§ 33) ; "Each one among us has his own wife, whom he has married according to law, and whom he uses as a wife, for the sole purpose of having children, and no further. There are also among us both men and women, who have grown old in celibacy, with the hope of a closer union with God. Now if the state of virginity draws us nearer to God, the very thought and desire of carnal pleasure draw us away from him. We therefore avoid those thoughts, and much more the acts themselves: and it is not in word but in deed that we carry out our principle, that *each one should remain in the virgin purity in which he was born, or should limit himself to one marriage ; for a second one is but a decent adultery.*"

Here is a considerable step in advance of the doctrine of the first century. Virginity takes a *far* more elevated stand than marriage, which is barely tolerated as a necessary evil, for the sake of offspring, and is restricted to the utmost. Second marriages are disallowed as virtually if not formally adulterous: and even in the one tolerated marriage, not even a thought of connubial enjoyment beyond the unfortunate necessity of it for the propagation of children, is deemed innocent!

We need not say that the Bible teaches no such sentiments. Second marriages are expressly allowed, and matrimonial enjoyments are subjected to no such unnatural restriction.* Christianity lays no unnatural, arbitrary, and useless restrictions upon human enjoyments. It wages no war against our natural appetites, but subjects them to such wholesome rules as are necessary to prevent evil consequences from the indulgence of them. There is no

* Rom. vii. 3. 1 Corin. vii. 3—5.

reason for the restriction mentioned by Athenagoras, which does not apply with equal force to the appetite for food and drink. According to his principles, we should eat and drink for the sole purpose of sustaining life, repudiating as evil every thought of pleasure from this source. Consistency did at last drive the devotees to this extreme, and the result was monkery.

Theophilus of Antioch lived near the same time. He wrote three books addressed to one Autolycus. Speaking in the third book concerning the corrupt practices of the Gentiles, he says:— "Far be it from Christians even to think of doing such things, among whom, temperance is present, continence is exercised, monogamy (only one marriage) is kept, chastity is guarded, wrong exterminated, sin eradicated, &c."

Here again we find ascetism gaining ground: for the Greek phrase [εγκρατεια ασκειται] translated *continence is exercised*, technically signifies that course of bodily mortification and prayer, which the monks afterwards practiced. Monogamy was commended in the first century as preferable to second marriages: now it was enforced as an obligation, upon the principle that a second marriage was but a decent or hidden adultery, as Athenagoras called it. This father seems to have been the inventor of a very subtle reason for calling it so. God made for Adam only one wife, and they two were one flesh. A second marriage therefore breaks this bond of unity by introducing a mixture of other flesh into the compound. The argument has no solidity, for the death of a husband or wife completely and forever destroys the marriage relation between them.. They are then in no sense *one flesh*. But Tertullian, some years later, in the true spirit of an old father, took up this sophistical argument, enlarged it, and refined and twisted it in all manner of ways.* These reverend guides of the Church were by no means scrupulous about the use of sophistry. Anything that would serve their turn was welcome.

Our next quotation is from the epistle to Diognetus, usually

* In his Treatise on Monagamy.

printed with Justin's works, but written in a style so different from Justin's as to be evidently the work of another hand. It was probably composed in the second century.

"What the soul is in the body, Christians are in the world. It dwells in the body, but it is not of the body. The flesh hates the soul and wars against it, but is unable to injure it. The soul is imprisoned in the body, but preserves it. The soul is ill-used by food and drink, but grows better, &c."

These expressions savor strongly of the oriental philosophy and a superstitious hatred of the body, as an enemy of the soul. But the author writes in so rhetorical a style, that possibly he meant nothing more than an exaggerated statement of St Paul's doctrine concerning the opposition between the flesh and spirit—that is, the good and evil principles in man. But one possessed of the oriental notions now spreading through the eastern churches, would be apt to misinterpret St. Paul's figurative language on this subject, as we think this author did.

Clement of Alexandria lived near the close of the second century. He was a great admirer of the Grecian philosophy, and mixed its doctrines with those of Christianity.

It is remarked by Schroekh,* that towards the end of the second century, the Ascetics came by Clement and Tertullian to be called *Εγκρατιτες*, in Greek, and Continentes in Latin—that is, *Temperate* or *Abstinent* people. Clement says that Continence consists not only in abstaining from venereal pleasures, but in despising all the possessions and pleasures of the world.† "We, therefore, (says he) from love to the Lord and from honesty, embrace continence, sanctifying the temple of the spirit. But he, who, from hatred conceived to the flesh, abstains from conjugal connection and convenient food, is indocile and impious, and continent without reason."

Again he says, "Now concerning those who abhor marriage, St. Paul says, In the last days many shall depart from the faith—

* Christliche Kirchengeschichte, vol. iii. p. 137.

† Stromata, L. I.

forbidding to marry, &c. And again, Let no one seduce you with a voluntary humility and neglecting of the body, &c. Some just men of old brought up children, having lived continently in marriage. Will they reprove the Apostles? Peter and Philip begat children. Philip also gave his daughter in marriage. *He who marries a wife to beget children, ought to exercise continence, that he may not lust after his wife, &c.*"

Again, he says, "We admire single marriages as honorable. Concerning second marriages, if you burn, says the apostle, get married "*

These extracts suffice to show that Clement found it necessary to defend the lawfulness of marriage and in certain cases the expediency of second marriages, against a strong party who were disposed to repudiate them. But lest he should seem to concede too much to a corporeal appetite, Clement takes care, like Athenagoras, to lay severe restrictions on its indulgence, even where it may be lawfully indulged.

His condemnation of those who exercise abstinence from hatred to the body indicates the existence of this hatred among the religious people of his time.

On the whole, Clement is less fanatical in his sentiments on the subject before us, than most of his cotemporaries were. Yet he, like all the rest, had a lofty admiration of virginity, considering it as a holier state than matrimony. He is the earliest of the Fathers who taught that Mary the mother of Jesus retained her virginity after the birth of her first-born son. As authority for this doctrine, which made a deal of senseless noise in the Church afterwards, he cites a spurious piece, full of "old wives' fables," called the Protevangelium of James. He often cited spurious gospels and other forgeries of the two first centuries.

Third Century.

Whilst we are at Alexandria, we shall quote a passage from Origen, of the same city, who flourished about 25 years after Cle-

* Same L. III.

ment. Origen was also a Platonist and like Philo the Jew, he adopted an allegorical mode of interpreting the Scriptures, that he might incorporate his philosophical opinions with the doctrines of the Bible.

The passage which we are about to quote is designed to show that virginity was considered as entitling the possessor to a higher degree of heavenly felicity than married persons could attain. In his nineteenth Homily on Jeremiah, Section 4, Origen says:

"I will venture to give an example of useful deceptions. There are some who thereby exercise chastity and purity, [that is, abstain from marriage]; and others who thereby exercise monogamy; the former believing that they are lost if they marry at all: the latter believing that they are lost if they marry a second time. Now it profits the person who is once married, if he or she expect everlasting punishment for marrying a second time, because their deception prevents a second marriage. For, let any one look at the consequences. It is better indeed to live unmarried or in widowhood without being deceived, and with a knowledge of the fact that *the twice-married may partake of a degree of salvation, but not so high a blessedness as one who has lived purely:* yet if this cannot be done, it is better to be deceived in the opinion that the twice-married are lost, and through the deception to live in purity, than to know the truth, and thereby to suffer the disadvantage of being *degraded into the rank of the twice-married.*"

Here the principle is clearly taught, that marriage, and especially a second marriage, is a comparatively impure state, whilst virginity has the merit of raising its possessor to the highest degree of heavenly felicity. But this is not all. Origen here avows the abominable doctrine that useful deceptions—or pious frauds, as they are generally called—are justifiable, when they promote true religion, or what the deceiver may happen to think is beneficial to his dupes.

This immoral and mischievous principle was adopted by the Christian Fathers from the heathen philosophers, who considered the ignorant and unthinking multitude incapable of being guided by philosophical truth and reason ; hence they deemed it necessary and proper to influence their minds by such false and superstitious notions as were best adapted to inspire them with salutary fear of the Gods and of future punishment for their crimes.

Brucker, in his History of Philosophy, when speaking of the Eclectics or New Platonists (Sect. xvi.) says, that the Egyptian priests—and to some extent those of other nations—held, that pious fraud and lying are justifiable, when they are useful to religion. "It was a saying of Timaeus Locrus, that as we heal bodies by certain medicines, so we may coerce minds to good by false speeches, when they are not affected by true ones. Even Plato was not averse to this principle. He allows princes especially to deceive and lie for the public good. The New Platonists gloried in these teachers and followed their example. What wonder then if they endeavored to sustain a falling superstition by fables and fictions. This they did by both feigned miracles and supposititious books. These philosophers and the Christian teachers of these times contended with one another in the use of these frauds"—each party trying to make the most out of these knavish impositions.

One would suppose that St. Paul's emphatic condemnation of the principle—Let us do evil that good may come,* would have deterred the Christian Fathers from resorting to dishonest means for the promotion of Christianity, which needed no aid from falsehood, and which taught a morality inconsistent with all manner of hypocrisy and fraud. But neither apostolic denunciation nor Christian consistency, could deter the corrupt teachers of an already corrupted Christianity from using fraudulent means for the promotion of what they conceived to be useful ends. In imitation of the heathen priests and philosophers, they made use of pretended visions, revelations and miracles, as well as forged writings, to impose on the credulous multitude, when they had a purpose to serve, whether it was to convert heathen unbelievers, or to establish some corrupt innovation in the Church, such as

* Romans iii. 5—8.

monachism, saint-worship, relic-worship, purgatory, and transubstantiation. We venture to say, that, since the creation of the world, there have never been among heathen nations more falsehoods propagated for religious purposes, than there were in the corrupted Church of our blessed Saviour from the rise of monachism in the fourth century, for the space of twelve hundred years, during the dark reign of Popish superstition. The reader will see in the following lives of some of the primitive monks only the *modest beginning* of this system of religious imposture. Yet if he has not previously read some of these ecclesiastical romances, he will be struck with wonder at the unprincipled boldness of their *sainted* authors and the stupid credulity of the believing multitude. But let him recollect, that the venerated Fathers of the fourth century only carried out Origen's principle of "useful deceptions," and quieted their consciences with the belief that "the truth of God more abounded through their lies to his glory," or if not "the truth of God," yet something else, which they supposed it would be useful to establish under that name.

Since the great Reformation under Luther, this system of imposture has been checked, but even to this day it has been frequently resorted to, chiefly among the Roman Catholic priests and monks, who "hold the tradition of the Fathers," and to some extent even among Protestant ministers, who in their writings and discourses too often conceal or discolor the facts of ecclesiastical history, fearing lest the undisguised truth should injure the cause of religion. We shall give those facts, so far as they come within the range of our subject, without concealment or disguise. Our divine Christianity needs no fraud nor concealment for its vindication; on the contrary, it does need a full exposure of the truth of history, for its purification from the inventions of men. But let us proceed with our quotations. We take a little more from Origen.

In his work against Celsus, (Lib. V.), Origen says, "We, when we abstain from flesh, do it to chasten the body and reduce it to servitude, wishing to extinguish our earthly members (passions)—whoring, impurity, lasciviousness, depraved affections, that we may put to death our corporeal actions."

On this extract we have two remarks to make; first, that like the Hindoos and Boodhists, all the Christian ascetics abstained from flesh and from wine, and most of them from marriage; and secondly, that the design of this abstinence was to extinguish the carnal appetites and passions.

In a book of uncertain date and authorship, but composed probably about this time, called The Apostolical Canons, we find (in Canon 51) the following rule;—" If any bishop, priest, or deacon abstain from marriage, flesh, and wine, not for (ασκησιν) exercise, but from abhorence, forgetting that all things are very good, and that God made man male and female, but blaspheming calumniates the Creator, let him be either corrected or deposed and cast out of the Church."*

From this rule as well from the extract which the reader has seen from Clement of the same import, it evidently appears that there was a strong tendency in the Church toward an excessive abstinence from all corporeal pleasures, not only for *exercise* in piety, but from a hatred of the body as an evil thing, and an enemy of the soul, insomuch that stringent discipline was necessary to keep it in check. We see in this tendency the influence of that Oriental philosophy of which we have spoken in the preceding chapters.

About this time excessive fasting became common among the *ascetics* or exercisers. Eusebius, the Church historian, (Lib. V., cap. 24,) quotes Irenaeus as saying, that some thought they ought to fast one day at a time, some two days, and some even more. But Dionysius of Alexandria says, that the ascetics fasted, some two days, some four, and some six days; showing that in his time fasting was carried to great excess in Egypt, where monachism began. It was this practice of much fasting, that gave these persons the name of ascetics. This Dionysius, was

* See Bingham's Ecclesiastical Antiquities. Book VII., ch. 3.

bishop of Alexandria, about the year 250, just before ascetism began to ripen into monachism.

Eusebius relates in his Church History, (Lib. IV., c. 23,) that Dionysius wrote an epistle to the Gnossians, in which he exhorted their bishop, Pynitus, "not to impose the heavy burden of virginity upon the brethren as *a necessary thing*, but to have regard to the infirmity of most people." Pynitus wrote back in answer, that "he received his advice with great respect," but he exhorted him in turn, that "he should at last administer strong meat, and and by a second epistle of more perfect instruction, so feed his people, that they would not always continue to use the mere milk of the word, and insensibly grow old in the nurture of infancy."

Eusebius remarks on this answer, that Pynitus showed in it not only a right faith, and a due care for his flock, but eloquence and skill in divine things.

The notion was now spreading in the Church, that the Apostolic permission to marry was merely a temporary concession to the weakness of babes in Christ, and that Christians would never attain the stature of full-grown saints, until they renounced marriage altogether. This was the opinion of Pynitus at least, and this we think was what he meant in his respectful answer to Dionysius, when he exhorted that prelate to administer strong meat to the Gnossians, instead of the soft, milky doctrine of his first epistle.

These extracts from the Alexandrian Fathers are sufficient to show the progress of ascetical opinions and practices in that part of the Church, down to the middle of the third century, when monachism was about to come forth in Egypt, of which Alexandria was the great capital.

Let us now turn back to the beginning of the century, and see what opinions on these subjects prevailed about the city of Carthage, the capital of the African provinces, far west of Alexandria. Here Latin was the language of the country, and here we find the earliest Latin Fathers, whose works have come down to us. The first is Tertullian, who flourished about the year 200, that is, twenty or thirty years before Origen.

He was a vehement advocate of ascetic austerity, an uncompromising monogamist, a rigid exactor of matrimonial abstemiousness—no Pythagorean philosopher or Greek father having imposed severer restrictions on married people—and an ecstatic admirer of virginity, as the nearest approach to angelic perfection, and the surest guaranty of angelic felicity in Heaven. He would have made a capital saint of the Catholic Church, had he lived a hundred years later, when his gloomy ideas of religion would have been considered orthodox. But he was not satisfied with what in his day was considered a Catholic degree of ascetic sanctity. He joined the sect of Montanus; which, esteeming its founder to be the Paraclete, or Comforter, promised by our Saviour, went as far as he desired, in the flesh-tormenting severity of its rules. Therefore Tertullian, is not Saint Tertullian. Nevertheless, he is good authority, admitted on all hands, for the facts which we are investigating. Most of his writings were composed while he was yet a good Catholic.

Like the Fathers generally of the Third and Fourth Centuries, he esteemed the merit of virginity as the highest of human merits. He exalted it above the merits of fasting and other mortifications of sense. So did the Fathers in general, probably because it was the most difficult to attain, and required the aid of all the rest. Virginity could not generally be maintained in its purity without a rigid system of corporeal maceration, exposure to the rudest hardships, nocturnal vigilance; in short, the whole corps of ascetic mortifications;—so to thin the blood, attenuate the flesh, enfeeble the nerves, dry up the marrow, and exhaust the constitution, as to destroy this natural appetite, and to conquer both the demon without and the demon within. No wonder then if this was deemed the most glorious of spiritual achievements; and if many who had the form of virginity were destitute of its power, that is, of the spiritual purity which it was supposed to infuse into the soul of man. Experience demonstrated even in Tertullian's time, that the state of virginity might exist, and yet the heart be as full of worldly vanity and unholy passion, as if those angels on the earth had been married! It was found too, that a large portion of professed virgins, were virgins only in name, and that indignant nature often impelled them to do worse than to marry!

What mortified Tertullian, Jerome, and other Fathers, more than the misconduct of the virgins, was the fact, that the institution of virginity, which *ought* to have been the peculiar glory of the Church, originated among the heathen idolators, long ages before the birth of Christ. Tertullian thus expresses his mortification, in his treatise on Monogamy, (Sect. xiii.)

"Since Satan affects to imitate the mysteries of God, it will be a shame to us, if we be slow to present that contenance to God, which some present to the Devil, either by virginity or by perpetual widowhood. We know the virgins of Vesta, and of Juno, in a town of Achaia,—of Apollo at Ephesus,—and of Minerva at several places. We know continent men also, particularly of the Egyptian God Apis. The African Ceres has women too, who, having renounced their marriage, will afterwards avoid the touch of a man, and refuse to kiss even their own sons. *See how the Devil, next to luxury, invented a destructive chastity!*"

He elsewhere complains that the Devil had anticipated the Church in other matters. "The Devil (says he,) who makes it his business to pervert the truth, imitates the divine sacraments by idolatrous mysteries. He baptizes some as believers and followers of his; promises them purification from sin, by baptism; and if I rightly remember, the god Mithras makes the sign of the cross upon the foreheads of his worshippers. And then too, he limits his chief priest to one marriage, and has also his virgins and his male professors of continence."*

We remark by the way, that St. Jerome, in his treatise against Jovinian, gives a long and learned account of the honors paid to virginity among the heathen, and observes afterwards, that true virginity suffers no prejudice from the fact that the Devil's virgins

* De Prescriptione Hereticorum, § XL.

imitated it. He says also in some part of his works, that the virgins of heretics ought to be deemed whores.

Tertullian says in his Treatise on the Resurrection, (§ 8):—"They are acceptable sacrifices to God, which the flesh offers by its own suffering;—I mean (says he) those conflicts of the soul, fasting, abstinence from flesh and wine; and the *dirtiness* annexed to it;—also virginity, widowhood, monogamy, moderation in connubial indulgences [that is, as he says elsewhere,—limited to the necessity of the case.]*

We shall take but one more extract from Tertullian. It is from his Treatise on the Veiling of Virgins, (§ 14.) It shows that the young women who professed to consecrate their virginity to God were much glorified by the Church, and, as might be expected, were made vain by the honors bestowed upon them. They were fond of showing themselves—went publicly unveiled—and did not neglect to set off their persons to advantage. Tertullian thus censures them.—"Where there is glory there is solicitude [to avoid vanity]; where there is solicitude, there is constraint [on one's inclinations]; where there is constraint, there is necessity [for its exercise]; where is necessity, there is infirmity [of nature.] Deservedly therefore, when virgins do not cover their heads, and thus for the sake of glory expose themselves to temptations, they are compelled afterwards to hide their shame.† It is vanity, not religion, that leads them to profess virginity; sometimes it is the belly, their god; they desire a free maintenance; *for the brethren gladly receive and support virgins.* They are publicly presented to the pastor of the church and consecrated;‡ their good deed is proclaimed; they are loaded by the brethren

* We give in Tertullian's Latin a sentiment which we do not choose to translate. Etiam matrimonii secreta *maculosa*. See his Address Ad Uxorem, Lib. II. § 3.

† Ventres tegere coguntur infirmatatis ruiná.

‡ This disproves the opinion of Bingham and others, that Tertullian *does not* here speak of professed or consecrated virgins of the Church. He does, most explicitly; but some Protestant writers are fain to hide such disgraceful facts. They have not forgotten Origen's "useful deceptions."

with honors and gifts. If one falls from the grace of virginity, she still appears with head uncovered, and makes no change in her dress, lest she should betray her condition. These apostates still claim to be virgins, and will not confess, until they are betrayed by the cries of their new-born children! Virgins of this sort are easy of conception and parturition, and bear children very like their fathers! Such are the crimes that spring from a constrained virginity! Then the desire of being seen and of pleasing the men does not become a virgin. However good her intentions may be, there is unavoidable danger in her exposing herself to the gaze of many eyes; whilst, at the same time, her vanity is tickled by the fingers that point at her,—whilst she is too much loved, and is warmed by the constant embraces and kisses of the brethren and sisters."—Thus far Tertullian. We remark that the warm salutations just mentioned were customary in the Church, and were not confined to the virgins, though naturally somewhat warmer in their case.

The passage just quoted gives us some insight into the much glorified institution of virginity in the Church about the year 200.

We shall obtain a farther knowledge of the subject from the extracts that we shall now take out of the writings of Cyprian, the good bishop of Carthage, who lived about 50 years after Tertullian. We shall first extract some passages from his book on the dress of virgins.

"Virgins (says Cyprian,) are the flower of the ecclesiastical tree,—the glory and ornament of spiritual grace,—a joyful race—the perfect and incorrupt work of praise and honor,—the image of God's holiness,—the most illustrious portion of Christ's flock. The glorious fecundity of mother Church rejoices in them, and flourishes through them; and the more copiously virginity adds to her number, the more does mother's joy increase."

Again, near the end of the book, addressing the virgins, he says:—"Since there are many mansions with the Father, one must afford better entertainment than the rest. You seek that best one, and by castrating the desires of the flesh, you will obtain in Heaven the reward of your *superior grace.* All indeed who come to the divine washing of baptism, by sanctification put off there the old man by the grace of the salutary washing, and being renewed by the Holy Ghost, are purged from the filth of the old contagion, by the second birth; but a greater sanctity and truth of the second birth belongs to you, *who have now no desires of the flesh and the body.*"

Such are some of the high-flown laudations, which Cyprian, like the other Fathers of these times, pours out upon the virgins of the Church. It should be observed that neither he nor the rest inform us that the virgins were distinguished from other Christians by superior virtue in a single particular, unless it was their virginity. This was the sole distinction by which they were to be raised to the highest and best mansion in Heaven.

Whether these angelic beings excelled other Christians in other respects, will appear from what this admiring Father himself gives us to understand of their behavior. From many passages of the same book, in which he so bepraises them, it is evident that they still had all the passions and infirmities of their sex. He told them that their hardest struggle was to tame the flesh; but many of them appear not to have girded themselves for the contest.

Many of them were very fond of dress and personal ornaments. They delighted especially in gay-colored clothes, against which he argues that God did not make scarlet and purple sheep, nor dye wool with the juice of herbs and shell-fish, nor did he set precious stones in gold, nor string pearls together for necklaces. He says that the fallen angels taught these arts; and taught women also to paint their cheeks and to draw circles of dark-red coloring round their eyes. He justly admonishes both virgins and wives, to abstain from spoiling their natural beauty, by such artifices. But he ought to have given a better reason.—"Dares any one (he asks,) change that which God made? They lay impious hands upon God's work, who undertake to reform and transfigure it;

not knowing that what is naturally produced is God's work, but whatsoever is changed is of the Devil."

The very pen with which Cyprian wrote those words, might have furnished his gay virgins with an apt retort. But he is wittily severe upon these virgin belles of the Church. "Are you not afraid (says he,) that when you rise from the dead, your Maker will not know you!—and that he will shut you out of Heaven with this strong rebuke?—You are none of my work; you have not my image; you have stained your skin with falsifying drugs; your hair is adulterated with dye; your face is disguised with falsehood; *your figure is transformed;* * your look is strange; you cannot see God when your eyes are not such as God made them, but are infected by the Devil. You have followed him; you have imitated the red-colored eyes of the old serpent; and having been decked out by your enemy, you shall burn with him."

After this severe rebuke, Cyprian warns these holy virgins from attending marriage-feasts, at which he says there was commonly a license inconsistent with a chaste and sober morality; and he makes no exception in favor of Christian weddings. The customs of which he speaks, seem to have been common to all classes of people in the diocese of Carthage, and probably throughout the Roman provinces.

"Some virgins (he says,) are not ashamed to be present when people are married, and to mix in the wanton sports and conversations of the occasion; and are observed to be present at the filthy speeches and drunken carousals, by which lust is inflamed, and the passions of the married couple are excited."

St. Chrysostom gives a similar account of the marriage customs of the Eastern provinces about the end of the fourth century. He says that marriages were celebrated with dances, immodest songs, hymns in honor of Venus, and representa-

* From this it would seem, that like our modern ladies of fashion, they endeavored to improve, by artificial stuffing and padding, the form which God had given them.

tions of adulteries. Prostitutes were invited to the entertainment; and after the feast, the guests, most of them intoxicated, led about the town the bride splendidly arrayed and painted, and sang scandalous ballads, offensive to Pagans as well as Christians. We would fain believe, that even in Constantinople, such abominable practices occurred only among the more depraved classes of the population.

To attend such marriage feasts was bad enough for consecrated virgins; but some of them did even worse: they were so immodest as to frequent the mixed baths, where the two sexes went naked into the water together. He supposes a virgin to excuse herself by saying that she went purely to bathe, not to see nor to be seen. But he justly rejects all excuse for so indecent a custom. We know that allowance should be made for the customs of different times and countries, and that practices deemed by us immodest, may not be so considered in a different state of society and manners; yet nature itself must condemn a virgin who would expose herself to the temptations of mixed bathing and of licentious songs and jests at a wedding feast.

Upon the whole, it appears that these consecrated brides of Christ—as they were called, were many of them in ill repute. "The Church (says Cyprian) often complains of her virgins, and groans at the infamous stories that are told of them. Thus the flower of the virgins is withered; the honor of continency and purity is destroyed; and all their glory and dignity are profaned."

But we have not yet mentioned the worst of all the infamous things which resulted from this institution of virginity, combined with the celibacy of the clergy, which had now become general.

In his sixty-second epistle, Cyprian mentions a practice, dishonorable alike to the petted virgins of the Church, and to some of the clergy. Pomponius, to whom the epistle was addressed, had consulted Cyprian about a case of this sort:—"You ask me (says Cyprian) to write you my opinion of what should be done with those virgins, who, after firmly resolving to live chastely in their virgin state, were caught lying in bed with men, one of whom you say was a deacon; and who confessed that they had slept with the men, but affirmed that they were yet pure virgins."

As a general rule, he advises that virgins should not be permitted to live in the same house with [unmarried] men;—much less should they permitted to sleep with them. He gives strong reasons for his advice: we only wonder that he should think any reasoning necessary to justify such advice.

The practice of unmarried men—some of them clergymen—and consecrated virgins living together, seems to have prevailed to a considerable extent, even at this early period; but then the parties professed that there was no harm in it, seeing that it was all the while a chaste familiarity, a purely spiritual conjunction!

"Let such be separated (says Cyprian) whilst yet they innocently may. *We have seen many grievous falls spring from this practice;* and through these illicit and dangerous connections, we have, to our sorrow, seen *a great many virgins corrupted.*"—From these words of Cyprian we can easily infer how common the practice was. If so many virgins, to Cyprian's knowledge, gave signs of having been corrupted—what numbers of them must have practiced this sort of concubinage!

He advised also that the men who had offended in this case, should be restored to the communion of the Church, upon due repentance and separation from their virgin concubines. As to these sweet virgins,—"the flower of the ecclesiastical tree"—he advised that they should separate from their chaste paramours, and that they should be diligently inspected by the midwives. If found to have the physical symptoms of virginity, they might be admitted to the communion immediately, although he had just before expressed the opinion that the inspection by midwives was not a reliable test. How indulgent this good Father was to "the brides o Christ." Had other females, married or unmarried, been guilty of such licentious behavior, we think that his sense of what was due to the honor of Christ, would have made him anathematize them to all intents and purposes.

We would fain say no more upon this nauseous subject. But, since we have undertaken to give a true history of those opinions and practices in the Church which led to monachism or were associated with it—and since we deem it important that the reader should have a just view of the state of religion in the Church, when monachism was in its prime, virginity and celibacy in the highest estimation, and when saint-worship and relic-worship and other corruptions of Christianity were coming forth—we must bespeak the reader's attention to a further development of this never-enough-to-be-praised institution of virginity.

One might be inclined to believe that the disgraceful practices of which we have spoken were confined to Carthage, where Tertullian and Cyprian lived, and to the third century in which they lived. But this was far from being the case. Celibacy led to the same evil practices throughout the Church, and throughout the long ages of monkish austerity, priestly celibacy, and Popish domination. We shall confine our remaining quotations to works which were written in the

Fourth Century.

It was in this century that monachism was established and many of the corruptions of Christianity were introduced.

We shall first quote a passage from St. Basil, bishop of Cesarea, in Asia Minor. It is in his LVth Epistle, addressed to Paregorius, a priest, who had kept a professed virgin in his house, and attempted to justify himself to Basil. The bishop answers him in this Epistle. Among other things, he says: "We are not the first who have decreed that [unmarried] women should not live with men. Read the canon published by our Fathers in the Council of Nice, which plainly enacts that there should be no [συνεισακτους] women kept in a man's house, who are not his near relations. The honor of celibacy consists in separation from women. Wherefore, if any one who professes it, does what married people do with their wives, it is evident that he follows virginity only in name, when in fact he abstains not from indecent pleasures."

This priest being 70 years old, Basil acquitted him of sinful intercourse with the woman; but, for the sake of example, required him, under the penalty of excommunication to put her away into a monastery.

What we have chiefly to remark on this passage of Basil is, that he informs us of a decree of the General Council of Nice, early in the fourth century, forbidding what must then have been a not unfrequent custom of the unmarried clergy—namely, the keeping of what were called *privately-introduced* women in their houses. But in vain did Councils forbid and Fathers censure a practice, which naturally grew out of the celibacy of the clergy and the professed virginity of young women. The practice continued to prevail to a scandalous extent, as will appear from what we shall now take from the writings of the most learned of the Latin Fathers, and, if we except Origen, of all the Fathers, whether Greek or Latin. This was Hieronymus, or Jerome, as he is commonly called. He was educated at Rome, resided a while in Gaul—travelled extensively in the East, resided again in Italy, and finally settled in Palestine, where he wrote the most of his voluminous works. He was, therefore, well acquainted with the state of the Church in both the East and the West. He flourished about the year four hundred, that is, one hundred and fifty years after the time of Cyprian.

Monachism was now in the full tide of successful experiment, and St. Jerome was a fiery advocate of the system, and an unsparing assailant of all who dared to oppose it, as some yet dared to do. Virginity was an object of his enthusiastic and never-ceasing admiration. Most of the one hundred and fifty epistles, found in his extant works, have monachism and virginity for their subjects. Many were addressed to professed virgins and widows professedly opposed to marrying a second time. Much of his anxiety was to keep these holy pets of the Church in order. The frequent exhortations, advices, cautions and rebukes, which he administered to them, prove that in his time, as well as in preceding ages, these terrestrial angels were difficult to manage, or at least found it difficult to manage themselves, and often acted like creatures of mere flesh and blood. Indeed, from his invectives against many of them, it appears that they were worse than even St. Cyprian's virgins.

In his long epistle to Eustochium, a favorite virgin, he exhorts her constant vigilance, fasting and avoidance of the sight of men, in order to subdue the natural desires of the constitution; and to show how difficult this was, he tells her of his own experience in warring against nature. Like other monks of his time, he had fled to the deserts, that he might get away from all tempting objects.

"Oh how often (says he,) when I was in that vast desert, scorched by the sunbeams, which affords a horrible dwelling-place to the monks, did I imagine myself to be amidst all the delightful scenes and luxuries of Rome! When I awoke from this day-dream, I would find myself sitting alone in the desert, and my soul was filled with bitterness. My limbs were covered with rough sackcloth; my shrivelled skin was black like an Ethiopian's. Day by day, my tears flowed and my groans broke forth; and when, in spite of my efforts to keep awake, an oppressive sleep overpowered my senses, my naked bones, that scarcely hung together, fell clattering upon the ground. I say nothing of my food or drink; even when sick, monks drink nothing but cold water, and anything cooked is to them an unusual luxury. Yet, even I, *who, from fear of hell*, had condemned myself to such a prison, and whose only companions were scorpions and wild beasts, *yes, even then, I often thought myself surrounded by choirs of beautiful girls, charming me with their songs and dances. Whilst my face was pale from fastings, and my emaciated body was as cold as a corpse, my soul yet burnt with desires and boiled with the flames of lust.* Therefore, when all other help failed me, I threw myself at the feet of Jesus, I washed them with my tears, I wiped them with the hairs of my head; and I subjugated my rebellious flesh by fasting week after week. Day and night I cried aloud, nor ceased to beat my breast, until the Lord rebuked me, and I became calm again."

"Then I grew afraid of my little cell, as if it were a witness of my thoughts. Angry at myself, and resolute, I started forth, and all alone penetrated the deepest recesses of the desert. Wherever I met with the hollow of a valley, the ruggedness of a mountain, or a precipice of rocks, there was my place of prayer; there was the penitentiary of my miserable flesh; and as the Lord is my witness, after many tears, and after long and steadfast looking up to heaven, I seemed to myself at times to be among bands of angels, and then I would joyfully sing—*we will run after thee for the odor of thy ointments.*"

Such in substance is Jerome's account of his hermit life. It is a picture of fanatical austerity, such as we often read of in the lives of *The Fathers of the Desert.*

Having thus warned Eustochium of the extreme difficulty of suppressing our natural desires—he afterwards supposes her to object, that, as she was of a noble family, and had been brought up in the delights of luxury, she could not live by such severe rules of abstinence. He answers, "Well then, live according to your own law, if you cannot submit to God's. Think not, however, that God, the Creator and Lord of the Universe, takes any pleasure in the rumbling of our intestines, the emptiness of our stomachs, and the scorching of our lungs with the hot air of the desert:—but observe, *chastity can in no other way be safe.*"—Again he admonishes her that "*even at home, not a face can be looked at with safety.*"

Then he warns her by the example of other virgins. "I am ashamed (says he) to mention *how many virgins are ruined every day;* how many children of her bosom mother Church loses; upon what lofty stars [virgins] the proud enemy sets his throne; in how many rocks the serpent makes holes for his dwelling place. You may see most widows, before they marry again, hiding their evil conscience only with a deceiving robe, until their manifest pregnancy and the cries of their infants expose them: but until then they walk with outstretched neck and mincing steps. Others produce barrenness or destroy the fœtus with drugs." Then, after speaking of the full feeding and drinking of others, he says;—"These are the sort who walk forth in the most public manner, and by sly winks draw after them crowds of young men. They dress only in thin purple robes, tie their hair loose that it may fall over their shoulders, over which a mantle is loosely thrown. They wear short sleeves and thin slippers, and go tottering as they walk. And this is all their virginity! Let them have flatterers of their own sort that they may perish more profitably. As to ourselves, we are willing to displease them."

"*I blush to say it; but alas! it is true. Oh! whence came that pest into the Church—of clergymen keeping mistresses?—unmarried women, not called wives?* Nay, whence this new sort of concubines? I will go further;—Whence these one-man whores? They occupy the same house, the same chamber, often the same bed; yet they complain that we are suspicious. The brother forsakes his virgin sister for another; the virgin spurns her unmarried kinsman, and seeks a brother of a different family; *though the brother and sister both pretend to have the same purpose of living in unmarried purity;* yet they seek spiritual comfort in a connection with others, that they may have carnal intercourse at home."

The professed purpose of these people to live in unmarried purity, proves that they were not merely single persons; they had made profession of perpetual virginity, or of celibacy at least, from religious motives.

Sulpicius Severus in his first Dialogue, of which the reader will find a translation in a subsequent part of this work, quotes a part of the foregoing passage. Speaking of St. Jerome, he says; "*But how truly and forcibly has he argued concerning the familiarities of the monks and even of the clergy, with the virgins!*" For this reason he is said not to be liked by certain persons whom I shall not name. These men are said to be enraged when they read the following words in that little work:—"The virgin despises an unmarried man who is a real brother; she seeks a connection with one who is not of her own family." From this passage of Severus it is evident that the same infamous practice of which Jerome spoke was not uncommon in Gaul, where Severus lived and wrote.

St. Chrysostom, cotemporary with Jerome, wrote two treatises against this practice—but we shall make no more extracts in relation to it. We have given facts and authorities enough to prove beyond controversy, that the celibacy of the clergy and the monks, and the institution of religious virginity among females, led to the most shameful practices, and that, instead of promoting holiness, it occasioned the most scandalous violations of the Divine law and of common decency. If, in these latter days, there is less *appearance* of the same scandalous practices resulting from the same causes, it may still be a question, whether this is a sign of purer morals, or of more cautious and ingenious methods of concealment.

Before we leave this famous order of ecclesiastical virgins, we must present the reader with another trait in their character, as drawn by St. Augustine. This celebrated Father, in his commentary on Psalm xcix. says;—"*You find consecrated virgins* (sanctimoniales) *who are disorderly. Many of them do not stay at home, but go from house to house, tattling, talking proudly, and getting drunk.* If they be virgins, what avails the chastity of their flesh, when their minds are corrupt? Humble marriage would be better than such self-conceited virginity. If they were married, they would not have the name of virgins to swell the pride of their hearts, and they would have a bridle to restrain their waywardness."

CHAPTER XIII.

OF EGYPT AND SOME ADJACENT COUNTRIES, IN WHICH CHRISTIAN MONACHISM FIRST PREVAILED.

CLIMATE and other physical circumstances have great influence on the feelings, habits, and institutions, of mankind. Egypt, in which Christian monachism arose, is a country of such uncommon characteristics, and was anciently so remarkable for the superstition of its inhabitants, that we are led to inquire, whether its geographical character could account, in any measure, for the early rise and rapid increase of monkery within its boundaries. We shall, for the general illustration of our subject, and for the particular illustration of this point of enquiry, give a descriptive sketch of Egypt and some other countries in which monachism prevailed in early times.

1. *The most extensive deserts of the earth* are found on the Eastern Continent, stretching in an unbroken, but somewhat irregular zone, from the Western coast of Africa eastwards through Egypt, Arabia and Persia, to the valley of the River Indus,—a space of not less than 5,000 miles in length. These immense tracts of dry barrens lie between the 18th and 34th parallels of latitude, but do not occupy the whole of this broad interval; for wheresoever a system of high mountains attracts copious rains, or fresh-water streams irrigate the lands, there the labors of agriculture are rewarded by good harvests. Rains, more or less, fall likewise on some favorably-situated plains, and pro-

duce some pasturage on which flocks and herds can be kept. But over a vast extent of these deserts, particularly in Africa, no rain ever falls, or if any, yet too little to cause any sort of vegetation to relieve the utter desolation of the scene.

2. *Three great rivers flow across these deserts* from interior mountains to the sea;—the *Indus*, at the eastern extremity; the *Euphrates*, of which the Persian gulf is a continuation; and the *Nile of Egypt*, the most remarkable of them all.

The waters of the Nile, descend from the high mountains of Abyssinia, where its thousand branches are fed by copious rains, from November till April. The streams unite in the low country of Sennaar, and form the great river, which then pours its swelling flood through the desert a thousand miles wide, receiving not a single tributary between its parent mountains and the sea. The upper part of its course is through a deep, narrow valley; but when it has passed over the rocks of Syene, the valley of Egypt begins to expand, and widens gradually to the breadth of ten or twelve miles, until it approaches the sea. Here the river divides, the mountains diverge to the right and left, and the low lands sink, till land, sea and river, are nearly on the same level.

In June, the swelling waters of Abyssinia reach the valley of Egypt, and continue to rise until all the low grounds of the valley are inundated with muddy water. The valley is then a sea bounded by mountains, and diversified by islets crowned with villages, and by promontories of barren sand! where the waters subside, they leave a deposit of slime on which the husbandman drops his seed. Then, in a few weeks, instead of an expanse of muddy water, the valley of Egypt becomes a smiling scene of exuberant vegetation, which ripens into abundant harvests. But whilst the watered valley presents such diversity and even contrast at different seasons, the deserts that touch this fertility on both sides, present at all seasons and through all ages, one changeless scene of sterility and desolation.

3. *The Egyptian Deserts* cover the whole space of the country not reached by the fertilizing waters of the river. The transition

is immediate from exuberant fertility to everlasting and irreclaimable barrenness.

Between the Nile and the Red Sea is a desert about a hundred miles wide, in part mountainous towards upper Egypt, and relieved in a few spots by fountains of fresh water, issuing from the bases of the mountains, and fertilizing a small space of low ground before they are absorbed by the sands, or evaporated in the dry, hot atmosphere of the desert. Wherever such watered spots occur, the date-palm grows, and, with its sweet, nutritious nut, supplies the nomadic tribes with luxurious food.

The Great Western Desert, between the Nile and the Atlantic Ocean, is the most dreary region of the earth, though dotted at wide intervals with Oases, where a low basin or vale is fertilized by springs of water.

Most of the fountains that occur in the deserts are warm and bitter, poisoning all that they touch, and making the sands through which they trickle incurably sterile.

4. Through all these dreary regions, *the mountains* are masses of barren sun-burnt rocks, the *valleys* and *ravines* are composed of drifted sands at the bottom, and naked rocks at the sides. *The plains* are covered with gravel and loose sands, which the breezes roll along in ripples, the whirlwinds gather and lift up in tall sandspouts, and the tempests hurl aloft in clouds that darken the atmosphere, and sometimes bury whole caravans, where they fall in cataracts upon the ground.

5. *The Poisonous Wind*, called *Simoon* or *Samiel*, is often distinguished by its purplish tinge. It comes sometimes silently stealing over the hot desert, blasting vegetation, parching the human skin, and curdling the blood, if inhaled into the lungs. At other times it drives along in a gale from the hottest regions of the desert, and though it is then less charged with the reddish blue poison of the silent wind, it is yet so hot and so loaded with pestiferous exhalations, that man, beast, and vegetable, languish and sicken under its scorching blast.

6. *The Heat of the Deserts* is far beyond anything known in

countries blessed with refreshing rains, shady woods, and green fields. Here are no clouds to intercept the sun's rays; here is no moisture to absorb and carry off the heat. A surface composed of naked sands and rocks for thousands of miles, receives day by day perpetually the full force of southern sunshine, till the sands are scorching hot, and the rocks almost glow with accumulated heat. During the night, as cloudless as the day, the sands and rocks continue to radiate their gathered heat into free space. This is a partial relief. The breezes on the highlands, sometimes also, feel refreshing to those who have been half-suffocated by the sultry atmosphere of the valleys.

The constant glare of the sunshine by day, and the fine sand which the wind drives through the atmosphere, are hurtful to the eyes and often cause blindness. Excessive heat and drought relax the human system, and weaken the digestive power of the stomach. Strong food and stimulating drinks are injurious; *abstinence from animal food and alcoholic liquors* is easy and natural, and moderate *fasting* is dictated by nature, and salutary.

8. In such circumstances there is a constant *tendency to indolent relaxation, melancholy fancies, and solitary contemplation.* The scenery of the desert is well adapted to aggravate this tendency, and to nourish those principles of the oriental philosophy, which produce a monkish hatred of the body and enthusiastic dreams of heaven.

The desert is the image of death. Over its dreary wastes scarcely a sign of life appears. All is solitude and silence and death, while the winds are still; but when the stormy winds are roused, they are messengers of wrath, their breath is poisonous, and the clouds which they drive are hot sands. The blessed sunshine that cheers the inhabitants of temperate climates, here quickens nothing into life so much as serpents and scorpions; it makes no fields green, no meadows bloom, no forest shady with verdure, no birds sing among the branches;—it is a fire that burns, a glare that blinds, a light that reveals the horrors of eternal desolation.

9. But here, where the earth is stripped of every attraction and converted into an emblem of hell, *the nocturnal heavens are ever bright and glorious.* By day the wretched traveller or dweller in the desert pants with thirst, and would fain seek in some cavern a refuge from the scorching sunshine, the sand-storm, and the dismal aspect of the scene around him. By night he can emerge from his hiding place, when the sad earth is shrouded in gloom, and behold the unclouded heavens, where all is peace and purity; where the moon and stars exhibit a soft and dewy radiance, and give the imagination a boundless range among worlds of glory and beauty.

The soul is thus led from earth to heaven, from the visible to the invisible;—and taking as a basis whatever religious ideas it may have imbibed, it constructs a fabric of the imagination, and converting its conceptions into realities, it peoples the deserts with malignant demons, whose moan is heard in the night wind, and whose changeful and horrid shapes are seen in the undefined shadows of the desert. Haunted by its own creations, the soul fights against its spiritual enemies, by prayer and fasting; and by the exercise of faith, sees visions of heavenly messengers, and scenes of celestial bliss. Animated by these, it labors to free itself from its fleshy prison, and from this dreary world of sin and death; and endeavors by the exclusion of all earthly thoughts, the suppression of all earthly sympathies and desires, and by perpetual dreamy contemplations of the spiritual world, to fit itself for an immediate entrance into the celestial paradise, whose outskirts are seen in the nocturnal heavens above the desert.

10. Now it is not difficult to conceive how such a country as Egypt, may predispose the soul to a solitary contemplative life, and how the desert into which the imaginative enthusiast retires, may breed in his soul all the feelings and fancies, that so remarkably distinguished the Egyptian hermits.

Nor is it wonderful, that in such times and circumstances, well-meaning, pious souls, should be carried away by one-sided views of religion; and neglecting the earthly relations and duties of man, should run the principle of devotion to God into error, by running it into excess. In a region where the earth is divested of its charms, and human life of its principal enjoyments, the soul naturally seeks a refuge in heaven from the dreariness of its mortal state. Society can afford little pleasure where desolation reigns, and all the powers of life are enfeebled by heat and drought. Hence the duties of society are often shunned as burdensome. Celibacy is preferred to marriage, and solitude to society, by those whose religious feelings incline them to take gloomy views of human life. Such views the climate and aspects of Egypt are well adapted to produce.

11. But it is only when certain principles of religious philosophy predominate, that monkery arises in a country like Egypt. The Bedouins of the desert do not resort to celibacy and solitude for relief, though they are great admirers of monkish saints, and always have been. They are lean, shriveled, red-eyed, black, diminutive creatures. Perpetual want makes them fierce and predatory. Necessity drives them from place to place for subsistence. They are prone to religious enthusiasm. Of this Mahomet took advantage—he fired their imaginations with the promise of a paradise filled with all the sensual delights which their passions craved, but their circumstances denied them. For these they fought bravely, because a speedy death would introduce them the sooner to paradise. Had Mahomet persuaded them that a life of monastic seclusion and mortification was a passport to paradise, the Bedouins would have been enthusiastically devoted monks.

12. From Egypt, monachism spread into Palestine. St. Hilarion, founder of the Palestine monasteries, selected as his place of exercise the desert of Gaza, which is but a continuation of the Egyptian deserts. His disciples spread Eastward along the border of the desert that bounds the fertile land of Palestine on the South and East. This desert extends northwardly along the Eastern border of Syria. The multiplying monks followed this border, being deterred from penetrating deeply into the Arabian and

Mesopotamian deserts, by the fear of the Saracens, who claimed possession of every spot on those barren wilds, where water and vegetation afforded subsistence for man. But the monks of Palestine and Syria, and afterwards those farther north, found more eligible solitudes on the mountain tops, where they were protected from disturbance, because the surrounding valleys were occupied chiefly by a Christian population. By the end of the fourth century, scarcely a high mountain in the eastern parts of the Roman Empire between Armenia and Arabia, was without a colony of monks.

12. To illustrate the lives of St. Antony and other Egyptian monks, we shall notice the chief divisions of Egypt and the chief localities of the monasteries.

Egypt has been usually distinguished into Lower, Middle, and Upper Egypt.

Lower Egypt embraces the broad triangle anciently called the Delta, in which the river divides and the low grounds spread out to a breadth of more than a hundred miles along the seacoast. At the north-western angle of this Delta are the seaport and once great city of Alexandria, now reduced to one-tenth of its former population. It stands on a sandy peninsula between the sea and a salt lake, anciently called Mareotis. Near the southern shore of this lake, and on the border of the desert, many monks of the fourth and fifth centuries established themselves. At no great distance farther south, were the Mountain of Nitria and the marshy grounds of Scetis, which were famous seats of monasteries.

Middle Egypt comprehends the broader part of the Valley of the Nile above the Delta. The average width of this part of the valley is some eight or ten miles; but a singular recess of the mountains on the western side, opens a large space of fertile low country, in which Lake Moeris is situated. The lake is connected with the Nile by the great canal of Arsinoe. On the southern side of this lake the Jewish Therapeutes had their monasteries. Christian monks also settled there in the fourth century.

Upper Egypt was usually called Thebaid, from the once great

city of Thebes, whose ruins are yet an object of wonder to travellers. The valley in these upper parts is narrow, the average width not exceeding four miles, or thereabouts; and the bordering mountains are higher and more abrupt than they are below. In Thebaid St. Pachomius founded his order of monks, in the district of Tabenna. The mountains of Upper Egypt as well as of the lower parts of the country, were filled with monks. It was in Middle Egypt, or the Lower Thebaid that St. Antony founded his monasteries, in the mountains bordering the valley.

---

13. The excessive superstition of the ancient Egyptians is well known. But they bore a bad character in other respects. Aelian says that they would endure the severest tortures without flinching, and that they would rather be racked to death than confess the truth.*

Ammianus Marcellinus says, that the Egyptians were swarthy, lean, and dry in their persons; fiery in all their motions; quarrelsome and bitter in their disputes. A man among them would be ashamed of himself, if he could not show on his back the marks of the whippings that he had gotten for refusing to pay his taxes. No torture could wring from a thief a confession of his name or crime.†

These were the sort of people to make great monks. What would be almost unendurably hard for others to bear, would come easy to them.

* Var Hist. vii. 18. † Amm. Marcell. xxii. 16.

CHAPTER XIV.

THE LIFE OF ST. ANTONY THE MONK.

Translated with some abridgment from the Greek of St. Athanasius.

PREFACE BY THE TRANSLATOR.

St. Antony was born in Egypt in the year 251, and died in the year 356, aged 105 years. St Athanasius, bishop of Alexandria, who wrote this life of Antony, was born about the year 296 and died in the year 373, after having been bishop of Alexandria for the space of 46 years, though he spent a part of the time in exile. Being an Egyptian by birth, having lived so many years cotemporarily with Antony, and been personally acquainted with him and with some of his most intimate disciples, he had good opportunities of learning the facts which he relates of the great founder of monasteries, and of investigating the truth of the wonderful things that he relates of him. Now, as no sober-minded man, in these days, can believe the stories of demons and of miracles which this sainted bishop relates of the sainted founder of monasteries, we must suppose that either St. Antony, or his disciples, or his sainted biographer, fancied or feigned these incredible things to have really happened. It is hard to accuse such glorified saints of wilful imposture, and quite as hard, if not harder, to account for such fables in such a case, without the supposition of both wilful imposture and superstitious credulity.

St. Athanasius wrote in a rather prolix, though simple style, and some parts of his narrative are of no importance. We have therefore somewhat abbreviated his work in the translation. We have also added some notes by way of explanation or comment.

LIFE OE ST. ANTONY.

1. *The Preface addressed to the foreign Monks.*

You gloriously seek to emulate the monks of Egypt in all their virtues: for among you also the institutions and usages of monachism now exist. You have requested that I should write the life of St. Antony, because he first instituted monasteries. You wish to know whether the reports concerning him are true; and you are desirous of imitating his holy zeal. With pleasure do I comply with your request; for it will do me good to remember St. Antony, and your admiration will cause you to emulate his holy example.

You need not scruple to believe what you have heard concerning him. You have probably heard but a small part of what he did; and what I shall write will yet leave a great part of his history untold; nor will the narration equal the dignity of the subject. To ascertain the facts, I have consulted those monks who were longest and most intimately acquainted with him. I have duly investigated the truth of what I relate, and have carefully recorded what I know of myself (for I saw him often), and what I have been told by those who were with him, and especially by one who acted for a considerable time as his servant, and poured water on his hands when he washed.

2. *The youth of St. Antony until he became a Monk.*

Antony was born in Egypt, of noble parents, from whom, as they were Christians, he received a Christian education. He was brought up in the house of his parents, and had no intercourse with other persons. When he approached the age of manhood, he was unwilling to go to school, because he disliked the company of other youth. His whole desire was to live like Jacob (Gen

xxv. 27.)—a simple life at home. But nevertheless, when he went to church with his parents, he was not a negligent hearer or worshipper, even in his boyhood. He was an obedient son and attentive to the lessons read in church, and applied them to his own practical use. He did not, as the sons of rich parents are apt to do, complain if he was not furnished with luxurious fare: he took no pleasure in such things, but was content with whatever was given him.

By the death of his parents, when he was eighteen or twenty years old, he was left in charge of the house and of a very young sister. Within six months afterwards, when he went to church one day as usual, and before the service began, he fell into a meditation on the apostles and primitive Christians,—how the former had left all to follow their Saviour, and the latter had sold their possessions for the benefit of the poor. Full of these thoughts he entered the church, while the lesson from the gospel was being read, and heard how the Lord said to the rich young man, *If thou wouldst be perfect, go, sell that thou hast and give to the poor, and come follow me, and thou shalt have treasure in heaven.* Antony felt this to be a divine admonition to himself Therefore, when he went home, he divided his inheritance, consisting of 300 acres of fertile land, among the people of the village; and having sold his moveables, he gave the proceeds to the poor, reserving only a small portion for his young sister.

When he went to church again, he heard the Lord saying, *Take no thought for the morrow.* Without delay he went and gave this reserved portion to the poor, and committed his sister to the care of some virgins of his acquaintance that she might be nourished in the Virgin-house.* He then left the dwellings of

* The Greek word is *Parthenon, Virgin-house.* Tillemont supposed it was a nunnery, and the earliest mentioned in the Church; but Fleury and Helyot with more reason took it to have been merely a virgin-house, that is, a dwelling, or part of a dwelling, in which two or three holy virgins lived together privately with their relations, according to the custom then prevalent in the Church. We venture to suggest that this one was

men, and devoted himself to an ascetic life of prayer and bodily mortification.

3. *He begins an ascetic course of Life.*

As yet no monasteries existed in Egypt or elsewhere; nor had any monk penetrated the pathless deserts; but each one who had a mind to devote himself to ascetism, retired to some solitary place near his own village.

Near Antony's village was an old man, who had, from his youth led a solitary life. When Antony found him and saw his manner of life, he began to imitate him beautifully. He presently took up his abode more remote from the villages; and whenever he heard of an ascetic distinguished for virtue, he sought him out as a bee seeks the flowers; and never left him until, like a bee, he had gathered something good to carry home. He never returned to his father's dwelling, nor took any interest in the affairs of the neighborhood, but devoted himself exclusively to his spiritual exercises. But he worked with his hands, after he had learned that *if any one will not work, neither should he eat.* He lived on a part of what he made, and gave the rest to the poor. He prayed continually, after he heard *pray without ceasing.* He gave attention to reading, that he might not loose anything of what was written; and he retained everything so well, that his mind afterwards served him instead of books.

Living after this manner, Antony was beloved by all. He subjected himself sincerely to the instructions of every good man whom he approached, and learned of each that virtue in which each excelled. He contemplated in one his gracious manners, in another his earnestness in prayer, in another his meekness or humanity, or love of reading; he admired this man's watchfulness, that man's fasting and lying on the ground; and another's self-denial. In short, he marked how pious all were towards Christ, how affectionate towards one another. Filled with these observa-

a sort of boarding-school for girls, since Antony's sister was too young to enter as a nun or professed virgin.

tions, he returned to his own place of exercise, and labored to reduce to practice all that he had learned. He had with his fellows no contest but this,—not to appear inferior to them in their several virtues; and this he did, not to grieve but to gladden their hearts. Therefore, all who lived in this vicinity, and whose company he kept, called him the beloved of God, and the elder saluted him as a son, the younger as a brother.*

4. *Antony's first contest with the Devil.*

But that hater of good, the envious Devil, could not bear the holy purpose of the young man, and set himself against all his pious endeavors. He first attempted to draw him away from his ascetic life, calling to his remembrance his former possessions, the care of his sister,† the nobility of his family, the love of money, the desire of glory, the pleasures of wealth and of ease; and on the other hand, the hardness of virtue, the laboriousness of his life, the infirmities of his body, and the long struggle before him. In a word, he confounded his understanding with subtle reasonings, that he might draw him from the right way. When he failed thus to shake Antony's purpose, and was baffled by his constancy, his faith and his unceasing prayers, he resorted to the weapons near the navel of a young man's belly—the most dangerous of all. He troubled him by night and vexed him by day, with unclean thoughts, which Antony drove away by prayer. He tickled his flesh, till the young man blushed, and had to fortify his mind by prayer and fasting. He assumed the shape, and *imitated the actions of a woman, by night*, that he might deceive Antony. But the young man thought of Christ and of his high

* From this chapter it is evident that many ascetics had retired into solitary places, before Antony began his course, but this is the earliest mention of the solitary mode of life in the deserts.

† This is one among many instances in the lives of monks, in which the struggling of natural reason and conscience against superstition, is considered as a temptation of the Devil. "The care of his sister," was so obviously a natural duty, that he could not abandon her without some uneasy feeling.

calling, and of the superiority of intellect over sense ; and thus he quenched the live coal of this temptation.

When the enemy again suggested the delights of sensual indulgence, Antony became angry, and called to mind the threat of hell-fire, and of the worm that never dies ; and so he escaped unhurt.

Thus was the Devil disgraced in all these contests. He thought himself a god, yet he was fooled by a youth.

The Dragon, when he found that he could not prevail by assaulting him with internal reasonings and imagined pleasures, gnashed his teeth with rage, and henceforth used the human voice, and thus addressed Antony. I have deceived and conquered many in my time ; but now in your case, as in that of many others, I am defied by your ascetic labors.

And who are you, (said Antony, surprised at this address) who talk to me of such matters ?

I am (said the Devil in a loud complaining tone of voice) the one who tickles the flesh of young men :—I am called the Spirit of Fornication. Ah ! many a one who desired to live chastely have I seduced : many have I hypocritically misled by tickling their flesh. I am he of whom the prophet speaks in these words —*The Spirit of Fornication deceived them.* (Hos. iv. 12.) Often have I disturbed you, and as often been driven away by you.

Then Antony gave thanks to the Lord, and taking courage, he said to the Devil :—Then you are a contemptible black-hearted fellow, and as weak as a boy. For the future I shall despise you. The Lord is my helper.

The black fellow was frightened at these words, and fled ; being now afraid to come near Antony. So ended Antony's first battle with the Devil.

5. *How Antony prepared for a second encounter.*

Because he had routed the demon once, he did not therefore become remiss ; nor did the Devil cease to watch Antony. He walked round him like a roaring lion, watching for an opportunity to assail him. Antony, on his part, knowing from the Scriptures that the Devil had many ways of tempting men, applied himself vigorously to his exercises, that he might be prepared at all points for his adversary. He subjected his body to a severer discipline; lest, having conquered in one way, he might be defeated in some other. He determined, therefore, to accustom himself to harder exercises. Many were astonished at the ease with which he bore them. But by long practice he had acquired a confirmed habit of bodily mortification. He would watch whole nights, at which people wondered. Often he ate but once a day, and then, after sunset; but sometimes he would eat but once in two days, or even four days. His usual food was bread and salt; his drink, water only. As to flesh and wine, we need not mention them, for they were not found among any of the ascetics. For sleeping, he was content with a mat at most—generally with the bare ground. He would not anoint himself with oil, saying, that young persons better adorned the ascetic life by cheerfully submitting to hardships, than by laboring for things that made the body effeminate. The mind, he said, was strengthened by weakening the pleasures of the body.

6. *How the Devil gave Antony a beating.*

Such being the manner of his life, he retired farther from the village and dwelt among the sepulchres. A servant was at long intervals to fetch him a supply of bread. Having entered one of the sepulchres, he shut the door upon himself and there abode. When his enemy, the Devil, saw this, he feared that the whole desert would soon be filled with ascetics. Therefore he came upon him one night with a whole troop of demons, and beat him so unmercifully, that he lay on the ground like a dead man. On the next day his servant came with bread for him, and found him there, apparently dead. He carried him into the village temple, and laid him upon the floor. Many of his relations and other people came and sat by his body, supposing it to be a corpse. In the night he revived; and perceiving that all the company were asleep, except his servant, he beckoned to him, and commanded him not to waken the rest, but to carry him back to the sepulchre. This being done, he shut himself up as before, and remained in the vault.

7. *What a hubbub the Devil raised against Antony in the Sepulchre.*

As he could not stand by reason of the wounds which the demons had inflicted upon him, Antony prayed as he lay on the ground. When he had finished his prayers, he said in a loud voice,—Here, Devils, here am I, Antony, ready for more of your wounds. Try your worst, for you shall never separate me from Christ. He also sang the Psalm, *Though a host should encamp against me, yet my heart shall not fear.*

This was the true spirit of an ascetic, and those were his words. But that black Devil, hater of good, wondering that Antony dared to return after the beating that he had given him, called to his hell-hounds, and bursting with indignation, said to them: Don't you see now? This fellow could not be restrained, either by the spirit of fornication, or by bangs and bruises. Nay, he comes against us only the more audaciously. We must assail him in another way. So spake the Devil.

It was no hard matter for him to devise other and still other schemes of malice. So that night they raised such a hubbub, that the whole place was shaken; the four walls of the sepulchre were broken, and the demons rushed in through the breaches, in all manner of fearful shapes. The whole room and the space around were filled with spectral lions, bears, leopards, bulls, serpents, asps, scorpions, wolves. Every one acted according to his character. The lion roared and sprang; the bull, bellowing, rushed with presented horns; the serpent crawled; the wolf howled and growled. In short all seemed to be in a threatening rage.

Antony, though he suffered yet greviously from the whips and clubs of the demons, now watched them with a calm mind, though he had to groan from the pains of his body. Feeling excited by this scene, he said in a mocking way: If you could do any harm, you would be satisfied to come one at a time; but being weakened by the Lord, you try to frighten me after a fashion by your numbers. It is also an evident token of your impotence that you put on the shapes of brute animals. Then after a pause, he said confidently: Come on now; do your worst! What is the use of all this vain uproar? If ye have power to hurt, why don't you? But you can't; for the Lord is my shield, and my wall of safety.

Then the demons attempted many things. They gnashed their teeth at him, being enraged to find how they deluded themselves, and only made sport for him. Now the Lord who watched over the contest, came to Antony's assistance. The saint raised his eyes, and saw through the open roof a ray of light descending upon him. Then the demons vanished, the pains of his body were mitigated, and the building became whole and sound.

When Antony perceived these tokens of God's help, he asked, Where wast thou? why didst thou not appear for my relief at first? Then a voice came to him, saying: I was here, Antony; but I wanted to witness your combat. Now you have finished it, without having flinched. Henceforth I will be your helper, and will make your name celebrated far and wide.*—When he heard this, he rose and prayed, and was soon sensible that he had gained strength by this contest.

8. *Antony's hermit-life in a ruined castle.*

He was now in the 35th year of his age. The day after the hubbub, he went to the old man before-mentioned (in Chap. III), and proposed they should go out into the desert and live together as hermits. The old man, either because he was too old, or because the scheme was a new one, refused. He determined then

* The love of fame, says Young, is the universal passion. Even the solitary ascetic felt it in his most secret feats of starvation, prayer, and demon-fighting. He was conscious of the fact, all the while, that his spiritual heroism would give him renown, and draw around him admiring crowds of spectators.

to go alone, and set off straightway for the mountain.* There again, the enemy, seeing his ardent zeal, endeavored to draw him back from his course. He threw the appearance of a large silver disk or coin in the way before him. Antony, when he saw this trickery of the unclean spirit, stopped, looked at it, and discerning the Devil in the disk, he said to it contemptuously:—Ho, you disk, how came you here in the desert, where there is no beaten way, nor a trace of any traveller having passed? If any had dropped you, you must have been missed; or if you had been lost, you could easily have been found again in this naked solitude. So this must be a trick. But, Mr. Devil, you shall not hinder my purpose by this contrivance. You and your money go to perdition together. Thus spoke Antony; and the words were no sooner out of his mouth, than away went the silver disk in fumes, like smoke from a fire.

Passing on, he saw—not a phantom—but real substantial gold, cast in the way before him. Whether this was done by the same enemy, or by some heavenly being, who would exercise the saint's piety, and show the devil that Antony cared not a straw even for genuine money—neither did Antony tell us, nor can we determine anything about it, except that the gold was real gold. Antony wondered at the great quantity of it; he would not touch it, however, but leaped over it as if it were fire, and ran hastily on without a moment's pause, that he might not know the place again, nor be tempted to return for the gold. Thus, with a confirmed purpose he reached the mountain. Here on the eastern side of the river he found the deserted ruins of an old castle, which, by length of time, had become a den of serpents. He took possession of it as an abode for himself, and no sooner had he done so, than the serpents took fright and scampered away forthwith. He blocked up the entrance, after having laid in

* That is the desert mountain bordering the valley of the Nile, probably in sight of his residence. His native town was Coma, near Heraclea Minor in upper Egypt, or Thebaid, where the valley is narrow.—SOZOMEN. Eccl. History. Book i., chap. 13.

a store of bread for six months, (as the Thebans of Egypt often do; for bread will keep there a whole year*); and having a spring of water inside, here ensconcing himself as in a sanctuary, he dwelt alone; making a monastery of the old castle, and neither going out himself, nor giving admittance to those who visited the place. Thus he lived a long time, secluded as an ascetic, only receiving once in six months a new supply of bread, let down to him from above. But those of his acquaintance who came to the place staid often whole days and nights outside. Then they would hear from within the noise of a multitude in a tumult, shouting and crying with a voice of distress. Get away, Antony, from our possessions. What business have you in the desert? At first those who stood outside supposed it must be men quarreling with him, who had gotten in by means of ladders. But afterwards, by looking through a crevice, they saw that there was no man with him: then they supposed that demons had made the noise. Then they became terrified, and called to Antony, but he heard them no more than he heeded the demons. Alarmed at receiving no answer they often broke in, and then they heard Antony sing psalms, such as, *Let the Lord arise and his enemies shall be scattered*, &c.†

9. *Antony comes forth a miracle-worker.*

Thus did Antony privately exercise himself during almost twenty years,‡ without leaving his old castle, or being easily seen

* Because in Upper Egypt the climate is exceedingly dry, no rain ever falling there. But this bread, so long kept in such a climate, must have become exceedingly dry and hard. So much the better for a monk, as Anthony would say; for then the eating of it would be unpleasant.

† On reading this story one is tempted to reflect, that *if* these reported noises in Antony's monastery were really heard by those outside, they must have been made, either by those spiritual beings called demons, who have no corporeal organs of speech or sound of any sort, or by *saint* Antony himself. Here is a hypothetical dilemma, which the reader may solve for himself.

‡ Twenty years' seclusion made a miracle-working saint among the Hindoos.

by any one. Many in the meantime desired ardently to imitat his ascetic mode of life, insomuch that some of his friends determined finally to break open his door, that they might get access to him. Then at last Antony yielded to their eager desire, and came forth from his sanctuary, like one issuing from a heathen temple, after having been initiated into the mysteries of the Gods. His soul was full of a divine inspiration; but as to his body, those who saw him for the first time wondered to see it as strong as ever, neither fat nor yet emaciated by his long fasting. He bore no mark of his long warfare with demons; for his appearance was unchanged, his mind was as vigorous, and his manners were as pure, as when he first became an anchorite in his castle.

By him, then, the Lord healed many of their diseases; others he delivered from evil spirits; and bestowing upon Antony the grace of speech, he comforted many who were in distress, and reconciled many who had been at variance. By his conversation he induced many to be mindful of their future welfare. He persuaded many to embrace a solitary life. Hence arose those monasteries in the mountains, and those seats and abodes of monks in the desert, who gave up their worldly goods that they might be enrolled among the citizens of heaven.

In one of his journeys to visit the brethren of middle Egypt, he had to cross the canal of Arsinoe, which was full of crocodiles.*

* The ancient geographer Strabo (Book 17, ch. 9.) explains why this canal, which let the waters of the Nile into Lake Mœris, was full of crocodiles. The people of Arsinoe, by this canal, had a great veneration for crocodiles, esteeming them sacred. They had tame ones in the canal, and the priests fed them with bread, meat, and wine, while they lived, and embalmed them after they were dead. Strabo once saw the priests feeding these divine pets, which were basking themselves upon the margin of the canal. Whilst some of the priests held open their monstrous jaws, others would put the dainty meats and drinks upon their tongues. No wonder that the canal of Arsinoe was full of crocodiles. Saint Antony, too, was not so lean as to be a despicable morsel for them. By this time also, it is probable that the veneration for them had nearly ceased, and as they were less fed by devout priests they would not scruple to devour a monk.

All he had to do was to pray, then he and all his companions passed over safely.

Afterwards he returned to his monastery, and strenuously applied himself again to his ascetic labors. Thus, by word and by example, he increased the zeal of his disciples for the monastic life, and incited others to the love of ascetism, so that by his influence a large number of monasteries were founded, over which he presided as abbot, or spiritual father.

One day, when he came forth, he was applied to by all the monks to give them a sermon. He consented, and spoke to them in the Egyptian tongue, after this manner.

10. *St. Antony's Sermon to the Monks. Part I. Exhortation to the Monastic Life.*

The Scriptures are sufficient for your instruction ;* yet it is a good thing for us to exhort one another to fidelity, and to exercise ourselves in teaching. Wherefore do you, as children, tell your father what you know, and I as the elder will impart to you what I know, and what I have experienced.

Now in the first place, let all of you aim at the same thing, and never flag in the pursuit, nor relax your labors, nor say, We have continued long in the exercise ;† but, rather, beginning anew, every day let us increase our diligence : For the whole of man's life is exceedingly short, compared with the ages to come ; so that all our time on earth is nothing to eternal life. Everything in this world is sold at its value, and exchanges are made of value for value received. But the promise of eternal life is bought for a small price : for it is written, *The days of our life are three score years and ten, and if by reason of strength they be fourscore years, yet is their strength labor and sorrow.* If then we should continue the whole eighty years in our exercise, we shall afterwards reign for ages of ages. Our labor is upon the earth, but

* An unpapistical sentiment. The necessity of oral traditions, and the supremacy of the Pope of Rome, were as yet undiscovered.

† τῇ ασκησει—the ascetic practice, fasting, watching, prayer, &c.

our promised inheritance is in the heavens. We lay down our mortal bodies, and again receive them immortal.

Therefore, my sons, let us not grow weary, nor think the time long, nor that we are doing a great thing: For the sufferings of the present time are not worthy to be compared with the glory that shall be revealed in us. Nor, when we look at this world, let us think it so very large; for the whole earth is small, compared with the whole heavens. Therefore, if we were lords of the whole earth, we should bid it all farewell, as unworthy to be compared with the kingdom of heaven: just as one would despise a brass penny, when he might gain a hundred golden guineas. If you give up a piece of land, it is almost nothing; or if you give up a house or a large sum of gold, you should neither boast nor be down-hearted. On the contrary, we ought to reckon that as nothing, which we give up for virtue. When we die, we often leave our possessions to others whom we would not, as Ecclesiastes says. Why then should we not leave them for virtue's sake, that we may inherit a kingdom?

For the same reason, let us not covet these things; for what profit is there in acquiring what we cannot carry with us to the other world? Let us rather gain durable possessions, such as prudence, righteousness, temperance, courage, understanding, charity, love of the poor, faith in Christ, forbearance, hospitality. If we gain these, we shall find hospitable entertainment among the meek of the earth. Let no one of us therefore think meanly of himself, especially when he considers himself as the Lord's servant, and as bound to devote himself to his master's service.

Now the servant cannot presume to say, Since I labored yesterday, I will not labor to-day; nor counting on the labors of his past days, will he cease for the days to come; but every day, as the Gospel says, he will show the same diligence to please the Lord. So let us continue daily in our exercise, knowing that if we lose a day, we shall not be forgiven on account of the past time; but the Lord will be angry with us for our negligence. So we have heard in Ezekiel (xxxiii. 12); and Judas in one night lost the labor of the time past. Let us therefore, my children, cleave to the exercise, and not flag; for in this we have also the Lord as a fellow-worker, as it is written, *To every one that chooseth what is good, God is also a co-worker for good;* * and that we may not be negligent, it is well to meditate on the Apostle's saying (1 Cor. xv. 31,) *I die daily;* for if we live every day as if we were dying, we shall not sin. The saying means this; when we rise in the morning, let us consider that we may not live until the evening; and when we lie down at night, we should consider that we may not rise in the morning. Our life is naturally uncertain, and is dealt out to us day by day; being duly affected by this, and living day by day with this upon our minds, we shall not sin, nor desire any earthly thing, nor be angry with any one; but as daily expecting to die, we shall possess nothing, forgive everything to all, have no desire for women, nor any sordid pleasure, but turn away from them as transient things, ever anxiously striving, and looking for the day of judgment: for the prevailing fear of future torments always dissipates the advantage of pleasure, and strengthens the soul against temptation.

Therefore, having entered upon the way of virtue, let us strive the more to reach the things before us, and let no one turn back to the things behind, like Lot's wife (Phil. iii. 14; Luke ix. 62); especially as the Lord hath said that no one, who, *having put his hand to the plough, turneth back, is fit for the kingdom of God.* To turn back is nothing else than for one to mind worldly things again, after he hath repented. Fear not when ye hear of virtue, nor think that the name signifies some strange thing. The thing is not far off, nor without us; it is within us; and the work is easy, if we be only willing. The Greeks travel over land and sea after knowledge: but we have no need to go abroad for the kingdom of heaven, nor to cross the sea after virtue; for the Lord hath said, *The kingdom of heaven is within you.* (Luke xvii. 21.) Virtue needeth only the consent of the will; since it is within us and originateth in the mind; for it is a part of the mind, which is

* There is no such text in the Bible.

naturally intelligent: the soul is therefore in its natural state, when it remaineth as it was originally created; for it was made beautiful and upright. Now that the Lord may acknowledge his work, let us keep the soul for him in its original state of virtue. If the soul vary from this, and turn from its original nature, this is called vice. The thing is therefore not difficult; for if we remain as we were originally made, then we are in a state of virtue. But if we entertain evil thoughts, then we are judged to be vicious. Now, if the thing had to be obtained from without, there would be real difficulty; but since it is within us, let us guard the soul as a precious deposit, which the Lord hath committed to our keeping, in order that he may acknowledge his work to be as he made it. Be it our task to prevent anger from tyrannizing, and lust from ruling over us.*

11. *St. Antony's Sermon continued. Part 2. Demonology, or the doctrine of demons.*

Living after this manner, let us watch, and as it is written, keep our hearts with all diligence; for we have keen and crafty enemies, the evil demons; and besides, as the Apostle saith, *We wrestle not against flesh and blood, but against the principalities and powers, against the rulers of the darkness of this world, against the spiritual things of wickedness in the heavenly places.* (Ephes. vi. 12.) There is therefore a great multitude of them in the air about us; but they differ much among themselves. But to ex-

* The foregoing somewhat metaphysical argument about virtue and the soul, savors more of the polemic bishop of Alexandria, than of the illiterate monk of the desert, into whose mouth he puts it. The doctrine is such as Pelagius afterwards taught,—attributing the sanctification of the soul to itself without the aid of Divine grace, and denying original sin and depravity in the soul. This was the general doctrine of the earlier monks; and was prevalent in the Church during the second and third centuries, and indeed until Saint Augustine hewed it down in his controversy with Pelagius. Its origin was not the Bible, nor even apostolical tradition; but the Platonism of the fathers from the time of Justin Martyr. Plato taught the entire moral ability of man to purify his soul from sin.

plain their nature and their differences, would require a long discourse, and greater ability than we possess. All that we need to know at present, is the arts which they use against us.

First then, we know that the demons were not created evil beings (for God made nothing evil), but were originally good, and fell from their heavenly wisdom, and were cast down to the earth.* They deceived the Gentiles by false appearances; but envying us Christians, they put everything in motion to obstruct our way to heaven, that we may not reach the place from which they were expelled. Hence the need of much prayer and exercise, that one may by the divine gift of discerning spirits, be able to know which among them are more, and which less, evil than others; what each of them specially studies to perform; and how each may be defeated and cast out; for, many are their evil devices and mischievous plots. Therefore the blessed apostle and his associates said, *We are not ignorant of his devices.* (2 Cor. ii. 11). But we when we are tempted by them, ought to assist one another. Therefore I, having had some experience of them, speak to you as children.

Now, when they see Christians, but especially monks, making progress by diligent labor, they first assault and tempt them by putting obstacles in their way. These obstacles are evil thoughts, which they suggest. But we should not fear their threats. They are baffled immediately by prayer and fasting, and faith in the Lord; but when baffled, they do not give up their attempts, but come on again with their tricks and devices; for when they cannot deceive the heart by what is manifestly impure pleasure, they change their mode of action. They endeavor to delude or to frighten us by visionary appearances. They put on the shapes of women, of beasts, of serpents, of huge monsters, and of an army of soldiers. But neither should we fear these fantastic re-

* St. Peter says that God *cast them down to hell, and confined them in chains of darkness, until the judgment of the great day;* which is inconsistent with this whole doctrine concerning demons, and all these stories about their tricks. See 2 Peter ii. 4.

presentations; for they are nothing, and soon disappear, especially when one fortifies himself by faith and the sign of the cross. But they are an audacious and impudent set; for though they be thus defeated, they will try to impose on you in another way. They pretend to foretell future events; and they swell themselves up to a prodigious bulk, making themselves as tall as a house, and of enormous breadth; that they may by such phantasms, carry off those unawares, whom they could not delude by reasonings. But if they find the soul secured by faith against this trick, they finally bring their prince with them.

Antony said also, that they often appeared such as the Lord described the Devil to Job (lxi. 18—21). *His eyes are as the appearance of the morning star, out of his mouth proceed burning lamps, and they are scattered as coals of fire, &c.**

Such being the appearance of the prince of demons, he terrifieth people—as I said before—the crafty braggart: as again the Lord showeth what he is, saying to Job, "*He esteemeth iron as stubble, and brass as rotten wood; he regardeth the sea as a pot of ointment, and the depth of hell as a prisoner; he counteth the deep as a playground.* (Job. xli. Septuagint). And by Moses (Exod. xv. 9.) *The enemy said, I will pursue, I will overtake:* and by Isaiah (x. 14.) *I will take away the whole earth, as a nest, and as forsaken eggs.*† Such are their boastings and pretences, that they may impose on the pious. But we who are faithful, should neither fear the Devil's empty phantasms, nor heed his words: for he is out

* Some of the Fathers thought this description of Leviathan in Job must mean the Devil, because there was so much fire in it: but some thought that Leviathan was the *Devil's father*, as Jerome tells us in his commentary on Isaiah, ch. xiii Athanasius quotes the text in Job from the Greek Septuagint.

† Here we have some fair specimens of the manner in which most of the Fathers interpreted and applied the Holy Scriptures. Any one who will read the passages from which these quotations are taken, may see that they have no more relation to "the prince of demons," than to the man in the moon. Yet the Romanists would have us rely implicitly upon these miserable interpreters!

and out a liar; and his visible shapes are as false as his words: for that is not true light which appears in them, but rather an image of the fire prepared for their punishment. The demons show themselves in the flames in which they are to burn, and try to frighten men with them; and when they vanish, they carry with them this image of the fire that is to burn them, hurting none of the faithful.

They are great cheats, and ready to turn themselves into every sort of shape, and put on every sort of character. They often pretend, without showing themselves, to sing psalms; and they tell us where passages of Scripture are to be found. Sometimes when we are reading, they repeat after us what we read, like an echo. Sometimes also, when we are asleep, they waken us up to our prayers, and that so often as to let us get hardly any sleep. Sometimes, too, they appear in the habit of monks, and talk very religiously, in order to gain our confidence, and then to seduce us.

But we must not give heed to them, even when they waken us up to prayer, or admonish us to abstain from eating, or pretend to accuse us of negligence, and charge us to lie on the ground; though they are sometimes very indulgent to us in respect to these things. It is not from piety that they do these things, but to drive the simple to desperation, and make them think the exercise a useless thing, and the life of a monk disgusting and oppressive. Our Lord would not suffer the demons to speak, even when they confessed the truth, lest they should defile the truth with their own uncleanness: so should we turn away our ears from them, even when they speak the truth: for it is unbecoming, when we have the Holy Scriptures, to receive instruction from the Devil.—For the demons do everything to deceive the simple; they put on false appearances; they make disturbance and noise, sometimes break out in loud laughter, and sometimes whisper in your ears. If you do not mind these things, then they will weep and lament, as if they were beaten. But let us not listen to them, nor obey them; but be the more strenuous in the exercise, and not suffer them to turn us aside from our path, whatever artifices they may use. Nor let us fear them, even when they make a show of attacking us, or threaten us with death; for they are weak and can do nothing but threaten.*

Thus far I have given you only a sketch of the subject; but now it will not be unprofitable to take a wider and deeper view of the nature and history of demons; the knowledge of which will be very useful to you.

When the Lord sojourned upon earth, the enemy fell and his powers were weakened. Yet the fallen tyrant, though powerless, will not rest; though all he can do is to threaten. Think of this, and you can despise the demons. If they had bodies like ours, men might hide from them, and thus escape injury; as we hide from one another by closing our doors. But such is not their nature. They can enter when the doors are shut; and they are everywhere in the atmosphere around us. Their prince is the Devil, a murderer from the beginning, and the father of wickedness, as our Saviour called him. So are they all malicious, and ready to do mischief. No place is free from their snares. If they spare us, it is not out of good will; for the more virtuous and devout we are, the more do they try to harm us. The reason why they do us no mischief is that they cannot: they can only threaten. If they had the power, they would tear us up in a moment: they would not leave a Christian of us alive; for in our assemblies we are always speaking ill of them; and they know that their power fails as our spiritual strength increases. Piety is an abomination to the sinner. Having no power against us, they wound one another, when they find that they cannot hurt those whom they threaten. Think of this and fear them not. If they had any real power over us, they would not come in crowds

* Yet they gave Antony a substantial beating in the sepulchre. We know of but one way in which his doctrine here can be reconciled with his experience there, and that is, to suppose that the clubs and whips in the sepulchre were wielded by demons of flesh and blood, such as are apt to be found in villages.

upon us, nor assume visionary shapes to deceive us; but, one of them alone would be sufficient to work his will; and especially because every one had effective power, he would not resort to a vain show—an airy nothing—nor fetch a crowd with him, to frighten us; but he would directly employ his power in fulfilling his purpose. But because they can do no harm, the demons play like actors on the stage, changing their forms and scaring the boys with the visionary appearance of a multitude of frightful shapes. Wherefore they are only the more contemptible. The angel of the Lord who destroyed the Assyrian host (2 Kings xix. 35), had no need of such vanities. But some one may say, Did not the Devil show power against Job, when he destroyed his flocks and herds, killed his children by tearing down the house over their heads, and then afflicted his person with a sore disease? Yes; but this was not Satan's own power; it was the power which God granted him for a time, in order to try Job's patience. Without this Divine permission, the contemptible enemy could have done nothing against Job. We read in the Evangelist (Mat. viii. 31) how the demons said to the Lord, *Permit us to go into the herd of swine.* So they have of themselves no power even over swine, much less over those who are made after the image of God. Therefore we ought to fear God only, and to despise the demons. Still, however, the more they attempt against us, the more zealously should we devote ourselves to the exercise: for an upright life and faith towards God are a strong defence against them. They are afraid of the ascetic's fasting, watching, prayers, meekness, quietness, contempt of money and of vainglory,—of his humility, love of the poor, alms, freedom from anger, and above all, piety towards Christ. They endeavor by all means to prevent men from obtaining the power to tread them under their feet, according to the Saviour's promise to his disciples (Luke x. 19.)

Therefore, when they pretend to foretell future events, let no one give heed to them. They often tell us, days beforehand, of brethren coming to visit us, and the brethren come accordingly.

They do this, not out of regard for those who hear them, but to persuade men to put confidence in them, that they may afterwards lead them to destruction. Instead of trusting them, we ought to drive them away, because we have no need of their predictions. They have in reality no foreknowledge. What wonder is it, if by means of their lighter bodies,* they are able, when they see men set off on a journey, to outrun them, and foretell their coming? A swift horseman might do the same thing, by out-travelling a man on foot. Only the omniscient God has proper foreknowledge of events. These roguish imposters, when they see and hear things among us, steal off to another place and tell it, before people can hear it by other means. Suppose one were to leave Thebes or some other place, to travel to another distant place on foot. Before he departs, they know nothing about it; but when they see him going, they run ahead and announce his coming. But sometimes their news is false, because the traveller turns back. So they babble sometimes about the overflowings of the river (Nile.) Having seen much rain fall in Ethiopia, and knowing that this causes the rising of the water, they run down to Egypt, and announce that the flood is coming.† Such were the Greek oracles, by which, through the agency of demons, men were in like manner led into error by pretended prophecies. But these deceptive oracles have ceased, since Christ came into the world and abolished the deceitful arts of demons. These often make plausible conjectures of coming events, without having absolute foreknowledge; as physicians learn by experience to make probable conjectures of the issue of diseases, and navigators and husbandmen, of the changes of the weather.

* It was the common opinion of the early Fathers, derived originally from the heathen, that spiritual beings and the human soul after death, were invested with material bodies, so refined as to be generally invisible. Still they might be made visible. Hence visible demons and ghosts of men.

† As the fertility of Egypt depends on the overflowings of the Nile, the people look for them in their season with great anxiety, as a failure would be fatal to their crops.

As for the predictions of the demons, we have no need of them. What does it profit us to hear of such things a few days before they happen? Such knowledge contributes nothing to virtue. None of us will be condemned for ignorance of these matters, nor rewarded for knowing them; but each one will be judged according to his faith, and his obedience to the Divine commands, Wherefore we should disregard these things, and apply ourselves to our exercise and our spiritual labors; not to gain foreknowledge, but the Divine approbation. We should pray, not for the knowledge of future events, as a reward for our labors, but for the help of the Lord, that we may gain the victory in our conflict with the Devil. If, however, we be solicitous to know future events, let us purify our minds; for I am fully persuaded, that a mind thoroughly purified, and calmly steadfast in its nature, is endued with a much clearer vision, by Divine revelation, than any of the demons possess. Such was the mind of Elisha, when he saw his servant Gehazi, and the host of angels standing by him (2 Kings v. 26 and vi. 17.) When, therefore, they come by night, to announce future things, or say, We are angels; believe them not, for they lie. Even if they praise the ascetic life, and pronounce you blessed; do not listen to them, nor accept their commendations; but rather fortify yourselves and the house by the sign of the cross, and betake yourselves to prayer: then you will see them vanish away; for they are timid, and are dreadfully afraid when they see the sign of the Lord's cross, since the Saviour spoiled them upon it, and publicly triumphed over them (Col. ii. 15.)

---

12. *The Sermon concluded. More about the Demons.*

Hear now in what manner we may easily distinguish the presence of the evil angels from that of the good. When good angels appear, there is no disturbance—no contention, no clamor,—but something so calm and gentle, that it fills the soul with gladness; for the Lord is with them. The thoughts of the soul are then subject to no agitation, but the soul is illuminated, so as to behold those who appear, and is so filled with heavenly desires, that it would fain fly away with them, when they depart. If at first sight men are afraid, when angels appear, these soon change that fear into love; as Gabriel did to Zacharias, (Luke i. 11,) and the angel at the Lord's sepulchre to the women. (Mat. xxviii. 5.) Such is the appearance of good angels.

But the rush and vision of evil demons is full of confusion with clamor, noise and shouting, like the noise made by a parcel of riotous young men, or a party of robbers in the desert. Hence our minds are affected with timidity, and our thoughts become disturbed and confused, our countenances downcast and sad, our ascetism hateful; we remember with sorrow the homes and friends that we left, and the fear of death invades our souls; finally, the desire of evil things, and the contempt of virtue, corrupt our hearts. Therefore when a vision appears, and you are at first terrified, but soon filled with unspeakable joy, and you feel delightfully tranquillized and refreshed, your soul enjoying peace, confidence, and love towards God;—then take courage and go to prayer: for the joy and self-possession of the soul manifests the presence of holy beings. So Abraham rejoiced when he saw the Lord (John viii. 56), and John Baptist leaped for joy at the salutation of Mary the mother of God.* (Luke i. 41.) But if, when superior beings appear, there be tumult and hubbub from without, a visionary show of worldly grandeur, and threatenings of death, as before described,—then know that this is an onset of evil spirits. Moreover, this is a further sign, when your fear of the apparition is permanent, then they are enemies who appear: for the demons do not take away your fear; on the contrary, when they see you afraid, they augment their visionary exhibitions, to make them more terrible, and then they come up to you, mocking, and

* *Θεοτοκος.* This impious title began to be given to Mary the mother of Jesus (as the Evangelists call her,) in this age, during the Arian controversy. Yet it is not more impious than some expressions occasionally heard among Protestants, as that "God the mighty Maker *died*," in Watts's Hymns.

say, Fall down and worship. It was in this way they deluded the Gentiles to idolatry, making them believe these demons were Gods. But the Lord has not suffered them to deceive us. When the Devil tried him with such arts, the Lord said, *Get thee behind me, Satan.* (Luke iv. 8.) Wherefore the old rogue ought to be more and more despised by us; for the Lord said that he had done this on our account; so that when the demons hear us utter such words, they may be driven away; the Lord having rebuked them in these words.*

But we must not be vain when we cast out demons, nor puff ourselves up when we heal the sick: for he who casts out demons is not alone worthy of admiration; nor should he who is unable to do it be therefore despised. But whenever one excels in the exercise of virtue, him we ought to imitate, and endeavor even to excel; for to work miracles is not of ourselves. The power is the Lord's. Thus he said to his disciples, *Rejoice not that the demons are subject to you; but rejoice that your names are written in heaven.* (Luke x. 20.) To have our names written in heaven, is a testimony of our virtue; but to cast out demons, is the Saviour's gift. But as I said before, we should pray for the gift of discerning spirits,—that, as it is written, we may not believe every spirit. (1 John iv. 1.)

I would rather not say anything of myself. But that you may not think I say these things simply, and without experience of their truth, but may be persuaded of them, though I *become as a fool* (2 Cor. xii. 11.)—but the Lord knoweth that it is not out of regard for myself, but out of love to you, and for your instruction that I speak of what I have seen concerning the devices of demons. As often as they blessed me, I cursed them in the name of the Lord. As often as they foretold the rising of the river, I said to them, What business is that of yours? Some-

*Let the reader compare this Christian account of good and evil apparitions with the fancies of the New Platonists on the same subject, as described in our 9th chapter, § 3, and he will easily see the heathenish origin of these notions among the Fathers and Monks.

times they would come threatening me, and would surround me in the form of an army of horsemen, fully equipped. Sometimes they would fill the house with wild beasts and serpents, then I sang the psalm, *Some in chariots, some on horses; but we will magnify the name of the Lord our God*—(Ps. xx. 7.)—so our prayers overthrew them. Sometimes they came in the dark, having the appearance of light, and said, Antony, we have come to give you light; but I shut my eyes and prayed. The light of the wicked was put out in a moment. A few months afterwards they came singing psalms, as it were, and speaking from the Scriptures. But I, as if deaf, heard them not. Once they shook the monastery like an earthquake, but I prayed that my mind might remain unmoved. Afterwards they came again, clapping, whistling, and dancing. But when I fell down, and began to pray and sing psalms to myself, straightway they began to whimper and cry, as if they had been unnerved. But I glorified God for thus openly quelling their audacity and madness. Once a monstrously tall demon came with a show, and had the audacity to say, I am the power and the providence of God. What shall I do for you? Then I spit at him, and calling upon the name of Christ, tried to strike him, and thought that I did strike him, and straightway this huge fellow, with all his demons, vanished at the name of Christ. Once, too, when I was fasting, he came in the shape of a monk—the hypocritical knave—carrying the appearance of loaves, and he counseled me, saying, Eat, and cease from your many labors. You too are a man, and your strength will fail. But I, perceiving his craftiness, rose up to pray. He could not stand that, for he walked off, and passed through the door in the form of smoke. Many a time in the desert he displayed the appearance of gold, that I might touch it, and look at it. But I sang psalms at the gold-fiend, and it melted away. Oftentimes they lashed me with whips, but when I said, Nothing shall separate me from the love of Christ, then they turned and lashed one another.* But it was not I who defeated them so, it was the

* We have a difficulty about this devil's bread, and gold, and whipping.

Lord, who said, *I saw Satan as lightning falling from heaven.* (Luke x. 18.) But I, my children, remembering the Apostle's word, *have in a figure transferred it to myself*, that you may learn, not to flag in the exercise, nor to fear the appearances of the Devil and his imps. And since I have become a fool in telling these things, take another instance as a proof that you may be safe and fearless. Believe me, for I tell no lie. Once on a time some one knocked at the door of my monastery. When I went out, I saw a tall, huge phantom. When I asked, Who are you? he answered, I am Satan. When I asked, What is your business here? he said, Why do all the monks and Christians of every sort slander me so? Why are they cursing me every hour? I answered, Because you trouble them. But, said he, it is not I that trouble them; they only plague themselves about me; for I have become weak. Have they not read, *The weapons of the enemy have failed forever, and thou hast destroyed their cities?*—(Ps. ix. 6.) Now I have no weapon, no city. Christians are found everywhere, and even the desert is full of monks. Let them keep watch over themselves, and not curse me for nothing.*—So spake the devil. Then I, admiring the grace of the Lord, said to him, You are always a liar, and never tell the truth; nevertheless, you have this time unwillingly said a true thing; for Christ has weakened and cast you down. When

If they were the real, substantial things, then the Devil is not so powerless as Father Antony would make out. If they were mere phantoms or optical illusions, they could not be eaten, touched, or felt: and what an old fool must the Devil be to try men with such unsubstantial things. If the men rejected them, and sung or prayed them away, the Devil was defeated, but if they offered to take them, and found that they were nothing, then surely the Devil would lose all credit with them, and be worse defeated than in the other case. To ascribe such silly tricks to Satan, is to make him as great a fool as that young devil was that the witty blackguard Rabelais represented as having been cheated by a clown.

* Here the author unconsciously satirizes his own "doctrine of demons" and silly fancies about the pranks which they play upon ascetic devotees. He puts into the Devil's mouth by far the most rational language in the whole sermon.

he heard the name of Christ, he was scorched by it and vanished. Now, since the Devil himself confesses that he can do nothing, we ought wholly to despise both him and his imps. Such as I have stated are the various devices of the enemy and his dogs. But let us keep in mind, that when the Lord is with us these enemies can do nothing against us. For when they come, such as they find us, such are they towards us, and *they accommodate their appearances to the state of our minds.** When they find us fearful and troubled, straightway like robbers they assault the place which they find unguarded; and whatsoever gloomy thoughts we have of ourselves, these they put into a visible shape with additions. Now, if they see us fearful and timid, they increase the fear by apparitions and threats, and so the unhappy soul is punished. But if they find us rejoicing in the Lord, and meditating or conversing on divine things, then demons have no power over the Christian, nor indeed over any one thus engaged: for when they see the soul secured by such thoughts, they turn away deeply ashamed of themselves. Therefore, if we would despise the enemy, let us always think of divine things and rejoice in hope, then we shall always see the pranks of demons dissolve like smoke, and the demons themselves flying rather than pursuing: for, as I said before, they are very timid, always expecting the fire prepared for them. Particularly this token of security you may always have against them. When an apparition presents itself, do not fall into a fright, but, whatever it be, boldly ask, Who art thou? and whence? Then if it be a holy vision it will show itself clearly,

* Here the author suggests a principle, without being aware of it, by which we may solve the phenomena of these visions of demons, so far as they were believed to be real by those who professed to have seen them. The brooding imagination of a solitary hypochrondriac would become so excited, one while with gloomy, another while with rapturous conceptions, that his mind would project these images into space, and make them ppear as objects of sense. The philosophy of these apparitions has begun of late years to be well understood, so that we can account for many things of the sort related in ancient books, without supposing them all to have been falsely reported.

and your fear will be changed into joy. But if it be the Devil, it will fade and vanish away, seeing the soul fortified; for, asking a question is a sign of self-possession. So Joshua, the son of Nun, learned the character of the vision by a question (Josh. v. 13): but the enemy could not conceal himself when Daniel asked him a question.*

END OF THE SERMON.

---

13. *Antony's conduct in the Persecution—his Miracles—and the crowds that resorted to his Monastery.*

All listened with delight to this discourse of Antony. The effect of it was, that in some the love of virtue increased, in others negligence was cast away, in others vanity was brought to an end, and all learned to despise the schemes of the Devil, while they admired Antony's gift of discerning spirits. Then were the monasteries in the mountains like tabernacles filled with the choirs of heaven, singing psalms, discoursing, fasting, praying, rejoicing in the hope of future things, laboring that they might give alms, having love and sympathy for one another; and truly the place looked like one set apart for religion and righteousness, for no one there either did or suffered wrong, and the tax-gatherer's voice was unheard. The whole multitude were ascetics, all engaged in the same pursuit of virtue; so that one beholding the monasteries and the order of the monks might exclaim, *How beautiful are thy dwellings, O Jacob, and thy tents, O Israel!* (Num. xiv. 5.)

But Antony, retiring again to his monastery, there shut himself up, and from day to day increased the severity of his self-discipline, and the fervor of his devotion. When he thought of the heavenly mansions, he longed for them, and groaned when he looked at the daily life of man. When he had to eat, and sleep,

* The author was mistaken here, if he meant that the book of Daniel mentions a vision in which an enemy appeared to the prophet. Perhaps the allusion is to a story in the apocryphal book of Susanna.

and comply with the other necessities of the body, he felt ashamed of himself, especially when he thought of the nobler exercises of the soul. Often, therefore, when he was to eat with other monks, and called to mind the food of the soul, he declined, and went far away from them, esteeming it shameful to be seen eating with others. He ate because it was necessary for the body, often by himself, sometimes too with the brethren. He was ashamed when he did it; but he took occasion to speak freely about such matters.

We ought (said he) to devote all our spare time to the soul, not to the body: a little time must indeed of necessity be given to the body, but let all the rest go in preference to the benefit of the soul, that it may not be degraded by the pleasures of the body, but rather make the body its own servant: for this is what the Saviour said, Take no thought for your life, what ye shall eat, nor wherewith the body shall be clothed: but seek ye first the kingdom of heaven, and all these things shall be added unto you. (Mat. vi. 31).

After this came the persecution which the Emperor Maximin raised against the Church. The holy martyrs having been led to Alexandria, Antony left his monastery and followed them to that city, saying, Let us also go down, that if called, we too may engage in the contest, or at least see them contending:—for Antony had a desire for martyrdom; but he was not willing to deliver himself to the persecutors.* He attended upon the confessors in the mines and prisons. He accompanied those who were summoned before the judges, and exhorted them to submit readily to martyrdom. When the judge saw the boldness of Antony and

* Because that would have been a sort of self-murder. But he chose to put himself in the way of being apprehended and put to death—which was very little better. Antony had a strong passion for renown, and like some military men, was willing to purchase it by voluntary martyrdom. Martyrs were more honored in the Church than even monks who died a natural death. Those who confessed Christ before heathen judges in time of persecution, were called confessors, and were greatly honored, though they escaped with life.

his associates, he forbade the monks to appear in court, and ordered them to leave the city. The other monks hid themselves for that day; but Antony not only disregarded the order, but washed his monk's coat* to render it more conspicuous; and took his station in a high place directly in front of the judge. He was seen, not only by the judge, but by the governor of the city and his officers, as they passed by. Everybody admired the boldness and intrepidity with which he stood there. He wished to be apprehended and martyred. But too his great sorrow, they took no further notice of him. The Lord preserved him for the benefit of many, that he might teach the ascetic life which he had learned from the Scriptures: For many, by the mere sight of his mode of life, were excited to imitate him. A second time he went, and after his own manner served the confessors; and as if bound with them, he underwent the labors and services to which they were condemned.

When the persecution was over, he left the city, and returned to his monastery, where he applied himself more intensely than ever to his ascetic practice. He fasted continually; he wore inside a hair shirt; outside, a skin. These he kept on to the end of his days. He never washed the dirt from his body. He would not even wash his feet, nor let them touch water when he could help it. No one ever saw him stripped, till his dead body was laid out for burial.

Having shut himself up for a certain time, then, with the resolution that he would neither go out himself, nor let anybody come in, it happened that Martianus, a military officer, arrived during the time, and troubled Antony no little about his daughter, who was infested by a demon. When he continued knocking at his door, and begging him for God's sake to come and pray for

* In Greek *Ependyte*, which seems to denote a sort of upper garment; but the fashion of it is unknown. Those who wish to see a discussion of the various opinions about it, may cousult Helyot's Life of St. Antony, B. I. ch. ii. Likely enough, as Bolland thought, it was a mellote, or white sheepskin overcoat or mantle. See ch. xxii.

his daughter; he refused to open the door, but getting up to a high place, he peeped down at him, and said, Man, why do you clamor so at me? I am a man as well as yourself. If you believe, pray to God, and it will be done. Martianus believed immediately; and having called upon Christ, he returned home, and his daughter was cleansed from the demon. Many other miracles did the Lord work by him, as he said, *Ask and ye shall receive.* For a great number of afflicted sat outside by the door of his monastery, and by believing and praying there, were healed. Afterwards, the crowd became troublesome to him, and he could not use secret retirement when he chose; he feared too that those things which the Lord had done by him, might make him think too highly of himself, and make others think so too. He therefore determined to go to the monks of the Upper Thebaid—the farthest part of Egypt—where they knew him not.

14. *Antony goes away into the heart of the desert. Plagued with demons.*

Having got some loaves of the brethren, he seated himself on the river bank, to watch for a passing vessel, in which he might go up the river. While he was looking out, a voice came to him from the air above him, saying, Antony, whither art thou going, and wherefore? He was not in the least disturbed, for he had been often called in this way. When he heard the questions, he answered, saying, Because the crowd will not let me rest. For this reason I wish to go into the Upper Thebaid, on account of the many disturbances that happen to me, and especially because they require of me things which are above my power. But the voice said unto him, Even if thou goest up to the Upper Thebaid; or if—as thou hast it in mind—thou comest down among the herds of cattle, thou hast to bear more—yea, two-fold more—labor. If thou wouldst really have quiet, go away now into the heart of the desert. Antony said, And who will show me the way? for I am ignorant of it. He straightway showed him a company of Saracens about to travel that way. Antony then went to them, and asked to go with them into the desert. They, as if by order of Divine Providence, readily received him When he had travelled three days and three nights with them, he came to a very high mountain. At the foot of the mountain, was a spring of clear, sweet, cold water :* a plain spread out from it, and a few wild palm-trees grew there. Antony, as if moved by Divine inspiration, was delighted with the place. This was the place signified by him who had spoken to him on the bank of the river. Therefore, as a supply to begin upon, he got some loaves from his fellow travellers, and remained alone by this mountain. Not a soul staid with him : for, from this time he considered the place as peculiarly his own : and even the Saracens, when they saw Antony's devotion to a solitary life, made it their business to pass that way, and carry him supplies of bread.† The palm-trees also afforded him some pleasant refreshment. The brethren, too, after they learned where he was, being mindful of him as children of a father, took care to send him bread.

But Antony, when he saw that this occasioned them much fatigue and labor, considered how he might spare them all this trouble. When he had fixed upon his plan, he asked some men who where passing that way, to bring him a spade, an axe, and a little wheat. When these were brought, he examined the land about the mountain, and found a suitable spot for cultivation, where he could water it plentifully. Here he sowed his seed. So he did every year, and thus supplied himself with bread : rejoicing that by this means he could support himself without troubling or burdening anybody.‡ Afterwards, when he saw that

* Such springs rarely occur in those dry deserts ; when they do, they are apt to become places of great resort for the Saracens, or wandering Arabs. Date-bearing palm-trees are apt to grow about them. The date is a sweet nutritious nut, and is an important article of food among the Arabs of the desert.

† The wild Arabs have always had great reverence for saints, especially for those who lived a solitary ascetic life, and were very dirty, as St. Antony was.

‡ Antony was a good old ignorant superstitious enthusiast, who, with all

travellers often came that way, he planted a few seeds of garden vegetables, that the traveller might have something to refresh him, after the fatigues of his difficult journey through the desert.

But the wild beasts of the desert, coming to the spring for water, often injured his crops. Having caught one of these intruders, without hurting him, he thus addressed them all: Why do ye injure me, when I do you no harm? Go now, all of you, in the name of the Lord, and never again set foot upon my premises. From that hour, the beasts, as if awed by the command, never again came near the place. So he lived alone in the mountain,* devoted to prayer and fasting. But the brethren, who ministered to him, besought that he would suffer them to come once a-month, and bring him olives, beans, and oil: for he was now old, and led a hard life there, and had many a battle with the demons: as we have been told by those who visited him: For they heard there tumults, and many voices, and a clashing, as of arms. By night, they saw the mountain full of wild beasts, and himself they beheld, as it were, fighting with the apparitions, and praying against them. On these occasions he encouraged his visitors; and himself fought upon his knees, praying to the Lord. He was truly worthy of admiration, because, being alone in such a desert, he dreaded neither the assaults of demons, nor the ferocity of the numerous wild beasts and serpents that were there. Then the Devil, as David saith in the Psalm, (xxxvii. 12), *watched him and gnashed upon him with his teeth.* But Antony, by calling upon the Saviour, continued unhurt by his trickery and subtile schemes. While Antony was watching by night, the Devil let loose upon

his erroneous notions, had, in some essential points, the heart of a true Christian, as the fact just related demonstrates. How different was he, in this particular, from the swarms of good-for-nothing, lazy, fanatical, beggar-monks, who long afterwards arose in the Church, and continue among the Roman Catholics to this day, doing no service (for their idle bead-roll mutterings are not worth a straw) and living upon the alms of the laboring population!

* This mountain stands near the shore of the Red Sea. Compare Jerome's description of the place, in his Life of Hilarion, § 31.

him the wild beasts: nearly all the hyenas of the desert came out of their holes, and surrounded him, grinning and threatening to bite. Antony, observing what the enemy would be at, said to them all;—If ye have received power against me, come on; I am ready to be devoured by you; but if the demons have put this into your heads,—then, not a moment longer, but begone with you! I am the servant of Christ. Hardly had Antony got out these words, before they scampered away, as if driven by the whip of his word.*

A few days afterwards, Antony was at work, making a basket, when somebody standing at the door, drew the string that he was using at his work. By the by, he usually gave the baskets that he made to his visitors, for anything that they chose to offer him. When he felt his basket-string pulled, he rose up and beheld a monster, like a man down to his thighs, but his legs and feet were like those of an ass. Antony only crossed himself and said; I am Christ's servant; if thou art sent against me; behold, here I am. But the beast with his demons fled in such a hurry, that he fell and broke his neck. Now the death of the beast was the defeat of the demons. Their scheme was, by means of him, to carry Antony out of the desert; but they were not able.

15. *More miracles, and some good advice.*

Having been besought once by the monks to come down and pay them a visit, and see the places where they lived, he travelled with the monks who had come after him. A camel carried their bread and water; for the whole of that desert is without drinkable water, excepting in the mountain where Antony lived. Their water failing by the way, and the weather being excessively hot,

* This story, like some novels, may be "founded on fact." The African hyena is a bold beast, and by night scruples not to come into houses, prowling for garbage. Several together may have entered Antony's cell, and been frightened away by his loud Quixotic speech. The old man's excited imagination may have multiplied them into "all the hyenas of the mountains," and of course sent by the Devil.

they were all in danger of perishing. They searched all around for water, but found none; and their strength failed, so that they were unable to walk, and had to lie down upon the ground. They let their camel go wherever he pleased, giving themselves up for lost. The old man seeing their desperate case, groaned for sorrow, then going a little way from the rest, he kneeled, lifted up his hands, and prayed. Straightway the Lord made a fountain of water burst forth at the spot where he was praying. So all drank and were refreshed. Then having filled their skins with water, they sought their camel and found him;* for his halter happened to be caught by a stone; so he was held fast. Having led him to the spring and given him a drink, they put the water-skins upon him and went their way. When they arrived at the outer monasteries,† all embraced and kissed him as a father; and he, as bringing them supplies from the mountain, entertained them with discourses, and made them partakers of the fruits of his experience. Again, there was joy in the mountains, zeal for improvement, and mutual exhortation through faith. Then he also rejoiced, seeing the ready-mindedness of the monks, and seeing also his sister, who had grown old in virginity, and presided over other virgins. After some time, he returned again to the mountain. Then at last many monks visited him, and others who had diseases ventured to come. The monks who came, he exhorted continually to faith, love, and purity of mind: he directed them to avoid carnal pleasures, and vain-glory; to pray without ceasing, to sing psalms before and after sleep; to repeat the Scripture commands, and remember the acts of the saints, that their minds might be excited to imitation. Above all, he admonished them to meditate continually upon the saying of the apostle, Let not the

* Camels can smell water in the desert, a long way off. But we dare not insinuate that this most wonderful fountain was discovered by the camel's nose, while Antony was praying. Even then a sort of miracle might have been made of it; but not near so good as the one which we have.

† That is, the monasteries on the outer verge of the desert, in the mountains that bound the Valley of the Nile.

sun go down upon your wrath. (Eph. iv. 26.) This he thought was meant, not of anger alone, but of every sin. Let every man, said he, daily call himself to account for his actions by night and by day. If he have sinned, let him cease; if not, let him not glory, but persevere without relaxing in his duties. Let him not condemn his neighbor, nor justify himself, but await the day of judgment: for a man is often unconsciously guilty of sins which God knows. Leaving the judgment to God, let us sympathize with one another, and bear one another's burdens. Let us examine ourselves strictly, and strenuously endeavor to amend our failings. A good way to detect and avoid sin, is for one to write down candidly his outward actions and his exercises of mind, as he would tell them to another; and he will assuredly feel ashamed of some of them, and sin no more. For why should any one, by sinning, wish to injure himself? Or who, after he has sinned, does not cheat himself by concealing it? Therefore, as we would not commit fornication in the sight of others, so, if we declare our thoughts to ourselves by writing them down, we shall better guard ourselves from filthy imaginations, being ashamed to expose them to our own eyes. Then let the writing serve us instead of the eyes of our fellow ascetics; that, blushing as much to write our evil thoughts, as to let others see them, we may banish them from our minds. By conforming ourselves to this rule, we shall be able to subdue the body, to please the Lord, and to frustrate the schemes of the enemy.*

Such were the precepts which Antony gave to those who met him. He sympathized and prayed with the afflicted, and *in many cases*, the Lord heard him, and healed them. But then he neither boasted when he was heard, nor murmured when he was not,† but always gave thanks to the Lord. He exhorted the sick to be

* With the exception of a little too much ascetism at the beginning, we can heartily recommend those rules to the reader's attention and observance.

† He often failed in his efforts to heal the sick;—and when by the power of imagination or otherwise, they got better, it was deemed a miracle!

patient, and to consider that to heal was not in his nor any man's power, but only in God's. Thus the afflicted received this benefit at least, that they learned from Antony's discourses to bear their sufferings patiently, and if they were healed, to thank not Antony, but God only, for the blessing.

16. *Miracles! Miracles!*

There was one Fronto, a courtier, who had a dreadful malady; for he had gnawed off his tongue, and appeared likely also to injure his eyes. He came to the mountain and besought Antony to pray for him. Antony prayed, and then told him to return to Egypt and he would be healed of his fits. Fronto at first refused to go, and staid several days; until Antony said to him, If you stay here, you cannot be healed. Go, and as soon as you enter Egypt, you will see a sign that will be given you. He believed and went. No sooner had he seen Egypt, than he felt himself to be a sound man.

Again, a certain virgin of Busiris had a sore and disgusting malady. Her tears, her mucus, and the moisture from her ears, when they fell to the ground, became maggots. Her body was paralyzed, and her eyes were not natural. Her parents, hearing that some monks were going to Antony, and believing in the Lord, who had once healed a woman's issue of blood (Mat. ix. 20), begged that they might accompany them with their daughter. The monks consented. The parents and child remained outside of the mountain with Paphnutius, a confessor* and monk. The others entered and had scarcely begun to tell Antony about the virgin, when he anticipated them, described the girl's disease and told of her having travelled with them. When they asked that she and her parents might come in, he would not permit it; but —said he—do you go out to the place, and you will find her

* Those who, in times of persecution, confessed before the judges that they were Christians, and were ready to undergo any punishment rather than deny Christ, were called confessors, if they were not put to death, martyrs, if they were.

either dead or cured: for, as I have no power to perform such a cure, it is useless to bring her to me, miserable man as I am. It is the Lord who has healed the poor woman, out of regard to her prayers, and he hath only revealed to me that he would do it in that place. The miracle was performed accordingly; for when they went out, they found her healed, and the parents rejoicing.

Again; two brethren were coming out of Egypt to see him; but their water having failed, the one was dead and the other almost dead, for he was unable to travel, and lay down, expecting to die. But Antony, sitting in his mountain cell, called two monks who happened to be there, and said, Take quickly a pitcher of water, and run down the road towards Egypt; for two brethren are on the way; one has died, and the other will die unless you make haste; for so it has been revealed to me when praying. The monks went accordingly; and found the one's dead body, which they buried; but the other they restored by means of the water, and brought him to the old man. The distance was a day's journey. Now, should any one ask, Why did not Antony send off the monks in time to save the other? He would wrong Antony; for the determination whether the man should live or die, was with God only; Antony could do nothing till the revelation came to him.

Another time, Antony was sitting in the mountain, and looking up he saw one carried up on high, and a joyful band meeting him. Filled with wonder, he pronounced them a band of the blessed, and prayed to learn what this might be. And straightway came a voice to him, saying, This is the soul of Ammon, the monk of Nitria, who led an ascetic life down to his old age. Thus spake the voice. Now the distance from Nitria to Antony's cell in the mountain was thirteen days' journey. Those who were present, seeing Antony filled with wonder, asked him the cause of it. He answered that Ammon had just ended his life. This monk was well known to Antony by reason of his frequent visits, and his numerous miracles; of which this was one. Ammon once having need to cross the river Lycus, when it was high, requested Theodorus who was with him, to go some distance apart from him, that they might not see one another naked, when they crossed the water. When Theodorus was gone, he still felt ashamed to see himself naked. Whilst he considered what he should do to avoid this shame, he was suddenly carried over to the other side. When Theodorus had crossed and met him there without wet, he desired to know how he had passed over; but he refused to tell. Then Theodorus embraced his feet, and vowed that he would not let him go, until he was informed. Ammon out of regard partly to his earnestness, and partly to his vow,—after charging him not to speak of it during his life-time,—explained the matter to him. He had been carried over the water without touching it, not by human hands, but by divine power. Theodorus told this after Ammon's death. The monks to whom Antony spoke of his death noted the day. Thirty days afterwards some brethren from Nitria arrived with the intelligence of his death. He had died the very day and hour in which Antony saw his soul ascending. The monks admired the purity of Antony's mind, who could see what had happened at such a great distance.

The Count Archelaus once happening to find him praying alone, outside of his cell in the mountain, asked him to intercede for Polycratea, an admirable virgin of Laodicea; for she was dreadfully afflicted in her stomach and side, and was altogether enfeebled in body, from excessive ascetism—that is, fasting and other bodily mortifications.* Antony prayed accordingly. The Count noted the day on which the prayer was made. On returning to Laodicea, he found that the virgin had got well on that very day.

He often predicted, days—sometimes even a month—beforehand, not only the coming of brethren, but also the cause of their coming. Some came simply to see him; others, because they were sick; and others again, because they were infested by

* Many persons thus destroyed their health and their lives, as we learn by occasional hints in the Fathers, most of whom, in their superstitious zeal for monkery, seldom alluded to cases of this sort.

demons. None of them esteemed the fatigue of the journey, either an annoyance or a loss; for every one felt the benefit of it.

Going down once again to the outer monasteries, he was asked to go on board of a vessel and pray with the monks. He alone perceived a nauseous and very strong smell. The crew of the vessel said that there was pickled fish in the vessel, and that this caused the smell. Antony replied that there was a stink of something else. While he spoke, a young man, who had a demon, and lay hid in the hold, cried out: but the demon, being rebuked in the name of our Lord, went out, and the young man was healed. Then all knew that the demon had made the stench.

There was another, a man of distinction, who was so possessed by the demon, that he was ignorant of his having come to Antony, and ate the excrements of his own body. Those who brought him, entreated Antony to pray for him. Antony, pitying the poor young man, prayed, and watched over him all the night. At day-break the young man suddenly ran at Antony and pushed him. Those that came with him were angry at this; but Antony said, Be not angry with the young man; for it was not he who did it, but the demon within him; who being rebuked, and ordered to be gone into dry places, raved and went. Therefore give glory to the Lord; for the demon's assault upon me is a sign to you of his departure. Whilst Antony was saying these things, the young man was restored to his right mind, knew where he was, embraced the old man, and gave thanks to God.

A great many monks have with one accord related numbers more of his miracles;* but these are not so wonderful as others of a different sort that appear still more wonderful.

* Yes, set monks to telling miraculous stories, and they will always have enough of them. Their lives are so monotonous and insipid; they have so little of nature, of reason, or of learning in them, or about them, and such dreamy fanatical notions of spiritual things, that miracles become as necessary a stimulant to them as brandy to a languid sot. Yet grave Fathers of the Church gathered up all their wonderful stories, and used all their authority to give them currency as sacred verities.

17. *Antony's wonderful visions about the passage of souls, and the Devil's attempt to seize them.*

Once when he was going to eat, and had risen up to pray, about the ninth hour, he felt himself rapt into a trance; and—strange to tell—he saw himself, as it were, carried out of himself, and conducted by certain ones through the air: then he saw certain malignant and terrible beings standing in the air and stopping up his way, so that he could not pass. When his conductors strove with them they demanded that he should give an account of himself, as if he were responsible to them. They wishing then to take up the account from the day of his birth, Antony's conductors forbade it, saying that the Lord had blotted out these earlier matters, but that they might begin their examination of him from the time that he became a monk and had consecrated himself to God. Then they brought accusations against him; but as they could not convict him, they gave way, and allowed him free passage. Then immediately he saw himself come back and stand near himself, and presently he found himself to be all Antony again. Then indeed he forgot to eat; and so he continued the rest of the day, and the whole night, groaning and praying: for he was astonished to see with what hosts we have to contend, and what hard work one has to get along through the air: and he remembered the apostle's saying—*According to the prince of the power of the air* (Eph. ii. 2):* for in the air the enemy has the power, by fighting and tempting, to hinder those who are passing. Wherefore he commended the saying, *Put on the whole*

* St. Paul here speaks according to the common opinion among those to whom he wrote. We are not to infer that he meant to teach it as a doctrine of revelation, no more than we are to infer, from a similar allusion of our Saviour, that the disciples of the Pharisees actually cast out demons. (Luke xi. 19.) In our account of the Greek philosophy and the opinions of Philo the Jew, we noticed this opinion concerning demons in the air. We take from Rosenmüller's note on Eph. ii. 2, the following extracts from Greek writers: Diogenes Laertius says, "The whole atmosphere is full of spirits, which are thought to be demons and heroes." And Plutarch says, "The air beneath and the heavens above are full of gods and demons."

armor of God, &c. (Eph. vi. 13.) Let us also remember the words of the apostle, saying, Whether in the body, or out of the body, I cannot tell. (2 Cor. xii. 2.)

Antony had, moreover, this gift. If at any time, when he was sitting alone, in the mountain, he doubted in himself concerning anything, this was revealed to him by Providence, while he was praying; as it is written, *The saint is taught of God.** (John vi. 45.)

After the vision just mentioned he was once conversing with some who were with him, about the way in which the soul passed into a future state, and what sort of a place it would have there. The next night some one from above called to him, and said, Antony, arise—come forth, and see. Then he arose (for he knew to whom he ought to give ear), and beheld a tall, gloomy, and terrible form, whose stature reached to the clouds, and other forms ascending as if with wings. The giant form stretched forth his hands, and arrested some of the ascending spirits; but others of them flew above him, and passing by, had then a free passage upwards. The monster gnashed his teeth when these escaped him, but rejoiced over those that fell.† Then came a voice to Antony, saying, Consider the vision. His understanding being opened, he perceived it to represent the passage of souls—the tall figure to be the Devil, who envies the faithful, and who seizes and stops those that are liable to his arrest, but cannot lay hold on those that fly above him, because they have not obeyed him.

After he saw this vision, considering it as an admonition to

* This is not correctly quoted here.

† It is pleasant to find among the vapid imaginings of monkery a truly poetical conception, like this of old Antony. His vast gloomy devil, with his feet on the earth and his head in the clouds, is not inferior to Camoens's Spirit of the Cape, so much admired by the critics. But in awfully descriptive power, nothing of the kind is equal to Job's vision of the night, when deep sleep falleth upon man, when a spirit passed before his face, and made the hair of his flesh stand up; when the image whose form he could not discern stood still before his eyes, and a voice sounded in his ears, "Shall mortal man be more just than God?" (Job. iv. 13.)

himself, he strove hard to make farther progress, every day, in his exercises of prayer and fasting. But as to the vision, he could scarcely be persuaded to tell it. But the long time that he spent in his prayers on that occasion, raised the curiosity of his companions, and their eager inquiries at length drew it from him—he believing that the narration would be useful to them.

18. *How Antony was taken to Alexandria to preach against the Arians.*

He held all clergymen in the greatest honor. He was not ashamed to bow his head before bishops and priests: and if a deacon at any time met with him, and discoursed in a profitable manner, he yielded him the precedence in prayer, for he was not ashamed to learn from any one. He often asked questions for information, and deigned to hear all who were present.

He possessed a wonderful grace of countenance, insomuch that a stranger visiting a company of monks, would at first sight be attracted by his look, and attach himself to him in preference to the rest. Yet he was not taller nor larger than the others: it was by his kindliness and ease of manner, and by the purity of his mind, that he won all hearts. His look was always serene and cheerful, showing a soul undisturbed by evil passions.

Excellent and admirable also were his faith and piety. For he would have nothing to do with the Meletian schismatics,* after he knew their wickedness and apostasy from the church. Nor would he associate with the Manichees,† or any other heretics, except

* Followers of Meletius, an Egyptian bishop, who was deposed from his office by a party headed by Peter, Bishop of Alexandria, but being sustained by a large minority, he made a schism which continued a long time. His enemies charged him with having sacrificed to idols in the late persecution. He alleged that the cause of their enmity was his opposition to Peter's indulgent policy towards those who had apostatized. The monks were of Peter's party.

† Followers of Mani, a Persian, who incorporated the Magian doctrine of two eternal principles with Christianity. According to the Manichees, the good principle is God, represented by light—the evil principle, matter,

so far as to admonish them, and exhort them to turn to the true religion: for he considered and declared that their friendship and society were destructive to the soul. He also abominated the heresy of the Arians, and exhorted the faithful never to go near them, nor to touch their corrupt doctrine. So when once some Arians came to visit him, and he discovered that they belonged to this impious sect, he drove them away from the mountain, saying, that their doctrines were worse than the poison of serpents: and when some Arians once told him, falsely, that their opinions agreed with his, he was filled with indignation and wrath against them.

Afterwards, at the request of the bishops and all the brethren, he left his mountain and went down to Alexandria, and preached violently against the Arians, saying that theirs was the last heresy and the forerunner of Antichrist. He taught the people that the Son of God was no creature, but the Eternal Word and Wisdom of the Father. Wherefore, said he, have no fellowship with these abominably impious Arians. You are Christians; but they who say that the Son and Word of God is a created being, are no better than the heathen, who worship the creature rather than the Creator. Believe me, that the whole creation is angry with them for putting the Creator and Lord of all things in the number of creatures.

The people all rejoiced to see so great a man denouncing and

endued with a living energy, called also the Devil, and represented by darkness. Matter being essentially evil, the body is therefore the prison of the soul, and the cause of its vice and misery. They denied the reality of Christ's body, supposing that a divine being would not unite himself with the evil principle. With such a foundation for their system, they would of course adopt ascetic rules of living. They divided their community into two classes, the elect, who were severely ascetic, practicing continence, and all the bodily mortifications of monkery, and the auditors, who were allowed to marry if they could not contain, but were taught to fast much, and live austerely. The Manichees rose in the third century, agreed in fundamentals with the Gnostics that preceded them, were diffused over Christendom, and continued for ages.

cursing this anti-Christian heresy. All the people of the city ran together to see Antony. Even the heathen part of the people, and those called their priests, came to the church, asking to see the man of God, as everybody called him. There, too, the Lord by him purified many of demons and of insanity. Many of the heathen, too, requested that they might only touch him, believing that it would do them good. Verily, as many were converted to Christianity in those few days, as we usually see in a whole year.*

When some supposed that he must be troubled by the crowds that surrounded him, he said that he was not; that he had struggled with quite as numerous crowds of demons in the desert. When he left us and we had attended him as far as the city gate, a woman came bawling after us, Stop! stop, thou man of God: my daughter is woefully vexed with demons; stop, I pray thee, or I shall kill myself with running. The old man stopped; and when the woman came near, her daughter was jerked to the ground by the demon. When Antony prayed, the unclean spirit

* Athanasius spent his life in battling with the Arians, who denied that the Son was of the same substance with the Father, though they affirmed his divinity and likeness to the Father. They were a strong party in Alexandria, as well as in other parts of the church, and several times got the emperor to banish Athanasius from the city. Hence he hated them with a perfect hatred.

He knew what he was about, when he brought the famous dirty old monk from the desert to work upon the minds of the Alexandrian populace, against the Arian party. The untaught multitude are always mightily taken with such characters. Many a wonderful report had they heard in Alexandria of St. Antony's doings in the deserts of Upper Egypt, four hundred miles away—of his fastings, prayings, miracles, battles with demons—and of his not having washed himself, nor changed his rough garments, nor cut nor combed his hair, or beard, for at least fifty years. Wonderful man! Wonderful saint! No wonder that they ran in crowds to see such a body and such a soul. The fact that he was totally illiterate was to them an argument that he was a heaven-taught expounder of the mysteries of the Godhead. Had he not conversed with the angels, and did he not know divine mysteries better than learned doctors of divinity? These sentiments were common to the heathen and the Christian populace.

went out, and the girl got up sound well. Then the old man departed for his own home in the mountain.

19. *How Antony out-witted the philosophers.*

It is wonderful how prudent and how sharp-witted Antony was, considering that he had never learned to read.

Two Greek philosophers came to him, one day, in the outer mountain [next to the Nile], thinking that they could confound him. When he saw them, he knew by their looks what they were.* He said to them, by an interpreter,† Heigh, philosophers! Do you put yourselves to all this trouble to visit a fool? They answered [perhaps ironically], You are no fool, but a wise man. Antony replied, If you have come to see a fool, you have lost your labor: but if, as you say, I am a wise man, then be what I am; for it is good to imitate a good thing. If I had gone to see you, I should have imitated you: but as you have come to see me, be Christians, as I am a Christian. The philosophers retired, admiring Antony; for they saw he was qualified to make demons afraid of him.

Others of the same sort came to him in the outer mountain, intending to make sport out of him, because he was illiterate. Antony said to them, Which is better, good sense or learning? And which is the cause of the other? good sense, of learning? or learning, of good sense? They answered, Good sense is to be preferred, and is the inventor of learning. Well, then, said Antony, he who has a sound mind has no need of learning. This reply confounded the philosophers, and they went away, wondering how an illiterate man could have so much wit.‡

* Professed philosophers distinguished themselves by wearing beards, and a cloak of singular fashion. The Platonic Christian philosophers generally adopted the same habit.

† Antony knew only the Coptic, that is, the Egyptian language.

‡ In both these instances Antony showed a ready wit: in the former, the turn that he took upon the philosophers was admirable; in the latter, it was ingenious, but by no means conclusive. If the philosophers had possessed half the mother-wit of old Antony, they could readily have

Another time, some, who were esteemed wise men by the Greeks, came to demand of him a reason for our faith in Christ, —thinking that they could turn his argument to ridicule. He paused awhile, and then said to them, through an interpreter, Which is better, to confess the cross of Christ, or to attribute adultery and sodomy to those whom you believe to be Gods? [NOTE.—Here Athanasius puts a long argument into the mouth of Antony. Most of it would be uninteresting to the reader; we therefore omit it all, except a few select passages, which contain something striking.]

"Which is better, to say that the Word of God assumed a human body, that, by partaking of human nature, he might make men partakers of a divine and intellectual nature; or to liken the Divine nature to brutes, and on that account to worship four-footed beasts, and reptiles, and images of men?* For these are objects of worship to your wise men. And how dare you scoff at us for saying that Christ appeared as man, when you yourselves say that the soul—which you consider a distinct thing from the intelligent mind—went astray, and fell from the circle of the heavens into a body; and that it transmigrates not only into the human body, but also into the bodies of beasts and reptiles?†

replied, that man has need not only of sound natural sense, but of the improvement in knowledge which is best acquired by means of books. In respect even to religion, what would it be without letters? And what would all men be without them, but savages? But perhaps the philosophers considered it useless to present such an argument to an illiterate monk, who could not appreciate its force, and who thought that this world, and these bodies, which God had made for us, were very contemptible contrivances; who thought, moreover, that the best way to please the Creator of the world, was to reject the gifts that he offered us, hate the pleasures that he had prepared for us, and to renounce, as far as possible, the earthly life which he had assigned us.

* Brute worship was a part of the old Egyptian superstition, but the philosophers did not adopt or advocate that absurdity. As to image worship, the Catholic Church had not yet borrowed it of the idolaters, as she did afterwards, in spite of the Divine prohibition.

† The philosophers held that the animal soul of man was earth-born,

You depend on demonstrative reasonings to establish your doctrines; and having this art, you would also have us not to worship God without argumentative proof. Now tell me: How are facts, and especially how is the knowledge of God, most accurately ascertained? Is it by demonstration of reason? or by energy of faith? Which is older, faith wrought in the soul, or demonstration by reason? The philosophers admitted that inwrought faith was older. You say well (continued Antony), for faith springs from an affection of the soul; logic from human art. Therefore to those in whom faith has been wrought, demonstration by reasoning is unnecessary, if not superfluous; for what we understand by faith, you endeavor to prove by arguments. We are often unable to express what we understand by faith; so that the operation of faith is better than the operation of your sophistical arguments."*

"Behold the martyrs despising death for Christ's sake. Behold the virgins of the Church, who, for Christ's sake, keep their bodies pure and unpolluted. These are sufficient tokens to show that the Christian faith is the only true religion. You are now unbelieving, because you demand [philosophical] reasons and

and that it was the rational soul, or intellect, which "went astray and fell." The doctrine of transmigration was common through nearly all the ancient world. It seems to have originated from the idea that this corporeal life is a state of punishment. The same doctrine became current among the Jews after the captivity.

* Learned infidels have laid hold of passages like this in the Fathers, in order to show that the early Christians repudiated reason, and relied solely upon the power of faith to establish the truth of their religion. It is true that the Fathers generally were unskillful reasoners, and often made use of silly and unfounded arguments. But it would be a great mistake to suppose that they disclaimed rational grounds of conviction, and relied solely on faith wrought in the soul by Divine Power. Even here, old Antony professes to exhibit external evidence of the truth of Christianity. His meaning—or rather that of Athanasius—was, that Christians did not prove their religion by that sort of abstract reasoning which the philosophers employed to establish the truth of their system of philosophy. He was right. Christianity comes by revelation: philosophy by reason alone.

arguments. We do not use the persuasive arguments of the Grecian philosophy (1 Cor. ii. 4), but by faith we give a clear confirmation of what we teach. Behold here are some men suffering from demons."

Then Antony brought forward several who were troubled with demons, and said, Can you heal these men by your reasonings? or by any art or magic, calling upon your idols? Saying these things he called upon the name of Christ, marked the demoniacs with the sign of the cross, a first, second, and third time. Immediately these men were perfectly healed of their insanity. The philosophers wondered at Antony's wisdom, and at the miracle which was performed.*

20. *Containing sundry matters.*

The fame of Antony extended even to the imperial court. The emperor Constantine, and his sons Constantius and Constans, wrote to him as a father, and requested an answer. But he had *no respect for the art of writing*, and took no pleasure in letters. He was unwilling, therefore, to receive the emperor's letter, because he was unable to write an answer. But being told by the monks that the imperial family were Christians, and if he thus cast them off they would be offended, he suffered the letter to be read to him, and dictated an answer to the effect that he was glad to hear they worshiped Christ. He admonished them not to

* The belief in demons, demoniacal possessions, and magic, was universal in this age, and for many ages both before and afterwards. To cast out demons from the possessed, who were generally lunatic or epileptic, was supposed to require the power of God, or of magic, by which the aid of a superior demon was obtained, or else the aid of some natural object which had an occult virtue to expel demons. Our Saviour exhibited divine power by healing instantly before his enemies those known to be incurable by human art. But this story of Antony's healing the demoniacs is very suspicious. He had his *professed* demoniacs ready for the occasion. It was easy to feign madness or epilepsy. If the philosophers wondered and suspected nothing, we should remember that philosophers are sometimes verv credulous and not very wise.

think highly of present things, but rather to remember the future judgment, and to know that Christ alone is the true and eternal king. He exhorted them to be humane and just, and mindful of the poor. They rejoiced when they received this letter.

After these things he returned again to the mountain, in the heart of the desert, and applied himself to his usual exercise. Often when he sat or walked with those present, he would be struck dumb with amazement, for the space of an hour, after which he would pursue his conversation with the brethren, who knew from this that he had seen a vision. For, oftentimes, when he was in the mountain, events then happening in Egypt, would be presented to him in vision.

Once when he was seated in company he fell into a trance, and groaned heavily at the vision he saw. After an hour, he turned to the company, groaned, trembled, stood up and prayed, and then falling upon his knees he continued long in that posture. When he rose at last, weeping, the brethren importuned him to tell them what the matter was. At last he said, Children, would that I had died before I saw this vision. Wrath is coming upon the Church; she will be delivered to men who are like natural brute beasts. I have seen mules standing round the Lord's table, kicking and leaping in wild disorder. You heard how I groaned, when a voice said, My altar will become an abomination. This was the old man's vision. Two years afterwards the Arians made that inroad upon Egypt which yet continues.* During the Arian persecution, a certain prefect, named Balacius, in his zeal for Arianism, treated the (Catholic) Christians with great cruelty. He beat the virgins, and, stripping the monks, scourged them with whips. Antony sent some brethren to him, with a letter to

* By a decree of the Emperor Constantius, Athanasius was banished for the third time from Alexandria, and the Arians were put in possession of the churches. They committed many outrages upon the Catholics. As to Father Antony's prophecy of this event, we suspect that it was not *published* before it was fulfilled. Antony, being a sagacious old man, may have expressed some apprehensions beforehand that such a thing would happen. If so, his disciples would believe that he prophesied it.

this effect: I see the wrath of God impending over you. Cease to persecute the Christians, lest it fall upon you, as it will in a very short time. Balacius laughed at the letter, threw it on the ground, spit upon it, and said insultingly to those who brought it, Go tell Antony, that since he takes the monks under his protection, I shall soon come upon him.

Five days had not passed before the wrath overtook him. He rode out of the city with Nestorius, President of Egypt. Both horses belonged to Balacius, and were the gentlest that he had. They had scarcely reached the open country, when the horses became playful, as horses confined in a stable are apt to be when they get out. Suddenly, the horse which Nestorius rode, in snapping at the other, gave the thigh of Balacius such a lacerating bite that he had to be carried into the city. In three days he died.

Such was the influence of Antony over those who visited him, that many, even of the soldiers and of the wealthy, left the cares and burdens of this life, and became monks. He was indeed as a heaven-born physician to Egypt. For who went to him in sorrow, and did not come back rejoicing? Who went to him in anger, and was not converted into a friend? What poor man met him, with a dejected heart, who, after he saw and heard him, did not go away despising riches, and content with poverty? If a monk was remiss, he excited him to diligence. If a young man went to the mountain and beheld Antony, he straightway renounced pleasure and embraced a life of temperance. Whosoever came to him, tempted by a demon, was relieved; or if troubled with evil thoughts and reasonings, was tranquilized. For this was the grand attainment of Antony's exercise, that, as I said before, he had the gift of discerning spirits, and knew all their movements, and what was each one's aim and inclination. Not only was he himself free from their delusions, but he could advise those troubled in mind how to defeat their designs, by describing to them the weakness of the inworking demons, and their villainous acts. Thus each one being trained for the contest, went forth courageously against the devices of the devil and his demons.

Many virgins already espoused* to men, by merely seeing Antony at a distance, remained virgins for Christ.

21. *Antony's Death.*

How he ended his life, it becomes me also to relate, and you to hear with diligent attention; for in this also he was worthy of imitation.

According to custom, he visited the monks in the outer mountain; and being providentially warned of his approaching end, he said to the brethren: This is my last visit, and I shall think it strange if we ever meet again in this life. It is time for me to depart, for I am nearly 105 years old. When they heard this they wept, fell upon the old man's neck and kissed him. But he, as if going home from a foreign land, conversed with them cheerfully, and exhorted them to persevere in their labor and exercise, to live daily as if they were dying, diligently to guard their hearts against evil thoughts, to be zealous for the saints, and not to go near the schismatic Meletians. And (said he) have nothing to do with the Arians, whose impiety is manifested to all.

When the brethren insisted that he should stay and end his days with them, he refused, principally for this reason: The Egyptians are accustomed to embalm the bodies of their dead, especially of the holy martyrs, and to wrap them in linen cloths, but not to bury them in the ground. They lay them on couches, and keep them in private apartments of their houses. But Antony disapproved of this, and had often remonstrated against it with the bishops, and people, as contrary to the custom of the patriarchs and the example of our Lord. Fearing that his body might be treated in this way, he hastened away to the interior mountain where he had usually resided.

Here, after a few months, he was taken sick. He had, during

* Virgins of the East were often espoused long before the marriage was consummated. Antony must have emitted a powerful anti-matrimonial influence, when a distant sight of him was sufficient to dissolve a marriage contract. What would a touch have done?

the last fifteen years, kept two monks here with him, who ministered to him on account of his great age. To these he repeated his frequent exhortations and charges to others—never to relax in the exercise, not to fear the demons, and to have nothing to do with schismatics and Arian heretics. He charged them not to suffer his body to be carried into Egypt to be kept in houses, but to bury it in the earth and conceal the place.* Finally, he made his will. "Distribute my clothes (said he)—Give one of my sheepskins to Athanasius, the bishop, and also my undercoat, which he gave me when it was new, and I now return to him well-worn. Give my other sheepskin to Sarapion, the bishop. Keep my hair-shirt for yourselves. Finally, children, farewell; for Antony is passing away, and will be with you no more."—So saying, he stretched out his feet, and with a smiling countenance, expired. They buried him, according to his directions, and to this day no one knows where his body is hidden, except those two brethren.

The sheepskins and coat which he had worn, were thankfully received, and are kept as things of great value.

From this brief narrative you may judge how great a man Antony was, who from youth to extreme old age, steadfastly persevered in his ascetic life. He never indulged his old age with better food, nor his infirmity with a change of clothing; nor did he ever wash his feet. Yet he continued sound in all his members. His eyesight was unimpaired to the last, and his teeth were sound, though worn to mere stumps by long use. He retained also the perfect use of his feet and hands; and in fine, was more sleek and vigorous than those who use variety of food, washing, and change of clothing. His fame spread through all the Roman Empire, from his remote habitation in the desert mountain. That which rendered him famous, was neither learning nor worldly wisdom, nor human art; but only his piety towards God. And let this be known to all the brethren, that them who live as monks ought to do, will the Lord not only lead to heaven,

* See Jerome's Life of Hilarion, § 31, near the end.

but render illustrious and renowned through all the earth, however deeply they may hide themselves in the desert.

APPENDIX.

From Socrates's Hist. Eccl. Book IV. Ch. 23.

A philosopher said to Antony: How can you live without the consolation of books? My books, O philosopher, said Antony, is the nature of the things created; and I can readily, when I will, read the word of God.

From the same, Ch. 25.

It is said that Antony, when he went to Alexandria on account of the Arians, met with blind Didymus; and finding out how sensible a man he was, said to him: O Didymus, let not the loss of your external eyes grieve you, for with such eyes even gnats and flies can see; but rejoice that you have the eyes with which angels see, and God himself is seen, and his light is apprehended.

Concluding Note.

Having gone through the life of St. Antony, we cannot refuse him the parting tribute of our admiration for the real greatness of his character. He was the prince of the hermits, and the founder of monachism among Christians. Perfectly illiterate, and a recluse in a desert for eighty years, the force of his mere example was such as to draw thousands after him, and to establish an institution that soon spread through the Church, and for 1500 years has continued to exert a powerful influence over the minds of men.

Those qualities in Antony which made his example so influential, were, first, his steadfastness of purpose, and secondly the natural strength of his intellect. Setting out upon the principle, that what he understood to be the commands of Christ, he would obey to the letter; he did so with an unwavering resolution during eighty-five years; denying himself every earthly comfort, which the soul naturally desires, and the God of nature benevolently offers. While we condemn the error of his views, we must admire the steadfastness of his adherence to what he conceived to be his duty to Christ.

He was conscious of a strength of mind, which he conceived to make the aid of other men unnecessary, either for his instruction, or his confirmation in the path of duty. He relied upon himself alone, and the occasional help of God, to conquer all the hosts of darkness and all the passions of his nature. And in his way he did conquer. Then he had a sagacity, a ready wit, a persuasive power of thought, which completed his character, and fitted him to be the captain of all who were disposed to war against nature.

www.ingramcontent.com/pod-product-compliance
Lightning Source LLC
LaVergne TN
LVHW020236110826
845151LV00003B/934